Official Stories

Stanford Studies in Middle Eastern and Islamic Societies and Cultures

Official Stories

POLITICS AND NATIONAL NARRATIVES IN EGYPT AND ALGERIA

Laurie A. Brand

Stanford University Press
Stanford, California

Stanford University Press
Stanford, California

Printed in the United States of America on acid-free, archival-quality paper

Library of Congress Cataloging-in-Publication Data

Brand, Laurie A., author.

Official stories : politics and national narratives in Egypt and Algeria / Laurie A. Brand.
pages cm — (Stanford studies in Middle Eastern and Islamic societies and cultures)
Includes bibliographical references and index.
ISBN 978-0-8047-8960-8 (cloth : alk. paper) — ISBN 978-0-8047-9216-5 (pbk. : alk. paper)
1. Egypt—Politics and government—1952-1970. 2. Egypt—Politics and government—1970-1981. 3. Egypt—Politics and government—1981- 4. Algeria—Politics and government—1962-1990. 5. Algeria—Politics and government—1990- 6. Propaganda—Africa, North—History—Case studies. 7. Authoritarianism—Africa, North—History—Case studies. I. Title. II. Series: Stanford studies in Middle Eastern and Islamic societies and cultures.
DT107.827.B73 2014
962.05—dc23

2014021438

ISBN 978-0-8047-9232-5 (electronic)

Typeset by Bruce Lundquist in 10/14 Minion

CONTENTS

PREFACE

As my 2009–10 sabbatical drew near, my research plan was to devote time to developing a better understanding of the periods of transition from colonial rule to the first independent Middle Eastern and North African governments. I became particularly intrigued by what seemed an interesting puzzle: why was it that, while nationalist movements often had memberships and programs that suggested an intertwining of religious and less religious (perhaps secular) elements, it was largely nonreligiously oriented leaderships that came to power following the independence struggles. Gradually, however, the project shifted and expanded into a quest to understand the components of postindependence national narratives and, more specifically, how state elites construct and reconfigure them to serve the goals of regime consolidation and maintenance.

Since I began this project, the use of the term "narrative" has proliferated both within but also outside academia to a degree I could not have imagined. That said, most references to or discussions of "the narrative" are short, superficial, and underspecified. For my study, I elected a comparative-case approach because I felt it could potentially tell us more than a single case about what has been at work: the dynamics behind change and the forces that have promoted (or been unable to disrupt) continuity in official narratives. Over a year into the project, I finally had the good sense to take my spouse's advice and reduce the number of case studies from three to four, leaving Lebanon behind, in hopes that I might actually finish it before I became eligible for social security. And as I moved to finalize the manuscript for publication, I had to remove yet another case, that of Jordan, for considerations of length. Still, the cases left out have helped to inform my analysis, even in this study of just two countries.

I am deeply indebted to the Carnegie Corporation for an "Islam and Muslim Societies" fellowship 2008–10, which enabled me not only to have time off from teaching, but also to make trips to Algeria, Egypt, and Jordan to conduct research for this project. I am also grateful to Carnegie for their understanding along the way as the study's case composition narrowed and the focus of the project shifted. Then, to complete the first draft of this manuscript, I was privileged to have a writing fellowship at the Rockefeller Foundation's Bellagio Centerin Bellagio, Italy. I am most thankful for the support of the Center and its wonderful staff, as well as of my fellow residents, during this period of reflection and intensive writing. The Dornsife College at the University of Southern California also provided significant support, from a sabbatical semester in fall 2009 and an Advancing Scholarship in the Humanities and Social Sciences (ASHSS) grant for course release in spring 2011 (which was then completely overwhelmed by my attempts to keep up with falling Arab dictators) to course release to enable me to take the Bellagio writing residency, which did not coincide with a normally scheduled sabbatical. Also critical for my ability to make progress, in spring 2011 when I was floundering, USC's Center for International Studies sponsored a research meeting to help me rethink the direction of the project. I am indebted to my faculty colleagues—Macarena Gómez-Barris, Deniz Cakirer, Robert English, Sarah Gualtieri, Dan Lynch, Ayşe Rorlich, Ramzi Rouighi, Ann Tickner, and Diane Winston—who took the time to look at a mass of empirical notes and comment on a draft theory chapter that, on reflection, must have read like everything plus the kitchen sink. I would also like to thank USC's School of International Relations for providing me with a research assistant for the final stages of preparation of the manuscript, and to Youssef Chouhoud for his tremendous help in this capacity.

In addition, even though I was ultimately forced to omit Jordan from this book, I am no less grateful to Kimberley Katz, who shared with me stacks of photocopied Jordanian textbooks when at first it appeared that the textbook museum in Salt, Jordan, would not be accessible. I also owe a *very deep* debt of gratitude to Nathan Brown, who had heard through the grapevine that I was working on Jordanian textbooks and forwarded me a link to an article in the *Jordan Times* announcing the reopening of the textbook museum. I would also like to thank my colleagues Nathan Brown, Jason Brownlee, and Robert Parks, who read and commented on the various country chapters once they were in relatively presentable form.

Then there are all the centers along the way. Robert Parks and Karim Ouaras at the Centre d'études maghrébines en Algérie (CEMAT) in Oran, Algeria, provided scholarly and moral support, and critical entrées into Oran's and Algiers' academic communities; indeed, they even tracked down textbooks for me. Special thanks goes to the indefatigable Abdennebi Mebtoul ('Ammo), who, as a former educator, took a special interest in my project and helped keep me going when it appeared that I might be foiled by the powers that be at the Académie d'Oran. Mr. Mohamed Tiliouine, the *chef de service* at the Archives in Oran, helped open what appeared hopelessly closed doors, and Mme. Khalida Attou assisted me with materials at the Archives, while making additional suggestions for sources. I am also indebted to Hassan Remaoun and Nouria Benghabrit-Remaoun for their help with my project though the wonderful Centre de recherche en anthropologie sociale et culturelle (CRASC) in Oran. In Cairo, my thanks go first and foremost to Nadine Sika (and to Bahgat Korany for introducing me to her). Nadine made the contact with the general in security, whom I never met, who (apparently) issued a letter, which we never saw, on the basis of which I was given access to the library of old Egyptian textbooks at the Museum of the Ministry of Education. The whole story is filled with one serendipitous event after another, but quite simply, without Nadine's help, there could have been no Egypt case study in this book. Thanks in Cairo also go to Lisa Anderson, president of the American University in Cairo, to Mustafa Kamel al-Sayyid, also of AUC, and to my dear friends Lisa White and Muhammad al-Qawasmah. Finally, in Jordan, thanks to my always supportive friends at the American Center of Oriental Research (ACOR) in Amman, especially Humi Ayyubi and Nasreen Amin, to Fatimeh Mar'i at the Jordan Museum, to Ni'meh Nsour at the Jordan Textbook Museum in Salt, and to the staff at the Jordan National Library in Amman.

Also critical, particularly in the final stages of manuscript revision and preparation, were the keen eye, wisdom, and patience of my editor at Stanford University Press, Kate Wahl. Her help and support as I grappled with more effective ways of framing and presenting my argument were invaluable. I am also most grateful to Peter Dreyer, whose work on this manuscript to catch my missteps and improve my prose went well beyond mere copyediting. Last, but by no means least, my husband, Fayez, helped in ways both large and small all along the way, from advice on case selection and discussions of his own work on authoritarian resilience to helping me secure access and materials in Amman to holding down the home front to enable me to carry out field research in the region and take up the Bellagio residency.

The final research and writing of this project took place in the aftermath of the dramatic changes brought by the uprisings and demonstrations that began in winter 2010–11. As the initial euphoria of the swift dispatching of Ben 'Ali and Mubarak began to recede, I was reminded of a time in the late 1980s when several countries in the region had also appeared to be on the verge of a new era.

Zayn al-'Abdin Ben 'Ali overthrew Tunisia's president for life, Habib Bourguiba in November 1987 and promised a more pluralist political system. The following month, the first Palestinian intifada against Israeli occupation began. By late the following year, severe riots had rocked Algeria and ended the period of one-party rule. Six months later, riots triggered by the reduction in fuel price subsidies in Jordan led the king to call for the first full parliamentary elections since prior to the 1967 war. And in 1990, the two Yemens came together to form a single country on the basis of a more open political system. There is no need to rehearse here how the promise of all these dramatic changes was denied or dissipated.

It remains to be seen whether, aside from Tunisia, any of the countries deeply affected by the Arab uprisings of 2011 will emerge from what have become increasingly brutal transitions with more open and just political systems. I take up post-2011 developments in the Epilogue. For now, suffice it to say that the documents produced today can be indicative of or lay the basis for important shifts in the state's approach to the critical areas of identity and citizenship going forward. The many attempts to reappropriate narrative themes and rescript historical symbols over the past several years underscore the fact that across the region both state leaderships and the people/citizenry understand this quite well.

It is to all those in the region who have been and/or currently are engaged in the battles to dismantle the authoritarian order and rebuild MENA political systems so that they respect and promote human dignity that this book is dedicated, with admiration, respect, and hope.

A NOTE ON *QAWMIYYA* AND *WATANIYYA*

The words for "nation" and "national" are particularly important in this study; they are also problematic in working from Arabic texts into English. Two words—*qawmiyya* and *wataniyya*—have, depending upon period and place, been used to convey the term "nationalism" as we use it in English. Each comes from a very different root in Arabic and hence carries different connotations. *Qawmiyya* is derived from the word *qawm*, which is most often translated as "nation," but in the sense of a people that is not confined or defined by borders. *Qawmiyya*, therefore, has, certainly since the mid-twentieth century, been used to refer to a sense of (pan)Arab nationalism, one that includes all Arabs, since it transcends territorial boundaries. That said, its use in earlier texts can carry a more restrictive meaning. For example, it was used in Egypt in the early part of the twentieth century to refer to a sense of Egypt-specific belonging.

Watani, on the other hand, derives from the root *watan*, which has a sense of territory, or land to which one belongs. *Wataniyya*, therefore, has generally been used to mean a sense of loyalty to a particular area. *Wataniyya* evolved to express the sense of affiliation that Arabs may have with the political entity in which they live; that is, state-based or territorial nationalism. It can also be translated as patriotism, just as *watani* can mean patriotic. Significantly, the word for citizen (*muwatin*) and citizenship (*muwatina*) both come from this root. Given the different kinds of belonging that each implies, *qawmiyya* and *wataniyya* operate simultaneously, if with perhaps different salience, for many Arabs.

Further complicating the picture, there are some phrases in which the word *qawmi* is always used instead of *watani*. For example, in talking about national security, the translation is *al-amn al-qawmi*, and while it may be used to apply to broader Arab concerns, it is generally understood to apply to country-specific interests.

Not surprisingly, national leaderships have given shifting preference to these terms over the years. Which term is selected often says a great deal about prevailing ideology or orientation. It is for this reason that I have elected in numerous places in the text to indicate which word is used in the Arabic original. My hope is that this will clarify rather than confuse. It was too important a distinction to allow to disappear in translation.

ACRONYMS

AUMA	Association des Ulama musulmans algériens/Association of Algerian Muslim Ulema
ALN	Armée de libération nationale/National Liberation Army
ANP	Armée nationale populaire/National Popular (People's) Army
ASU	Arab Socialist Union
CCE	Comité de coordination et d'exécution/Committee of Coordination and Enforcement
CGT	Confédération générale du travail/General Labor Confederation
CNEH	Centre national d'études historiques/National Center for Historical Studies
CNRA	Conseil national de la révolution algérienne/National Council of the Algerian Revolution
EF	École fondamentale polytechnique/Basic polytechnic school
ENA	Étoile nord-africaine /North African Star
FFFLN	Fédération de France du Front de libération nationale/Federation of France of the National Liberation Front
FFS	Front des forces socialistes/Socialist Front Forces
FIS	Front islamique du salut/Islamic Salvation Front
FLN	Front de libération nationale/National Liberation Front
GPRA	Gouvernement provisoire de la République Algérienne/Provisional government of the Algerian Republic
HCE	Haut comité d'État/Higher Committee of State
IMF	International Monetary Fund

IPN	Institut pedagogique national/National Pedagogical Institute
MCB	Mouvement culturel berbère/Berber Cultural Movement
MENA	Middle East and North Africa
MNA	Mouvement national algérien/Algerian National Movement
MOE	Ministry of Education
MTLD	Mouvement pour le triomphe des libertés démocratiques/ Movement for the Triumph of Democratic Liberties
NDP	National Democratic Party
OAS	Organisation de l'Armée secrète/Secret Army Organization
OERA	Original Education and Religious Affairs (Ministry)
ONEM	Organisation nationale des enfants de moudjahidines/National Organization for the Children of Mujahidin
ONM	Organisation nationale des moudjahidines/National Organization of Mujahidin
PAGS	Parti de l'avant-garde socialiste/Socialist Vanguard Party
PPA	Parti du peuple algérien/Algerian People's Party
RADP	République algérienne démocratique populaire/People's Democratic Republic of Algeria
SCAF	Supreme Council of the Armed Forces
UAR	United Arab Republic
UGEMA	Union générale des étudiants musulmans algériens
UGSA	Union générale des syndicats algériens/General Union of Algerian Labor Unions
UGTA	Union générale des travailleurs algériens/General Union of Algerian Workers
USAID	United States Agency for International Development

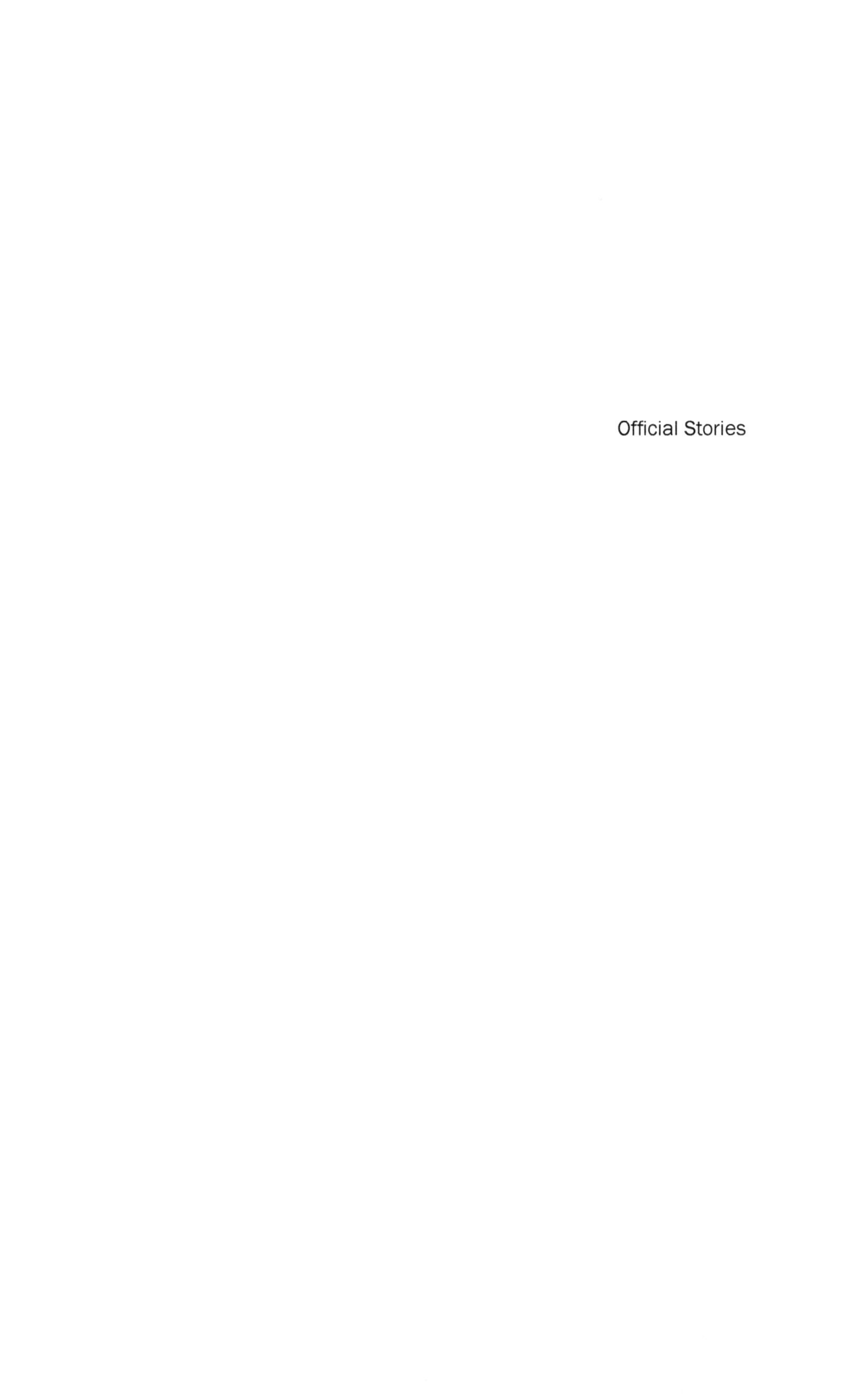

Official Stories

1 RESTOR(Y)ING THE STATE

National Narratives and Regime Resilience

PRIOR TO THE ARAB UPRISINGS IN SPRING 2011, much ink was spilt by academics, pundits, and journalists in an attempt to explain the resilience of the range of authoritarian regimes in the Middle East and North Africa (MENA) region. Although successive waves of democratization[1] seemed to wash over other parts of the world, the MENA states appeared impervious to the same forces of history. Politicized, polemical, and often ill-informed writing offered a variety of ahistorical arguments focused largely on the purported resistance of a disembodied "Islam" or an essentialized Arab culture to any movements toward more meaningful participatory political systems.[2]

Eventually, over the din of the dim, scholars of the politics of the region made more sophisticated analyses heard. Careful single-case and comparative studies pointed to a host of factors having nothing to do with religion or the broader and even more problematic concept of culture. These analyses instead looked for answers in the political economy of the region, in the intervention of external actors, the role of the Palestine conflict, and the development and entrenchment of the security forces.[3] In the economic sphere, the development of rentier economies or states was used to explain the ability of elites in some political systems to buy off potential opposition through distributive policies made possible by wealth accruing from oil or natural gas revenues, or strategic rents. Other analyses focused on the involvement of external or extraregional actors, most centrally the United States. Despite initiatives purported to promote democracy, U.S. aid, often to MENA military or security forces, privileged the stability seemingly guaranteed by dictatorships in order to protect the free flow of oil and thwart threats to Israel.[4] Finally, the exceptional strength of coercive apparatuses—the military, the police, and other internal security forces—as well as the patrimonial character of state institutions and low levels of popular mobilization were also shown to be of central importance.[5]

All of these are critical variables in analyzing political stability and change, regardless of regime type or region. Depending upon country case, singly or in combination, they constitute compelling explanations for the resilience of authoritarian regimes in the MENA region. Nevertheless, they do not exhaust the range of strategies or tools upon which a leadership can draw to maintain or reinforce its power and legitimacy. While its influence on regime resilience may not be as immediately obvious or as easily explored as these other factors, the content of state discourse is another element worthy of study. Official narratives and pronouncements asserting the right to rule, seeking to justify policies, or combatting opponents also deserve careful exploration if we are to understand the full range of tools available to leaderships as they respond to crises—whether chronic or acute—that threaten their hold on power.

It is precisely these narrative tools that this study explores. Specifically, it attempts to discern the forms of scripting and rescripting of elements of the national story and identity, and the way they have been used in constructing or reinforcing legitimacy, "national unity," and stability in postindependence Arab states. To do so, a range of official texts is analyzed to trace how key elements of the narratives have evolved or been reformulated in the context of major economic and political crises since the 1950s. In order to provide the basis for comparison and grounds for drawing broader inferences, the experiences of two countries—Egypt and Algeria—are explored in detail.

AN INTRODUCTION TO THE CASES

A brief examination of the histories of Egypt and Algeria reveals both similarities and differences that are critical in trying to understand the use of official discourse or narratives as a political instrument. First, both had colonial pasts, albeit of quite different natures. The invasion of Algeria by France in 1830 gradually developed into a brutal settler colonial regime, and the armed liberation struggle in 1954–62 that ended in national independence was subsequently adopted as the postrevolutionary state's founding story. Egypt was occupied by Britain in 1882, and its finances and foreign affairs came under European control, yet it remained nominally a part of the Ottoman Empire until London made it a protectorate in 1915. It gained formal independence in 1922, following a national uprising called the 1919 revolution, although it continued to be ruled by a monarch from the line of Mehmet Ali,[6] the Ottoman viceroy who had come to power in Egypt in 1805 following the defeat of the Napoleonic invasion. Not until after July 1952, when a group of military men known as the Free Officers overthrew the king, was the founding story for the Egyptian postcolonial state, that of the 23 July revolution, established.

In terms of their respective political systems, both Algeria and Egypt were long variations on "republican military" authoritarian regimes.[7] Egypt was built on the basis of a state that had arguably been initiated by Mehmet Ali during the first half of the nineteenth century.[8]Algeria was constructed on the ruins of what little infrastructure the French colonial regime had left behind. Following their respective revolutions, each country faced significant problems of socioeconomic development and political institutionalization, and each witnessed the emergence of a strong role of the military in politics. Confronted with a host of challenges to power consolidation and stability, their postrevolutionary leaderships subsequently drew heavily on their respective revolutionary credentials—Algeria's born in a bloody liberation war and Egypt's through a coup that promised equality and justice—as sources of domestic legitimacy and regional influence.

As for significant differences, the two present important variations in terms of "ethnic" composition and its potential challenges to national identity construction. The majority of the population in both is Muslim, but each has had a small Jewish community, and in Egypt there is also a Christian (largely Coptic) population, totaling perhaps 10 percent of the population. In Algeria, in addition to religious diversity, there are communities of Arabic speakers as well as a significant part of the population (referred to generically as Berbers) whose maternal language is not Arabic, and who have their own regional and tribal affiliations. Beyond that, there has been the issue of the role of French, the language of the colonizer, which had been so important to the limited educational opportunities offered Algerians prior to independence. In Egypt, homogeneity is generally proclaimed, yet some historic differences have existed between the south (upper Egypt) and the north (lower Egypt), along with the separate identities of Nubians and Arabs (in this context meaning desert or non–Nile Valley peoples).

Dramatic events or crises in each country serve to illuminate when and in what way(s) the leadership may have introduced changes into the content of state discourse. In Egypt, we have the initial challenge of consolidating the postmonarchy military regime, the Israeli-French-British invasion known as the Suez war in 1956; the termination in 1961 of the United Arab Republic, the Egyptian-Syrian union concluded in 1958; the disastrous June 1967 war, which destroyed the Egyptian military and led to Israeli occupation of the Sinai Peninsula; and the sudden death of President Gamal Abdel Nasser in 1970. Then came the decade of Anwar al-Sadat's presidency: the beginnings of charting a new political and economic course with the expulsion of Soviet advisors in 1972, the launching of the October 1973 war against Israel and the initiation of the Open Door economic policy in 1974. Bloody economic riots in January 1977 were followed by Sadat's trip to Jerusalem the following November, and ultimately the conclusion of a peace treaty with Israel, the first between the Jewish state and an Arab county, in March 1979. Sadat's assassination in 1981 brought another unexpected transition at the level of the presidency, beginning what would be Husni Mubarak's thirty-year rule. Under his presidency, stability was challenged by the violence of Islamist groups, the continuing movement toward ending the remnants of the welfare state, and a fuller opening to international capital and investment.

Turning to Algeria, there is a similarly significant list: the brief post-independence war in the summer of 1962 between rival forces seeking to control the new state; the 1965 coup against President Ahmed Ben Bella by his vice president and minister of defense, Houari Boumedienne; and the 1979–80 transition from Boumedienne to President Chadhli Bendjedid. Algeria also witnessed an ethno-political uprising in 1980 known as the Berber Spring, a popular explosion in October 1988 triggering the end of one-party rule in 1989, the rise of militant political Islamism, the dark decade of internal insurgency of the 1990s; and the move to national reconciliation in the 2000s.

These crises unfolded quite differently across the two countries; however, there are also a number of similarities that provide grounds for potentially fruitful comparison. For example, both Egypt and Algeria have suffered major economic crises that provoked serious riots. Both have experienced the unexpected death of a defining leader (Boumedienne and Nasser); a coup (Boumedienne ousting Ben Bella) or coup attempt ('Ali Sabri et al. against Sadat) as part of a leadership change; and have had to deal with domestic Islamic insurgencies (if of different orders), as arguably the most significant domestically generated challenges to the state.

In sum, there is significant and interesting variation in a number of variables that may be salient in challenging a founding story or in constructing national unity and identity, including ethnicity, language, religion, and region. The list above is intended neither to be exhaustive nor to establish that the two countries constitute "comparable cases" from a social science perspective. Moreover, in both cases, economic distributive policies, external assistance, and the coercion of the security forces were central elements in maintaining or restoring order, or enabling the leader or ruling group to survive in power, depending on the episode. Nevertheless, shifts in the portrayals of particular historical episodes or in the definitions of national mission and values found in speeches, official documents, government schoolbooks, and other texts provide strong evidence from the highest levels of leadership that discourse was viewed as an important tool in reinforcing or (re)legitimating political power.

STATE DISCOURSE AS A POLITICAL TOOL

No political leader or elite, even in authoritarian states, rules solely through the threat of coercive violence. All leaderships need some level of support, or at least acquiescence, from the people over whom they rule. Indeed, even the most brutal regimes manifest a strong desire to secure and maintain legitimacy, acceptance by the people of their right to rule.[9]

In considering the bases of acceptance of a given political system or leadership by the population, the political theorist Antonio Gramsci's formulation of hegemony is particularly salient. He argued that in order to understand the power of the state, it was necessary to explore far more than direct forms of control, such as the police, laws, and the courts, which he referred to as "domination." Less tangible elements that shape state authority are also central. Here he was referring to a complex configuration of values, customs, political principles, and social relations accepted throughout society and its institutions at a given historical moment. In his view, it was this set of elements that constituted what he called "hegemony," an indirect form of authority that arose from their broad acceptance in a given polity.[10] While Michel Foucault's notion of hegemony departs significantly from Gramsci's, he also argued that there had been an historical shift in the exercise of power, away from juridical forms that often involved corporal coercion and violence to more complex, and ultimately more effective, technologies of power.[11]

One element key to both Gramsci's formula of hegemony and Foucault's technologies of power is discourse. Ernesto Laclau and Chantal Mouffe define discourse as the means used to organize a society into a structured reality, in order to give it stability and meaning. Some meanings tend to become dominant in the sociopolitical imaginary, and thereby contribute to strengthening a particular cause, political position, or power structure. Discourse, which shapes cultures, identities, and ideologies, is indicative of power relations.[12] However, unlike more tangible material factors like distributive policies or the role of the security forces discussed above, the effect of discourse is generally indirect: "it operates though the 'minds' of people . . . typically exercised through persuasion or other forms of discursive communication, or resulting from fear of sanctions" for noncompliance.[13]

That the control of discourse has been a central concern of authoritarian leaderships is obvious from the experiences of many countries around the world, and certainly those in the MENA region. Algeria's second postindependence president, Houari Boumedienne, made clear that historians were to follow his directives in narrating Algeria's past, and both he and the Egyptian president Anwar al-Sadat established institutions aimed at controlling research and studies on historical periods deemed critical to their image or claim to rule. In addition, in authoritarian political systems like those of Egypt and Algeria, ministries of information, public guidance, press and publications, and the like have been established with the central task of constructing, controlling, and propagating messages, stories, and symbols aimed at generating support, or in some cases, silence, among the citizenry. Although their impact has waned with the rise of alternative information sources, before the globalization of electronic media, authoritarian leaderships exercised significant, and in some cases monopoly, control over such messages through state information outlets, various forms of cultural production (cinema, theater, and literature), educational curricula, and associated pedagogical materials.

A number of concepts help to link the exigencies associated with maintaining political power and the production of official narratives, whether in speeches, policy statements, and national charters, or in perhaps less immediately obvious forms, such as government school textbooks, and museum displays. Studies of China use the term "thought management," defined as activities geared toward making people's thinking conform to the dominant ideology to describe government efforts.[14] The term "linguistic engineering," meaning attempts "to affect people's attitudes and beliefs by manipulating the language that they hear, speak, read, and write," has also been used.[15] While it addresses only one kind of state discourse, the literature on propaganda also offers important lessons for understanding the intent behind and the mechanisms involved in producing official narratives.

Much of the literature on propaganda, defined by Karel Berkhoff as "a deliberate and systematic attempt to shape perceptions, mental states, and above all, behavior, so as to achieve a response that furthers the propagandist's intent,"[16] examines its use in addressing specific challenges. Wartime is one obvious example of a crisis in which a leadership will see a clear need to shape public attitudes and actions. For example, in his classic study *The Birth of the Propaganda State*, Peter Kenez argues that propaganda played a large role both in the 1917 victory of the Bolsheviks and in their retention of power during the subsequent civil war. Their successes, he contends, owed to the fact that they better understood the exigencies of the moment and the nature of the struggle than their enemies did, and adjusted their message and policies accordingly.[17] In a very different case, Lillian Guerra argues that during the Cuban revolution official discourse, far from being simply a backdrop, shaped events and outcomes, in particular in early confrontations with Washington.[18]

As for the role of propaganda in legitimizing colonial ventures, Matthew Stanard notes that wide use of propaganda by imperial powers suggests "that this pro-empire device was an integral and necessary component of overseas rule in the twentieth century as governments and others attempted to manufacture consent in societies of mass politics."[19] Focusing on Belgian colonization of the Congo, he stresses the importance of education, especially at the elementary level, in official efforts to instill an "imperial spirit," arguing that the initiative to introduce "imperial education" was in fact an indicator that the state and its supporters viewed colonial rule as weak or under threat.[20]

The flexibility and multivocality of political messages is another central theme in the literature on propaganda. For example, in his study of Britain during World War I, David Monger explains how different definitions of patriotism were used to appeal to various understandings of duty or purpose among the British population.[21] Anne-Marie Brady uses the example of the relationship between Confucianism and the Chinese Communist Party (CCP) to demonstrate the flexibility of symbols in the context of changing challenges to the regime. She characterizes Confucianism and the CCP as "old foes," yet she shows that in the initial period following Mao's death, when the country faced an identity crisis as it began to open up again to the outside, the party began to selectively reintroduce elements from the Confucian classics, in part to appeal to the large and wealthy Chinese diaspora and in part to expand its tourism market.[22]

Other studies of propaganda illustrate an element that is particularly important for this study: how and why particular narratives or their constituent elements can be changed, even in a relatively short time. In his study of Soviet propaganda, Berkhoff shows that even though in the aftermath of the 1917 revolution, patriotism had been deemed ideologically heretical for its focus on the state and not on class, in the lead-up to World War II patriotism was rehabilitated as a way of generating a sense of duty to defend the homeland.[23] He also details changes in the Soviet encouragement of hatred toward ethnic Germans. Stalin's decision to promote such hatred came, not immediately, but months after the start of the war, suggesting that he had become concerned about levels of domestic loyalty. Then, with the end of the war, this theme disappeared after the Soviet-friendly occupation zone that became the German Democratic Republic was established. Accordingly, when wartime propaganda was subsequently reprinted, the word "fascist" was used to replace "German."[24] Although her focus is on the changing portrayal of Ivan the Terrible, Maureen Perrie makes similar points: "The image of Ivan the Terrible—largely a negative one in the early 1930s—was reconstructed thereafter in order to provide a legitimation for Stalin and his policies through the creation of a positive historical parallel and precedent."[25]

As these examples demonstrate, during episodes of crisis and challenge such as revolution, war, and imperial expansion, leaderships of varying types and of different political systems all understood or at least believed in the importance of constructing, controlling, and at times reshaping elements of the national history, identity, and mission. In some cases, in order to mobilize the population or (re)relegitimize their rule, they drew on earlier historical events or traditions, demonstrating how flexible such elements can be when appropriately framed; in others, they counted on the multiple resonances inherent in well-known concepts. Whether one terms these efforts thought management, propaganda, or something else, the official construction and reconstruction of elements of discourse to serve the ends of leadership survival or regime maintenance have a long history across regions, cultures, and political systems.

THE CONCEPT OF THE NATIONAL NARRATIVE

The national narrative is one key instrument in a leadership's discursive "tool box" to address what are likely to be multiple challenges of legitimation. The term "national narrative" has commonly been used to mean "national history" or "national story," although few of the many authors who invoke it have attempted to provide a clear definition. According to Yaacov Yadgar, "In its simplest sense, the national narrative is the story that a (national) collective tells about itself. It tells the individuals constituting the nation (and anybody else who is interested) who they are, what comprises their past (the national, common one), the structure of their characteristics as a collective, and where they are heading—that is, how they should act in the political realm."[26] Its multiple strands therefore aim at establishing the traits or characteristics—cultural, linguistic, ethnic, religious, and confessional—that are the identity markers of the national community.

It is important here to clarify that although there may be overlap, the national narrative should not be confused or conflated with the concept of collective memory, about which there is an extensive literature.[27] In the first place, collective memory may be the product of the "remembering" or "commemoration" of any group of people, not just those who consider themselves, or are portrayed as, a "nation." Second, and more important, collective memory may be limited to a particular historical episode or event, whereas the national narrative, as Yadgar's definition indicates, generally includes a much larger set of events, as well as components related to a people and/or country's identity, mission, and goals. Depending upon case, the official narrative also, whether implicitly or explicitly, offers a vision of economic and development philosophy, of the relationship between religion and state, the military and the state, and state and society, in addition to a portrayal of the country's (aspired to) regional and international roles.

Perhaps most basic among the narrative's multiple strands is the historical one. While there are certainly variations, official national histories tend to follow similar lines: the story of an ancient past or mythical origin is generally followed by a period of decline, and then a modern movement toward revival. The accounts also include a set of identifiable heroes—past and perhaps present, individuals or collectives, real or mythical. In order to establish the group's distinct identity vis-à-vis others, this strand of the narrative will generally highlight particular events marking the emergence of the national collective. Where possible, the portrayal may reach into the very distant past to claim the glory of earlier civilizations that lived on what has become the nation-state's territory, just as it will likely include examples of both "national" struggles and glory along the path to the present.

Because of the tendency to reach back into a people's distant past and to glorify elements of its identity and mission, some writers have used the term "myth" to refer to the story lines of some national narratives aimed at legitimation.[28] Although drawn from his study of an extreme case, that of Nazi Germany, Ernst Cassirer's work on myths is relevant, for he contends that in the context of challenges that are dangerous and require exceptional efforts, "man will always have recourse to desperate means—and our present-day political myths have been such desperate means."[29] In other words, a focus on major crises or challenges is critical in understanding the content of a narrative; in fact, a political leadership's resort to constructing or evoking heroic narratives, perhaps even bordering on the mythological, is to be expected in such circumstances.

Edmund Burke III's observations regarding former colonies' nationalist histories highlight an additional element particular to the Algerian and Egyptian postindependence national narratives: story lines intended to counter the basic contentions of the colonial narrative, often those related to lack of or fractured identities or to purported backward essences of the population. In reaction, postindependence elites generally embraced the language and practices associated with an unexamined "modernization." Just as potentially problematic, the need to counter the colonial narrative has often led to an internalization or unreflexive adoption of its epistemology. For example, colonial historians generally attribute a progressive character (*mission civilisatrice*) to colonization which is then contested by nationalist movements and histories. However, rather than constructing new categories, the colonial dichotomies were generally retained, the most important change being that the heroes and villains simply change places: "If, for the French writers, France was the bearer of progress and resisters were coded as obscurantist reactionaries, nationalists told the opposite story, in which the French appeared as oppressors and Algerians as noble defenders of their way of life and cultural patrimony."[30]

Whatever its structure and features, the primary goal of the narrative's historical presentation is not accuracy but creating what has been called "a usable past":[31] a set of heroes, events, and/or story lines that can be marshaled to serve the needs of the leadership, whether the goal is securing or reconsolidating power or facing down internal or external challenges. The official scriptings of both the past and the present are intended to shape popular understandings and responses to the socioeconomic, political, and religio-cultural environment in ways that will serve regime ends. Thus, they must be understood as closely intertwined with the leadership's claim to legitimacy and the polity's (and their) presumed collective future.

NATIONAL IDENTITY AND UNITY IN THE NARRATIVE

The most basic task of an official narrative is—through a combination of simple exposition and more complex construction—to establish the identity markers of a unified national community, and to do so in a way that presents them as natural or given. Most scholars currently writing about identity and nationalism agree that there is nothing primordial about the existence of modern nations,[32] yet they disagree on the extent of identity *construction* that has been required to shape them. At one end of the spectrum is Eric Hobsbawm, who wrote about what he called *invented* traditions: those symbolizing membership in groups, real or artificial; those establishing or legitimizing institutions or relations of authority; and those whose main purpose was the inculcation of beliefs and value systems.[33] At the other end is Anthony Smith, who asks why, if the nation is simply invented, it has had such deep resonance across cultures, regions, and time.[34] The most critical point for the purpose of this presentation is to stipulate that although many themes in the narrative likely draw on elements that resonate with the populace, some aspects of national identity and its markers may in fact be of more recent origin.

The first step toward establishing the parameters of national membership involves distinguishing between insiders and outsiders. The physical boundaries of the nation-state are one obvious place to start, but geography alone is rarely sufficient to frame "the people." In her discussion of the Israeli national narrative, Yael Zerubavel emphasizes the importance of constructing a different kind of "great divide" between the target people and all others, which is then used both to undermine any denial of the group's legitimacy and to justify its claim to a distinct unity.[35] Such insider-outsider status is generally constructed on the basis of language, religion, historical experience, and the like. Smith's point that nationalism cannot be conjured up without reference points that resonate with the population is very important; this study nonetheless assumes that there is no necessary "natural" or given basis of unity in a territorially bounded modern nation-state. The elements that are selected or emerge to define the unity of "the people" are contingent upon a set of historical and material factors that are related to the challenges of regime legitimacy and state-building. Rather than looking for a standard set of elements across cases that serve as the bases of national unity, we should expect that key elements in the official narrative regarding unity will be the product of distinct histories and experiences.[36]

One way to construct unity among a large population is through least common denominators or flexible parameters. For example, a regime may appeal to a relatively broad base of "the people" by adopting a notion of unity that admits of various elements of diversity. In the case of Egypt, references to the area's pharaonic past provide a more inclusive basis of identity than one based on the country's Islamic heritage.[37] In the Syrian case, historical aspects of Ba'thist ideology have been "intentionally vague in order to help incorporate disparate groups into a nation-state, minimizing conflict and promoting consensus."[38] To the degree that official national symbols and prescribed identity markers offer multiple interpretations, points of entry, or affiliations, they can underpin a notion of the nation and national unity which is relatively broad and inclusive. Nonetheless, such flexibility has its limits, and must in any case be understood as marshaled to serve the kind of unity envisioned by its initiators.

James Wertsch argues that, unlike other collectivities, modern states attach a special importance to establishing a set of shared natural characteristics or essences, such as language, religion, or history, which define a national group as distinct from others. These essences, which are understood as binding the people together, are defended, not only by the state, but by the citizenry as well. "The temptation for states to inculcate such views is very strong and such practices can be found the world over."[39] As a result, a flexible basis of national unity has often been deemed insufficient. Instead, what is often demanded of the people is in fact *homogeneity*, whether on ethnic, religious, linguistic, and/or ideological grounds. In such cases, leaders expect, not just unity in the form of loyalty to the state (and to them), but an actual homogenization of identity along narrower, more exclusivist lines.

In support of this same point, Ernest Gellner argued that industrial society requires a culture that is disciplined and homogenized, and that only the central state has the ability to undertake this task. Moreover, "the only way a given culture can protect itself against another one, which already has its particular protector-state, is to acquire one of its own. . . . The state-cultures live in competition with each other."[40] According to this formulation, then, homogenization is, in effect, a requirement of national/cultural survival in a competitive international system. Michael Hechter, on the other hand, examines the drive for homogenization from the perspective of state-building, and contends that it has been the growth of direct rule in multinational polities that has militated for cultural homogenization. Under the indirect rule of many colonial regimes of an earlier era, cultural diversity did not threaten the social order. Not until the coming of political systems based on greater centralization of power did such diversity appear as a threat, and the state therefore undertook the task of promoting new traditions, symbols, and ceremonies in order to transfer attachments away from traditional local authorities to the new central state.[41]

In countries characterized by a paucity of "natural" bases of national unity—as is often argued, for example, in the cases of Lebanon, Iraq, and Syria, where multiple confessional, ethnic, or linguistic groups were forcibly united into a single national entity by agreements made by external powers—such potentially centrifugal identity forces are likely to appear all the more threatening to a leadership. Given the resultant fragility of the bases of a unitary national identity among such peoples, the quest for stability has often led states to engage in coercion to preempt potential challenges. In the process, however, many voices may be marginalized or silenced. Burke argues that nationalist narratives have particular difficulty in accepting the legitimacy of differing interests or conflict among the population.[42] In practice, this lack of flexibility in constructing identity results in a repressive homogeneity that is more inclined to villainize those regarded as "others." Postcolonial national narratives may have an even greater predisposition to this coercive homogenization than others because the defensive nationalism of anti-imperial movements often produced a strong negative othering of anything associated with the colonial past. As a result, ethnic, religious, or linguistic characteristics of the population that were politicized by the former colonizer as part of a divide-and-rule strategy, as was the case of the Kabyle/Berbers in Algeria, may then be suppressed by the nationalist leadership as the bases of postindependence unity are determined.

Whatever basis or bases may be selected or emerge as the parameters of unity, challenges in constructing and policing such a unity will inevitably continue to arise, and in order to maintain power and legitimacy, the leadership will be forced to respond. Even in the context of repression, the state is never able to eliminate alternative or competing visions of the nation. "The most successful states are able to contain these conceptions within relatively depoliticized spaces; but even where such states are older, as in Western Europe, there are overt challenges to the established national form in almost every nation."[43] Thus, as Homi Bhabha has argued, the nation is really an "impossible unity":[44] not only does it comprise myriad actors and forces, but they are continually changing.

Finally, even if national unity or the need for it is proclaimed by a leadership and promoted by the official narrative,[45] ruling groups often engage in divide-and-rule strategies aimed at different sectors of the population. An obvious example of such an approach in the MENA region is Jordan, where alongside proclamations insisting upon the unity of the people of all backgrounds, the government engages in a range of discriminatory practices against Jordanians of Palestinian origin. In such cases, asserting unity based on one set of characteristics may be used to obscure the intention of the regime (or a part of it) to instrumentalize existing fracture lines as a way of maintaining control.

LEGITIMACY AND LEGITIMATION IN THE NARRATIVE

The first task of a national narrative is defining the people, but this is not an end in and of itself. Rather, it serves to specify the boundaries of the political community, which is then the subject of or subject to the broader narrative's collective mission or goals. One of the most important of these goals is legitimation, the process by which a leadership secures the people's acknowledgement of its right to rule. In some countries in the so-called developing or postcolonial world, in which national borders are relatively recent and were often imposed by the former imperial power, the problem is more acute than elsewhere, for the ruling elite need a narrative that legitimizes, not only their role, but the very existence of the country as a single, unitary entity. As part of the legitimation process, the leadership, which may well have come to power through other than a recognized, institutionalized process, must succeed in constructing its interests as coincident with those of the public and the public good. It must, therefore, obscure the actual differences between state-building efforts intended to serve the citizenry in general, on the one hand, and policies aimed at regime consolidation—the reinforcement of the hold on power of an interconnected set of leaders or elites (political, economic, religious, etc.)—on the other. Without such a link, masking the distance or difference in interests between the ruling elite and the people, a key part of the narrative's legitimizing project will fail.

Once that link is made, or at least asserted, the task is then to mobilize support for the leadership's guiding ideology and the policies that flow from it. In some countries, it may be possible to construct a "national" history that suggests approaches to present challenges. In other words, implicit parallels may be drawn with past historical threats or events, which then serve as morality tales for the present. In both Algeria and Egypt, heroic episodes of struggle against invaders in past centuries were marshaled as evidence of the two peoples' ability in the present to confront whatever threats might arise. In other cases, what may be required is less a direct use of history and more a construction of the bases of the people's obligations to the nation or country. Here, presumptively shared values and goals may be instrumentalized. Such was the approach used by the Algerian leadership in the 1990s as it sought to construct a long-standing national value of tolerance derived from Islam in the face of a violent domestic insurgency that based its violent opposition to the state in purported Islamic values.

By scripting challenges as deep and perhaps even existential, the official narrative establishes the bases of responsibility to the country and the nation (and by implication the leadership), exhorting the people to serve, protect, and even die for them. The threats prompting such mobilization may be external, such as the shadow of armed conflict or attempts by foreign powers to infringe upon domestic sovereignty, as in Egypt in response to defeat in the 1967 war. Or, as both the Egyptian and Algerian cases amply demonstrate, crises may also proceed from the domestic front: economic challenges, such as industrial development, agricultural reform, educational expansion, and poverty reduction; sociocultural ones related to ethnicity, language, or religion; or political ones related to power sharing and resource access. Whichever the case, the official narrative must articulate a national identity, generally presented as unity, that is capable of mobilizing "the people" to confront such threats, whether real or fabricated. It must concomitantly make the case for why those in power are deserving of loyalty or allegiance, that is, legitimate, as these challenges are faced.

In his classic formulation, Max Weber distinguished three types of authority or legitimacy: charismatic, traditional, and legal-rational.[46] A leadership may draw on more than one of these sources of legitimacy, just as the legitimacy formula (and the narrative accompanying it) may shift from one type to another or involve a different mixture of elements over time. Although a national narrative generally specifies national heroes, it is rarely about a single leader. Hence, according to Weber's formulation, a narrative constructing a charismatic basis for legitimacy is likely be found in states where the heroic role of a particular leader is central to the national imaginary or identity. Egypt's Nasser certainly fits in this category, as do Tunisia's first president, Habib Bourguiba, and the founder of the Turkish Republic, Mustafa Kemal Atatürk. In systems based in traditional authority, on the other hand, one would expect to find strong religious and cultural or patrimonial elements, perhaps in the form of tribal or royal heritage, as crucial to the definition of national unity. Here from the MENA region, one could cite King 'Abdallah of Saudi Arabia or King Muhammad VI of Morocco. As for legal-rational leadership, one would expect unity to be constructed at least in part around values of citizen participation and democracy, although leaderships legitimized in other terms often attempt to associate some of the trappings of legal-rational authority with their rule as well.

One legitimating formula for national unity that Weber's classification misses, and that is critical for studying politics and narratives in the postcolonial world, is revolutionary legitimacy. Here, a coup or a protracted struggle has brought a new leadership or a new political entity to independence, and those who come to rule it base their right to do so on having led or participated in that struggle. They may or may not be charismatic, or hail from traditionally powerful or influential segments of society (tribes or religious figures); they may, once in power, engage in various forms of patrimonial politics to reinforce their position. However, their prior claim to rule derives first and foremost from their role in the revolution. Here again, Egypt's Nasser and Sadat, as well as all four of Algeria's postindependence presidents, may be considered examples.

Other bases of legitimacy have also been invoked by postindependence leaderships, as will be seen in the case studies. In Algeria, for example, a battle, both political and discursive, was waged between those who claimed "historic legitimacy," based on their role in planning and launching the war of national liberation in 1954, and those who claimed "revolutionary legitimacy" for having fought in the war, even if they had not been among the planners. In the case of Egypt, we see a shift from Nasser's post-1952 revolutionary legitimacy (at least until the debacle of the 1967 war) to what his successor, Anwar al-Sadat, called institutional or constitutional legitimacy, which he claimed as he gradually set the country on a different economic and political course. Most recently, following the highly contested removal of President Muhammad Mursi in July 2013, the latter's supporters insisted upon Egypt's first civilian president's electoral or constitutional legitimacy, while his opponents claimed popular legitimacy based on the massive street demonstrations that called for early elections.

Finally, it is important to note that although the narrative may present a president, general, or king as the symbol of national power, its legitimizing task need not be limited to any one particular leader. What is generally at stake is the power, not of a single individual, but of a broader ruling group. In cases where the target of legitimation efforts is a set of political, economic, or cultural relationships, it is the broader regime that the official narrative will seek to reinforce.

THE HOW AND WHY OF NARRATIVE RESCRIPTING

If one accepts Bhabha's contention, noted above, that nations are impossible unities because of the presence of competing and ever-changing forces among the population, then one should expect that the national narrative, whose tasks include promoting a particular notion of national history, identity, and mission, will also periodically be contested. Economic crisis, domestic opposition, the rise of new social, cultural, or political forces, foreign intervention, increased literacy, rural-urban migration: all of these factors and many others can challenge existing official constructions of who belongs to the nation and who does not, on what bases inclusion or exclusion should rest, how economic resources and political access are secured, and who has the right to rule.

When such developments occur, challenging some aspect of the legitimating narrative, a leadership would be expected to respond to protect or reinforce its position. Political scientists most often read responses in policy shifts, and often, in the case of authoritarian regimes, the expectation is that some type of overt coercive force will be brought to bear. However, as noted at the outset, leaderships have a range of instruments at their disposal and although they may well view changes in discourse alone as insufficient to ward off a particular challenge, that does not mean that they regard narrative shifts as without significant political value. As a result, the emergence of such challenges may prompt a reconstruction of constituent elements of the narrative. Boumedienne's and Sadat's institutional efforts to control the historical narrative as part of their struggles to secure or maintain legitimacy were noted above, and there is clear evidence of similar efforts by other leaders, such as Saddam Hussein[47] and Mustafa Kemal Atatürk,[48] facing state-building or state-threatening challenges.

Given the importance that such leaders attributed to shaping the official narrative, such political strategies demand closer examination and more careful study. What types of crises may trigger leaderships to introduce narrative reconfigurations, and what forms/content will the changes assume? Which elements may be appropriated for construction, reinterpretation, introduction, or exclusion, and which will remain intact? These are the questions this study seeks to answer.

Cases from other regions demonstrate ways in which national stories can be modified, but much of the literature focuses on collective memory, not on official narratives. None of the works concerned with the state systematically explore the relationship between the sociopolitical environment and rescriptings of the official narrative. Some suggest the importance of economic transformations, changes in state leadership, and the like for possible changes in the official narrative, but the nature of the relationship between regime and narrative is not a central empirical or theoretical focus. Indeed, the very concept of national narrative is underexplored and certainly undertheorized in academic literature in general, regardless of discipline or region of study.

This is not a work of historiography. The only contribution to the historical narratives offered here is in perhaps substantiating over time when and how the official narrative itself played a role in legitimizing successive regimes. Thus, there is no attempt to evaluate the truth claims of Egyptian or Algerian national historiography, or to correct errors in the portrayals of episodes of national history as read through the official sources consulted. Instead, this study is intended most broadly as a contribution to the literature on change and resilience in authoritarian regimes, as it focuses on the relationship between narrative rescriptings and regime maintenance. It attempts, in the first instance, to discern the content of the themes of founding story and of national identity and unity as they have evolved over time in government sources. Then, using that content, the official narrative's evolution since independence is analyzed against the backdrop of episodes of national political or economic challenges.

It is also important to stress that this study does not attempt to argue that the implementation of changes in various aspects of the narrative caused a particular change in political behavior among the target population. Such a focus would have required a different set of questions, sources, and methods, and previous studies have indicated how difficult a proposition this is. For example, in his study of the content of British propaganda and the National War Aims Committee that produced it, Monger argues that to have also attempted to gauge the impact of state propaganda on civilian morale—solely for the period 1917–18—would have required a much longer study.[49] Berkhoff also underlines the problems involved in determining the impact of Soviet propaganda, citing a survey of Soviet citizens who had recently left the country and whose assessments of the effects of the state efforts differed.[50] Similarly, Stanard notes the difficulty of gauging the impact of colonial propaganda on Belgian public opinion under King Leopold II (1865–1909).[51] Thus to reiterate, the focus here is on explaining the implementation of narrative change, not regime success or failure in its discursive efforts.

There are numerous factors to consider in studying crises and possible official narrative response. Among the most obvious are: the nature of the crisis—precipitous or gradual, economic, political, or cultural; its source—foreign, internal to the regime or from within society; and its severity—does the challenge threaten regime survival, or does it open up possibilities for extending control? All of these may play a role in determining which elements of the narrative remain untouched, which may be marshaled to new ends, and whether new themes may be introduced. Some story lines may have such a long history in the official narrative that it would seem heretical—that is to say, be impossible—to remove them. In other words, it may be that as a result of the success of earlier strategies of narrative consolidation or implantation, certain elements simply cannot be eliminated without undermining a basis of the elite's legitimacy. In such cases, one alternative is rescripting or reinterpretation, as we shall see in Sadat's successive adaptations of the meaning of the 1952 Egyptian revolution. On the other hand, a leadership may introduce modifications while pursuing policies that effectively empty a problematic element of its content, as with the continued invocation of "socialism" in both the Egyptian and Algerian narratives well after it had been abandoned in practice as a guiding economic policy.

Although they do not have the same focus, some previous studies of national narratives and propaganda offer some hints as to what we may find. Ann Anagnost's work on China underlines the fundamental contention that it is particularly during periods of crisis that gaps in the national narrative may appear, and new forms of representation of the past may be needed to reinforce a unity in the present.[52] Wertsch suggests that the changes introduced will in part depend upon the nature of the crisis, showing that whereas in the pre-Gorbachev era narrative rescripting had been caused by intra-elite struggles, under Gorbachev, changes in the narrative resulted from a dramatic change of regime, which transformed what had formerly been identified as evil into good, and vice versa.[53]

Sam Kaplan's work on Turkey illustrates how the nature of the narrative reshaping may also depend upon whether the crisis is sudden or more gradual, showing that changes in government, first in 1946 and then in 1980, led to shifts in the place of religion in the curriculum. After having been excluded as a school subject under Atatürk, religious studies were reintroduced in 1946, although Turkey's 1961 Constitution left the decision as to whether to take such classes to the student's family. After the coup in 1980, the military came to regard a particular construction of religion as an ally against the political Left, and the new Constitution of 1982 made instruction in religious culture and moral education compulsory in the primary and secondary school curriculum, thus further integrating Islam into the state's portrayal of Turkish identity.[54]

Nels Johnson's work on the evolution of Islamic content in the Palestinian national movement helps explain how such reinterpretations or reconstructions are possible. He argues that because they are not organic systems, ideologies (which underpin national narratives), are innately flexible and hence can and do change: "their constituent symbols do not share such close functional relationships that a change in one aspect leads inevitably to changes in the whole system . . . ideologies can easily change in several domains while still preserving an overall illusion of order and internal coherency." It is the multivocality of ideologies' constituent symbols that accounts for this flexibility enabling them to apply to a variety of situations, "yet still maintain recognizable boundaries and limitations."[55] Therefore, when entrenched power relations underpinning the dominant ideology are challenged, what results is more a change in emphasis or meaning than a completely new order of narration.[56]

Before concluding this section, several other works on aspects of national narrative and state discourse in countries in the MENA region should be mentioned. Without question the most extensive work has been done on Israeli narratives, or, rather, on the competition between Israeli and Palestinian narratives.[57] For Lebanon, Kamal Salibi's landmark study *A House of Many Mansions* discusses competing subnational narratives between different confessional groups.[58] Besides Kaplan's *The Pedagogical State*, cited above, there are several other works that address aspects of national identity and the official narrative in Turkey.[59] Also worthy of mention is Ofra Bengio's *Saddam's Word: Political Discourse in Iraq*, which seeks to discern the implications of changes in the political use of language.[60] The concerns of all of these studies overlap to some degree with this book, but none takes on the same set of questions regarding the rationale and impetus for official narrative shifts over time.

SOURCES FOR READING THE NATIONAL NARRATIVE

The focus here on the official narrative does not imply a lack of recognition of the existence of actors and forces outside the state that contribute to the production of other, often competing, story lines or values. Nor does it suggest that such alternative narratives have no power of their own. However, the goal here is to understand when and how a national political leadership uses elements of the narrative to consolidate or legitimate its power. States have at their disposal many possible texts or instruments for inculcating particular elements of the official narrative, or simply patriotism more broadly, including films, music, and television serials.[61] While in no way discounting the potential impact of these cultural vehicles, the focus here is on official texts or statements promulgated directly by governmental bodies, leaders, and recognized spokespeople.

State documents are tangible, broadly circulated or available at the time of their publication and use, in some cases produced over time in successive iterations, and generally accessible to researchers. Among them, perhaps most basic are national constitutions, which, as Prasenjit Duara has observed, "authorize" or remake the people.[62] In their preambles, they generally define the contours of the nation, and in the introduction or through subsequent articles, they embody key social, political, cultural, and economic values. In other words, they "constitute" the people.[63] Governments also periodically issue major summaries of or proposals for the (re)construction of state-society relations, often called "national charters." These documents are generally drafted as part of a process of national or political elite reflection to learn from the past or to chart a new course for the future. Hence, they, too, tend to comment on elements of national identity, just as they frequently reconstruct the national mission or signal significant shifts in political practice or official ideology. A third category of critical documents are those issued by the head of state or other leading officials, either in the form of speeches on key occasions or major discourses on policy or philosophy, such as Muʿammar al-Qaddafi's now infamous *Green Book*, or as will be examined in this study, Nasser's *Falsafat al-thawra* (Philosophy of the Revolution).

Obviously, these documents are not all created equal, whether in terms of level of saliency, shelf life, popular consumption, or impact. Speeches are more likely to be heard by large parts of the population, and they are also the most responsive to sudden developments or crises. Preambles in constitutions or historical introductions in national charters, on the other hand, are not produced with the expectation of regular revision in response to short-term challenges. Yet, precisely because they may be among the most enduring, because parts of them may be studied in schools, and because they are often subject to popular referendum, their portrayals of the nation are extremely important subjects for analysis of the way a leadership seeks to define the people and national goals. They can serve either to underpin the content of subsequently issued documents or to create cognitive dissonance if leaders decide to move away from their bases or principles.

It is certainly important to take into account the type of document from which one is drawing when analyzing its contribution to the national narrative; however, it would seem a mistake to exclude any of these sources based on the different roles they play or their shelf life. Indeed, a wide variety of sources was consulted for this study precisely to permit as thorough a portrayal of the parameters of the narrative as possible at any given time. All of them contribute *in their own way* to shaping its contours and content: unequally, unevenly, and in some cases, as we shall see, even contradictorily.

In addition to these documents, school textbooks are an obvious, rich source for reading the official narrative, and this study draws extensively on them. "Schools are more than bureaucratic institutions serving the public. They are state projects, both totalizing and individualizing, in which various forms of knowledge are deployed, imparting a sense of purpose and coherence to a population," Kaplan writes.[64] Ernest Gellner even went so far as to revise Weber when he claimed that for a state, "The monopoly of legitimate education is now more important, more central than the monopoly of legitimate violence."[65] At least in the highly centralized educational systems such as those found in most postcolonial political systems, there is a bounded set of textbooks, all children in public schools use them, and students are exposed to their content repeatedly over many years. As a result, the opportunities for inculcating a state-sponsored version of history, identity, and mission through textbooks are much greater than through perhaps any other source to which broad sectors of the population, in this case, children, the vital next generation, are exposed.

This central role of educational institutions in propagating official messages and ideologies is widely accepted by scholars. For example, in the Soviet case, Kenez highlights the importance of literacy campaigns as one instrument in the Bolsheviks' struggle to mobilize the population and spread their ideology.[66] Başak İnce examines the importance of literacy campaigns in Turkey, specifically the role of the so-called People's Houses, which were part of state efforts to control the areas of education, history, and language, three elements that were seen as key to forging a national identity and preventing the emergence of unwanted other identities among the citizenry.[67] The goal was to secure cultural legitimacy for the new regime, in part by eliminating the Islamic and Ottoman heritage, but also by creating a new culture that fused Western and older Turkic elements.[68]

A number of other studies of MENA countries have specifically examined the content and role of textbooks.[69] Valuable as they all are, most have focused on a relatively short period of time, have been ethnographic in nature, and/or have been single-country studies. None have attempted to use school texts to explore larger questions of narrative transformation over time and their relationship to regime maintenance.

Several words of caution are in order, however, regarding government textbooks and the narrative. First, a model that assumes a well-functioning educational system over which the state or its agents have full control is an ideal type, far removed from the reality of many state school systems around the world. In Egypt and Algeria, countries in which universal education was an explicit goal, the questions of how successful educational infrastructure expansion and delivery have been, and what percentage of the school-age population actually attends school, loom large. At independence, training sufficient numbers of teachers and providing quality physical infrastructure were major challenges in many countries; and in the new millennium, after decades of "Washington consensus" policies of starving social service line items in state budgets, such problems have recurred or been exacerbated.

Another issue is the production of teaching materials. Some analyses assume an infrastructure capable of crafting such materials, when such a set of institutions may well not exist, may be staffed by incompetent bureaucrats, or may include cadres who hold competing views of the state or the nation. Just as important is the question of how teachers conduct their classes and use textbook content, as Gregory Starrett, Fida Adely, and Linda Herrera and Carlos Torres point out, documenting examples of teachers refusing to teach certain elements or transcending them through class discussions.[70]

Finally, school textbooks generally are not recrafted overnight; indeed, the process of reforming or rewriting any curricular elements (whether they have import for the national narrative or target changes in pedagogy) is often contentious and drawn-out. Therefore, changes in interpretation, orientation, or content of the narrative may first be expected to appear in other government documents, such as speeches. In the meantime, traditional elements continue to be inculcated through schooling, thus at times creating dissonance between different official texts, potentially affecting the outcome that narrative changes are intended to achieve.

One may reasonably respond that in attempting to understand the content of all these official documents, a prior question arises regarding the identity of those responsible for crafting them. If we take the national story as presented in history textbooks, speeches by national leaders on key occasions, constitutions, and other key state documents as the primary sources of the state-sanctioned narrative, we have a host of potential sources of input. Beyond the leader, his political confidants, and perhaps high political party officials, there are also functionaries in relevant ministries (education, religious affairs, information or guidance, etc.) and perhaps specialized committees that determine or have input into the content of school curriculum and other salient national documents. Such an approach then begs the question of how those who help craft the narrative and those to whom they must answer—political, economic, cultural, and religious elites—have come to conceive of the national story in the first place. I examine aspects of the broader institutional context, as well as the ideological inclinations of some of the key personalities involved in shaping regime approaches to history and national identity. However, a more detailed sociology of those involved in the production of the narratives over more than half a century in two different countries is beyond the scope of this work.

Relatedly, it is clear that there is rarely complete unity regarding societal and political goals, even in centralized and coercive authoritarian systems. Therefore, the process of determining narrative content and change is likely to involve at least some contestation, and the end products may therefore manifest incongruities. Indeed, I provide evidence of such inconsistencies in several episodes. This lack of coherence or contradictions does not in any way undermine the rationale for this study. Rather, it further underlines some of the challenges a leadership faces in attempting to use narrative rescripting as a way of confronting crises.

WHAT LIES AHEAD

National narratives have many strands or elements, and it would have been impossible to trace all of them for a study covering more than sixty years of Egyptian and Algerian history. Therefore, three central narrative themes were selected for close examination over time: the founding story, the elements that have been promoted as constitutive of national identity, and the construction of the concept of national unity. The presentation is organized into country case studies, each comprising two chapters that proceed chronologically. The country cases begin with a brief summary of key episodes of crises since their respective revolutions. Basic historical background follows so that the reader can appreciate the origins of certain narrative themes that predate the respective revolutions. The chapters then proceed to establish how each theme was initially presented by the immediate postrevolutionary leadership. Those portrayals in turn serve as a baseline of sorts for the chapters' detailed explorations of speeches, national charters, constitutions (as well as postage stamp series and museum content), in addition to a particularly careful examination of textbooks and educational reform programs. The goal is to discern and then analyze changes in the construction of key elements of the official national narrative in order to understand how these rescriptings may have been expected to serve the interests of the leadership. To that end, the socioeconomic and political context is drawn upon for insights into how the changes in portrayal or use of the founding story or national identity may have seemed a useful tool in addressing the challenge. Chapter 6 attempts to draw broader lessons about the nature of crises and narrative rescripting. The Epilogue then examines post–spring 2011 developments and their implications for the argument.

Admittedly, an attempt to determine intent after the fact raises some issues, the most obvious of which is the temptation to attribute causality where there may have been none. How can we intuit what a leadership's intent was, as opposed to attributing it post facto based on the subsequent historical record? One partial check on this is prior familiarity with the regimes and countries in question—that is to say, outside of this study of their narrative production. Previous knowledge of the crises and challenges faced by the Algerian and Egyptian states helps mitigate the possibility of arriving at conclusions based solely on the explorations for this study. That said, one could argue that such familiarity may also have set particular frames or parameters—kinds of knowledge—that are difficult to escape or interrogate. All I can say in response is that, in looking at a wide range of both primary and secondary sources, I have tried to read in an informed fashion, but also to remain open to new information and interpretations. Short of claims in memoirs or interviews in which deliberate intent is conveyed, we must admit that such findings may be suggestive, but perhaps not always conclusive.

Another check on *post hoc, ergo propter hoc* conclusions is to remain cognizant of the fact that, although coercive, these regimes are neither all-powerful nor necessarily efficient or effective. In making decisions regarding narrative content, a leader or leadership is certainly seeking to employ symbols with emotive power. Yet elites are not always capable of predicting what will and will not be effective. Indeed, they may be clumsy, out of touch, or not particularly perceptive: they can and do make mistakes. One need only recall a few of the many political blunders made by regimes across the MENA region in their quest to stay in power. The disaster of the June 1967 war for Egypt, and the Algerian military's decision to overturn parliamentary election results in 1991, which triggered the outbreak of the more generalized violence of the 1990s, are only two of the most damning examples.

In sum, in trying to control elements of the national narrative and discipline the nation's unity and national identity, a leadership may skillfully reconfigure its components as one of a series of policies to enable itself to survive a political or economic challenge. It may, on the other hand, clumsily misread the lay of the land and attempt to introduce changes that fail to reinforce national unity; or, in resisting change, it may unintentionally set in motion unseen forces that it is unable to control. Both country cases offer examples of apparently poor intuition or understanding of the nature of the challenges and their possible solutions. It is to a careful, comparative examination of the historical record of these processes of narrative rescripting and their implications for regime and leadership maintenance in Egypt and Algeria that we now turn.

2 EGYPT UNDER NASSER

The Evolution of Revolution

THE EGYPTIAN FREE OFFICERS REVOLUTION OF 23 JULY 1952 marked the end of millennia of control of what had become modern Egypt by nonindigenous rulers and dynasties. Power relations among the coup makers themselves took some months to stabilize, but the new military leadership nonetheless moved ahead swiftly to consolidate its rule. One instrument in the consolidation process was the propagation of a narrative of the revolution with dimensions that both exceeded a mere coup and aspired to introduce change well beyond the initial abolition of the monarchy. Although it proudly proclaimed Egypt's 7,000-year history, and was mindful of the development of the state under the Ottoman viceroy Mehmet Ali (1769–1849),[1] who launched an ambitious program of economic and military modernization, the new story did not simply build on the past. Instead, it sought to justify both the ouster of the monarch and the drive for broad-based development in the context of a truly sovereign and independent Egyptian state ruled by Egyptians. Indeed, ensuring sovereignty, striving for social justice, and, as regional politics evolved, leading a transnational Arab people or community (*umma*) all became central to Egypt's mission and definition as constructed and practiced between 1952 and 1970.

To provide context and a basis for comparison, this chapter begins with a brief discussion of the Egyptian national narrative *prior* to the 1952 revolution. It then examines in detail the discursive responses by the Free Officers and their supporters to the first and most basic challenge to the postmonarchical regime: that of legitimation, establishing the right to rule. From there the chapter is organized around subsequent episodes that constituted potential challenges or threats to President Gamal Abdel Nasser's leadership: the 1956 Suez war, the

Syrian-Egyptian union, the 1961 Syrian secession, and the disastrous 1967 war. Drawing on a range of official texts produced in the wake of each event, the presentation seeks to discern what, if any, changes in the narrative—founding story, elements of identity, construction of national unity—appeared.

IDENTITY AND NATIONAL STORY PRIOR TO 1952

The lack of agreement among historians regarding the founding of the modern Egyptian state—with some dating it to the beginning of the Ottoman period and others to Mehmet Ali—is noted in the preface to an Egyptian history textbook published in 1991.[2] In the late nineteenth and early twentieth centuries, however, the debate was more about the broader roots of Egyptian identity than the origins of the Egyptian state. During this period, there were several different trends, from those who argued that Egypt's pharaonic heritage was a precursor to Greek and Roman civilization, making the country Mediterranean or Western in character, to those who viewed pharaonic civilization as unconnected to what they variously regarded as a primarily Islamic, Egyptian-Islamic, or Arab Islamic society, shaped most basically by the Arab conquests of the seventh century CE.

On the question of the role and appeal of Egypt's ancient heritage, Elliott Colla has pointed out the association of pharaonic society with tyranny in both the Jewish and Coptic traditions. For Muslims, this was the pre-Islamic period of ignorance, or *jahiliyya*, although there was recognition of the scientific and technological achievements of the ancient Egyptians.[3] The symbols of ancient Egypt were relatively marginal to the 1919 revolution, which forced the British formally to end their protectorate over Egypt and allowed for the promulgation of a constitution. However, they soon took on importance for the nationalist leaders of the period, because they suggested that Egypt had long ago been sovereign, and that "Egyptian national identity predated and transcended the religious, class and regional differences of modern Egyptians."[4] Indeed, during this period, adherents of ideologies across the political spectrum made "thematic use" of ancient Egypt, thereby demonstrating the flexibility of pharaonic history and symbols,[5] which included the possibilities of marshaling them to undermine Islam as a primary form of identification and open the way for a new identity.[6]

These discourses were about identity and not necessarily *nationalist*, but pharaonism did figure in the evolution of various strands of Egyptian nationalism as well.[7] Israel Gershoni and James Jankowski have argued that different visions of Egyptian identity and nationhood emerged in the first half of the twentieth century and gradually evolved from a territorially defined nationalism with a strong pharaonic component in the 1920s to supranational identities that drew on Egyptian society's Muslim and Arab identities by the 1930s. "[U]rbanization, educational expansion and the formation of new occupational groups," with reference points that were more Arabo-Islamic, led several supranational or transnational ideologies to displace the more limited, territorially based nationalism of the small Westernized and less religious political elite. First came what Gershoni and Jankowski term Egyptian-Islamic nationalism, which rejected pharaonism as a European-inspired "revival of paganism."[8] What followed, they argue, was the emergence of two other ideologies, which they label integral Egyptian nationalism and Egyptian Arab nationalism. The focus of the former was on Egyptian greatness, regardless of historical period; far from rejecting the pharaonic past, it regarded it as the earliest stage in Egyptian greatness, which continued at least until the arrival of the Ottomans.[9] As for Egyptian Arab nationalism, language was key and preceded religion as a basis of identity, although there was no real contradiction, since Islam was seen as an Arab product. Adherents of this view saw no contradiction in being both Egyptian and Arab, although they regarded Egypt as a center of Arab cultural development and a natural political leader of the Arab world, at very least primus inter pares.[10]

In his careful critique of their work, Charles Smith argues that Gershoni and Jankowski's evidence suggests, not the emergence of successive identity-related movements, but rather, "the ability of multiple 'imaginings' to coexist around a core vision of an Egyptian territorial state, whatever the dominant ideology of the moment."[11] In any case, echoing the earlier work of P. J. Vatikiotis, Smith agrees with Gershoni and Jankowski that what later came to be known as Nasserism "was the heir of Egyptian Arab nationalism of the 1930s and that Egypt's Pan-Arabism of the 1950s and 1960s owed much to the supra-Egyptianism of previous decades."[12]

As for official historiography, Anthony Gorman's work on the late nineteenth and early twentieth centuries shows that the historians of the era were part of the state administration, not independent scholars. Their dependence upon royal patronage therefore virtually ensured that they would produce works praising Mehmet Ali and his successors, thus legitimating the ruling dynasty.[13] In state documents of the period, we can "read" the elements of an official narrative. The first relevant administrative document is that establishing a consultative council (*majlis shura al-nuwwab*) in 1866 under Khedive Isma'il.[14]

However, this document stipulates only that those who were elected had to be sons of the homeland (*watan*), with no further comment defining "the people" or explaining their history. Perhaps its most interesting element is that in setting the dates for the convening of the council, it uses neither the Islamic nor the Western calendar, but the Coptic one.[15] The highly touted, but also short-lived, Constitution of 1882, promulgated in the wake of the 'Urabi revolt,[16] also lacked an historical preamble. However, it did specify that Arabic was to be the official language to be used in the council and its records[17]—a significant provision, given the non-Egyptian (Turkish and Circassian) origins of the ruling family and much of the officer corps at the time.

Not until after the 1919 revolution, which forced the British to accord nominal independence to Egypt, do we begin to see state-level elaboration of a national identity, key early elements of which were, not surprisingly, sovereignty and independence. A decree of 1922 referred to Egypt as an independent, sovereign country and established the line of Mehmet Ali, whose titles had been khedive (viceroy) and more recently sultan, as kings of Egypt, commencing with Fuad I, who promised to work "to return to Egypt the memory of its glorious past."[18] The Constitution of 1923 then went much further. Its preamble alluded to the greatness of Egypt's ancient history and talked about preserving the national spirit (*al-ruh al-qawmiyya*).[19] The country's sovereignty, freedom, and independence were asserted in article 1, which also affirmed its character as an hereditary monarchy (with a parliament). Article 3 introduced the notion of Egyptians' being equal before the law, enjoying political and civil rights, with no differentiation among them in terms of public responsibilities because of origin, language, or religion. The Constitution also made clear that only Egyptians were permitted to hold public jobs, whether civilian or military, and then expanded upon the ways in which Egyptians were protected from abuses regarding residency rights, no doubt in response to the discrimination they had faced under the British occupation and then protectorate (1882–1922). These provisions are all easily understood in the context of a country with a long history of nonindigenous ruling classes, foreign occupation, and the special legal and commercial concessions that had been accorded to resident Europeans.

As for identity elements such as language, religion, and ethnicity, article 13 protected religious practices and beliefs "according to Egyptian customs as long as public order or morals are not hurt." Article 16 guaranteed freedom to use any language in private meetings and commercial transactions, religious matters, and the press, and stipulated that the members of the upper chamber of parliament (*majlis al-shuyukh*) could be spiritual leaders. Not until article 149 (out of 170), under "general laws," was Islam specified as the religion of state and Arabic as the official language. One final identity element concerns two articles on Egyptian rights in the Sudan and the then ongoing negotiations over its political future.[20] These articles made clear that at least in terms of the official imagination, the territorial boundaries of the Egyptian political entity included the Sudan.

A new constitution was introduced in 1930, but its purpose was to assert greater control over freedom of the press and assembly, as well as to reinforce the king's prerogatives and limit opposition by changing the requirements for membership in parliament. It did not introduce any changes relative to identity or historical narrative, and, owing to continuing popular opposition to it, in 1935 the government was forced to reinstate its 1923 predecessor. In 1951, laws 176 and 177 amended the 1923 document, further asserting Egyptian rights in the Sudan, calling the two one country and making the royal title "King of Egypt and the Sudan." Otherwise, the 1923 document remained unchanged until the 1952 revolution.

In the realm of education, there was the well-known opposition to educational reform of Lord Cromer, Britain's consul-general in Egypt (1883–1907).[21] As in other cases of imperial control, the goal was to develop in the student an affiliation with and admiration for the colonizer and train the required number of government bureaucrats and administrators, not to educate a people, much less create a nation. In 1888, to weaken Arabic, the British mandated that the official language of instruction be either English or French. They also elevated the status of colloquial Arabic, presumably to reinforce distinctions among speakers of different dialects.[22] Not until the tenure of Sa'd Zaghlul as minister of education (1906–10) was there an attempt to reinstate Arabic as the language of instruction.

British policy also reflected the colonial priorities of largely ignoring indigenous history, so to the extent that Egypt was studied, it was only on the margins of what was overwhelmingly a focus on Europe. Indeed, many students graduated from high school without knowing anything about their country's past.[23] Not surprisingly then, when independence was declared in 1923, English was replaced by Arabic as the formal language of instruction.[24] Beginning in 1925, a new subject, civics (*tarbiyya qawmiyya*),[25] was introduced at both the primary and secondary levels of schooling, with the goal of "presenting the student with a faithful picture of the society in which he lived, and reinforcing societal and national values and concepts."[26]

The 1923 Constitution also made basic education (initially only four grades) obligatory and free in government schools for boys and girls. In addition to these primary schools, the state established what were called elementary schools for the poor, which stressed religion, reading, writing, and arithmetic. The traditional religious school system supervised by Al-Azhar, a mosque and university in Cairo that historically had been a preeminent center of Islamic learning and scholarship, also continued to function alongside the slowly expanding government system, which included secondary education. Nonetheless, literacy levels remained quite low. On the eve of the revolution, fewer than two million children out of a total population of over twenty-two million were in school.[27] As a result, the educational system was too limited in its reach under the monarchy to play a major role in propagating an official narrative of state or society among broad sectors of the population.

THE END OF THE MONARCHY AND THE FOUNDING NARRATIVE OF THE REVOLUTION

It has often been pointed out that the military officers who overthrew King Farouk I, Fuad's son and successor, were generic nationalists, lacking an articulated guiding ideology. What their early declarations did establish, however, was the basis for a new foundational story for Egypt. General Muhammad Naguib's letter of 26 July 1952 to King Farouk in the name of the Free Officers listed what would gradually become a robust narrative of justifications for his overthrow: the chaos that had become widespread in the country; his disregarding of the Constitution and the will of the people; the affluence of the elite at the expense of a poor and starving population; the defeat in the 1948 Palestine war and the king's role in the scandal of the faulty weapons provided to Egyptian troops fighting there.

Over the next several months, the Free Officers issued four other major declarations that further fleshed out the emerging new founding narrative. The declaration of 10 December 1952 from Naguib was addressed to "sons of my homeland" (*bani watani*),[28] suggesting not just a familial, but almost a tribal affiliation among the people. It proceeded to elaborate upon the background of decay and corruption that justified the revolution: "Instead of the executive power being responsible to the parliament, in various periods the parliament was subject to the executive, which in turn submitted to a king who was not accountable," 'Isam 'Ashur writes. "The king found holes in the Constitution that, with the help of others, enabled them to run the country as they pleased." The declaration of 10 December also introduced a second theme that became central to the narrative: ensuring the bases for a dignified life that focused on freedom, justice, and order so that the "sons of the people" (*abna' al-sha'b*) would be able to engage in productive work for the good of the country and its children. This declaration also introduced a new construction of national unity: "You need to forget yourselves as individuals and exert yourselves and your money and your efforts to ensure glory, happiness and strength for your country. There are no individual interests or political party inclinations after today: the homeland is one, the goal is one."[29]

Shortly thereafter, on 16 January 1953, a declaration announcing a three-year transitional period introduced two additional elements key to the portrayal of unity and national identity: the destructive role of political parties in the past and the nefarious role of foreign powers. In the case of the latter, one can see the underlying theme of insistence upon national sovereignty, inasmuch as the text asserts that the first goal of the revolution was the withdrawal of foreign troops—which was a new aspect added to the narrative of reasons for the revolution—and charges that some elements had been in touch with foreign powers to try to take the country back to the corruption and chaos of the past. After accusing the parties of having used destructive means that ignored the interests of the country, Naguib announced the dissolution of all political parties and the confiscation of their resources "for the good of the people." He connected this order with the emerging narrative of unity, claiming that the parties had spent their money to sow the seeds of sedition (*fitna*) and division. Those who would try to take the country back to chaos "forget that we stand as observers of all those who talk about departing from the popular consensus or the futility of its future. It has been ordered that the strongest and toughest measures be taken against any traitor who seeks sedition among the ranks of our unified people [*umma*]."[30] On 10 February 1953, a third declaration referred to the people as the source of all authority.

A fourth declaration, on 18 June 1953, terminated the monarchy, proclaimed a republic, and added more elements to the growing list of justifications for the revolution, including the first reference to imperialism: King Farouk had not only been corrupt, but was "a cornerstone on which imperialism depended." Moreover, a clear note of populism was added to the founding story, inasmuch as the text proclaimed that "the people unanimously called for an end to the monarchy."[31] The history of Mehmet Ali's family (although, significantly, not his rule itself) was characterized as a series of betrayals of the right of the people. First, Khedive Isma'il had submerged Egypt in debt, then, under his successor, Khedive Tawfiq,[32] foreign forces had entered the country to preserve the throne, which became "the curtain behind which imperialism operated." However, Farouk was the worst of all, "in tyranny and *kufr*;[33] he wrote his destiny, his end, himself." During this period, the theme of the Egyptian people breaking the chains of prerevolutionary oppression was also visually portrayed by a number of stamps issued in commemoration of the revolution of 23 July and celebrating the 18 June 1953 declaration of the republic.[34]

While the authors of the revolution were seeking to generate broad legitimacy for their revolution through this emerging narration of past ills, an internal power struggle was under way between the supporters of Naguib on the one hand and those of Colonel Gamal Abdel Nasser on the other. The stakes were not just who would ultimately take the reins of leadership, but the type of system that would emerge. The details of the many steps, retreats, and personnel shifts of the 1952–54 period are beyond the scope of this study. By April 1954, Nasser appeared to have won the battle, and in November, he forced Naguib to resign the presidency. In the meantime, in addition to discursive initiatives, consolidating power required a series of concrete measures that eliminated or neutralized opposition. Some steps were solely coercive: purges of municipal and provincial councils and the press of "undesirable elements."[35] Others, however, served two functions: to enhance the narrative of the revolution *and* to undermine key opponents. The most prominent example is the Agricultural Reform Law of 1952, which limited the size of landholdings: it supported the emerging narrative of a revolution seeking social justice, while at the same time breaking the back of landed interests that were among the most likely opponents of the revolution. Similarly, the dissolution of political parties and the decree depriving former ministers from the pre-1952 political parties of their political and civil rights for ten years both underlined the narrative's theme of the corruption of the politicians and parties under the monarchy and circumscribed their range of maneuver going forward. Because of the close relationship it enjoyed with some of the Free Officers, however, the Sunni religio-political Muslim Brotherhood (Al-Ikhwan al-Muslimun) was not shut down in 1953.[36] Not until a member attempted to assassinate Nasser in October 1954 did the new regime suppress it as well.

The Philosophy of the Revolution

Most important in solidifying the evolving foundational story and narrative of national identity and unity was Nasser's own 1953 widely distributed and studied manifesto *Falsafat al-thawra* (Philosophy of the Revolution).[37] This helped establish the regime's initial legitimacy, based on having both overthrown the king and adopted a broad revolutionary program. Even before securing the presidency, Nasser enumerated six fundamental revolutionary goals: achieving social justice; putting an end to imperialism and its supporters; eliminating feudalism; ending capitalist control of the government; developing a strong national army; and establishing a strong national democratic life.

Falsafat al-Thawra was "a work of discovery, to discern who we are, what our role is in Egypt's history of successive stages, and to explore the past and present to know on what road to proceed," Nasser wrote (5). Part of the historical narrative underlined the theme of the struggle for sovereignty, the successive attempts by Egyptians to take the reins of governance, a goal finally achieved by the 1952 revolution. However, Nasser also drew on the larger framework of Egyptian history to explain how he had discovered the roots of the revolution in himself. He denied that the cause of the revolution had been the 1948 defeat in Palestine, the scandal of the faulty weapons, or the crisis of the Officers' Club elections.[38] These had hastened, but did not justify, a revolution (10). Instead, he traced the revolution's origins to his birth; the necessity for it had been imprinted on him by the previous generations, suggesting that it was the culmination, not just of the corruption of the decades prior to 1952 or the failure of the 1919 revolution to fulfill its promise, but of centuries of struggle against the same kinds of forces that were aligned against the Egyptian people in the first half of the twentieth century.

Nasser's experiences as an officer in the Palestine War did play an important role in his developing political consciousness and identity, but the most critical and poignant line here is "we were in Palestine, but our dreams were in Egypt" (11), meaning that what they saw happening in Palestine, they felt could also happen in Egypt, and that Palestine was not viewed as a foreign country. He characterized his response to the tragedy in Palestine, not as an emotional one, but as one produced by a sense of responsibility for self-defense (62).

One admission in *Falsafat al-thawra* that was never integrated into the founding story was Nasser's surprise that the Egyptian people were not prepared for revolution and were certainly not unified. He had thought that all that would be needed was a vanguard, in the form of the military, to open the way. Instead, he realized that the task of the vanguard did not end with the revolution—here meaning simply the overthrow of the king—but in fact only began with it (21). The officers needed order, but found only chaos; they needed unity, but found behind them only differences (22–23). People came with complaints, most of which were demands for vengeance: "The word 'I' was on everyone's tongues." At this point, at least, according to Nasser, there was no sense of national unity or purpose.

In addressing the way forward, Nasser introduced the notion of two revolutions, one political and the other social. This distinction was regularly repeated, but then ultimately reinterpreted, under his successors. Here, the political revolution was defined as returning rule of the country to Egyptians, while the social one involved class struggle, which would ultimately be stabilized through achieving societal justice. He argued that the 1919 revolution had failed precisely because it had gotten lost between these two kinds of revolutions (28). The political revolution required the unity of all elements of the people (*umma*) for the sake of the entire country. The social revolution, on the other hand, at its beginning, involved a shaking up of values and a convulsing of beliefs, and a struggle among the citizens themselves as individuals and classes. Corruption, doubt, hate and egoism ruled: "One revolution requires that we unite, while another, regardless of what we want, imposes differences and divisions" (27). Other countries had preceded Egypt along this revolutionary path, but, in his analysis, they had not had to confront two revolutions at the same time. The frank admission of the existence of a wide gap between social classes is the one constant example of lack of unity that one finds in the narrative at this stage: overcoming it is recognized as a key task for the revolution (27).

In crafting a way forward, all of the episodes of the past had to be taken into account: Egypt's pharaonic history, the impact of the Greeks and the Romans, the arrival of Islam and the waves of Arab immigration that followed (42); the Crusades, the Mongols, and the Circassians, who came to Egypt as slaves and became princes. Not until the arrival of the French (45) had the "iron curtain" that the "Mongols" had imposed been brought down. At that point, he said, under Mehmet Ali, Egypt had to try to catch up with the caravan of human progress, because it was five centuries behind. This was the reason behind the absence of a strong united public opinion in the country: the difference between individuals was great, and the differences between generations extreme (48). Yet he insisted that Egyptians would come together in a strong harmonious unity. They just had to bear the period of transition (49).

Finally, in *Falsafat al-thawra*, Nasser proposed three circles of Egyptian affiliation or identity—Arab, African, and Islamic: "We cannot ignore that there is an Arab circle that surrounds us and that it is of [from] us and we are of

[from] it, our history is mixed with its history and our interests are linked with its interests. There is also an African continent of which we are a part. And there is an Islamic world to which we are tied" (59). In this way, he made a case for basing Egyptian national identity in three spheres of regional or international politics (60).

Thus, in this text, Nasser further elaborated the narrative of the background to the revolution, as well as the work ahead, as specified by the six goals and the contrast between the political and social revolutions. Although he acknowledged a range of past influences, identity markers in the present—beyond the Arab, Islamic, and African ones—were not addressed. What it meant to be ethnically Egyptian was taken for granted. Instead, the challenges to unity were to be found in the demands of the social revolution. Here Nasser was as clear as any leader could have been about the inevitability of conflict. As an admission of the difficulties ahead, and in terms that did not at this stage villainize anyone, it was quite remarkable. Finally, this seminal document suggested that Egypt was destined to play a leading regional political role.

Educational Reform and the Emerging Narrative

Among the six goals of the revolution, education was regarded as essential for achieving social justice through its role in helping to dissolve class differences. New state policies therefore aimed at generalizing primary education, lengthening the compulsory period, supporting technical education, planning education according to the needs of the country, providing equal opportunities and justice in the distribution of the educational budget, and achieving state control over foreign education.[39] Laws 210 and 211 of 1953 combined and reformed primary and elementary schools, and made education compulsory for both boys and girls from age six to age twelve. The regime then set about expanding the number of such schools with the goal of creating a new generation with the skills and training to respond to the country's social, economic, and political needs. It is worth noting here that the short-lived Liberation Rally (1953–56), the regime's first attempt, following the abolition of political parties, to establish an institution to mobilize popular support, also focused on students and youth activities.

Part of the broad-based reforms involved revising school texts. The Ministry of Education moved quickly to form a committee to rewrite all national textbooks, but history books were seen as the most pressing issue.[40] Isma'il Qabbani, minister of education under Naguib, instructed Dr. Abu al-Futuh

Radwan, the dean of education at ʿAyn Shams University in Cairo, to construct a curriculum that would choose elements from Egyptian history based on how they would serve to clarify that history. He wanted national history to be "freed of falsehoods," to highlight the role of the people as opposed to just a few prominent individuals, and to address Arab history in the framework of Egypt's belonging to the Arab people (*umma*) and homeland. In this way, the history of the Arab world would assume the place that European history had occupied in the previous curriculum. The committee, composed of prominent historians, decided that the text for the second year of secondary school would cover the history of the Islamic states and their civilization, while the curriculum for the third year would be a detailed study of the Arab *umma* in the nineteenth and twentieth centuries.[41]

In the introduction to the 1954 *Taʾrikh Misr f-il-ʿasr al-hadith* (The History of Egypt in the Modern Period), a secondary school book that served as the basis for a series of texts over the years, the authors explained that the desire to issue a new book on Egyptian history after the revolution was natural, because the revolution had brought new tendencies to Egypt, one of which was highlighting the importance of the people in the past and the present: their role had not received this same attention before the revolution, whether in public life or in history books. The text then offers many insights into the elements of national identity that the new regime sought to reinforce or cultivate. The preface began by suggesting that there may be no history older than that of Egypt and the Egyptians, which goes back thousands of years before Christ, thus acknowledging the pharaonic past, if not specifically in those terms. However, there was no mention of Coptic Egypt as a significant period or culture; only a brief mention of Christianity as having entered the Sudan through Egypt. The text then moved quickly to insist that in the seventh century CE, Egypt had been transformed into an Arab Islamic homeland (*watan*), and Egyptians became part of a large family, the Islamic Arab people (*umma*). Arab Islamic Egypt became one of the strongest and most glorious fortresses of Islam and Arabism, participating fully during its periods of greatness and power in building Arab Islamic culture and in defending Arabs and Islam in the face of Crusader and Mongol invasions (11). Thus, even at this early point in the history of the new regime, before the Arab nationalist surge that followed, the centrality of Egypt's Arabo-Islamic identity to the narrative is clear.

A number of the lessons or themes from Arab and Islamic history—the importance of sovereignty, the need for strength, and united Egyptian opposition and fierce resistance to the invader, yet also openness to the wider world—were implicit, and were used as "past echoes" or early examples of themes of more recent history the state sought to underline. For example, chapter 1 notes that from the time of the Fatimids until the Ottomans,[42] Egypt was independent and became a great empire (11); thereafter, however, Egyptians lived for centuries in social and economic subjection and turmoil, especially under the Turks and the Circassians. Egyptians of various backgrounds (merchants, craftsmen, peasants) had resisted the oppression of the Mamluks (26),[43] during whose rule almost all contact with the outside world was lost. They resisted the French invasion (42–43), and then fought their Ottoman overlords for several years after that (47). The people did support Mehmet Ali, however, and he relied on them in consolidating his rule over Egypt (51). However, he was an authoritarian leader who rejected the proposition that the people should participate in decision-making (59).

On the question of national identity and unity, the text admitted that until the beginning of the nineteenth century, Egyptians had been divided into classes (*tabaqat*) and *tawa'if*,[44] and they had felt sectoral affiliation (*ta'ifiyya*) or regionalism (*iqlimiyya*) more than nationalism. However, "today with the ease of communication among the sons of one country, these barriers between *tawa'if* and classes have come down. . . . Egyptians are all citizens in a single Egyptian community [*umma*] whose individual members feel one strong sentiment: that of belonging to this eternal homeland" (8–9). The identity theme of common and prolonged struggle against foreign imperialism was also stressed: Generation after generation Egyptians gave their blood, sweat, and tears. "This book is the story of that struggle . . . so that the young generation will continue the work for the sake of the standing and glory of the homeland" (10).

The book then traced the beginning of Egypt's modern history to the Napoleonic invasion of 1798, and the origins of the modern state to Mehmet Ali, with national consciousness (*al-wa'i al-qawmi*) first emerging in the context of his coming to power in 1805 and subsequently repelling the British invasion of 1807. As the preface promised, the people (*al-sha'b*) are major actors throughout. In one of the few references to subnational identities, the text mentioned that the army established under Mehmet Ali had been one means of creating national unity, since both Muslims and Copts were conscripted (68).

Turning to the topics of outside intervention, the text addressed Egypt's isolation under the Ottomans, the foreign capitulations, and the mixed courts under the Europeans. Positions taken in opposition to Khedive Isma'il by those pushing for a constitution were characterized repeatedly as patriotic (*watani*), but the first (*watani*) movement—and here *watani* can be read as meaning both "patriotic" and "national"—is traced to Ahmad 'Urabi. The discussion of 'Urabi is then used to construct an example of the unity of the people and the army for the sake of the nation: the echoes of the 1952 revolution could not be clearer. The text claimed that 'Urabi felt that the people supported him and that they were certain that the army, led by him, was their hope for saving the country from foreign intervention and for eliminating absolute rule (163). The entire period from 'Urabi until the issuance of the 1923 constitution is referred to as "the national movement and resisting occupation."

Whatever the evils of Mehmet Ali's descendants, the text nonetheless insisted that Egypt made great strides during the 150-year reign of this dynasty, more than most countries in such a period. The text then turned to the theme of Egypt's openness to the outside world for examples, not only of processes of cultural exchange and enrichment, but also of cultural (if not political) independence and sovereignty. Egypt's progress during this period was in no way mere borrowing from the West. What Egypt learned was part of a world culture to which Egypt and many civilizations contributed. Whatever it adopted, it then changed or amended according to its own needs and situation (216–17).

When the text presented July 1952, it provided extensive details reinforcing the narrative already set out in the early documents of the revolution. First, it elaborated upon the corruption under Farouk: he took advantage of the weaknesses of the political parties to subjugate them; he violated the Constitution in many ways, including taking over religious endowment (*waqf*) lands; and men in the government who wanted to preserve their positions engaged in corruption to appease him. The country experienced a period of terrorism and mass arrests of young intellectuals. Most elections were not clean, and then there was the disaster in Palestine. The text then juxtaposed the accomplishments of the revolution to date with this background of corruption and chaos. At this early stage, land reform was the centerpiece, because it purportedly eliminated the huge gaps that had existed between social classes. It had also put an end to the old titles from the days of the monarchy,[45] so that everyone became *sayyid* (mister), and all were free citizens. The revolution also established a range of public services—health, educational, building, social, and so on (249). Further examples of signature achievements were the proposed Aswan High Dam and the Evacuation Treaty of 1954, which removed all remaining British troops from Egyptian territory. It concluded that the revolution had accomplished a great deal in only two years, working to achieve the national/patriotic (*watani*) hopes of the *umma*, the people of the Nile Valley in Egypt and the Sudan for independence, freedom, and complete sovereignty. It called Nasser, who by this time had marginalized Muhammad Naguib, the Hero of the Evacuation, and put him in the same line of nationalists as 'Urabi, the heroes of the 1919 revolution, Mustafa Kamil, Muhammad Farid, Sa'd Zaghlul,[46] "and all those who have given their souls in sacrifice to this country" (254).

In this way, the text participated in inculcating a legitimizing narrative for the revolutionary regime, not only through exposing the errors and corruption of the past, but also through underlining the new rulers' many achievements in such a short time. Key among them for the broader population were those aimed at social and economic justice. However, the historical record was also constructed to portray the 1952 coup as an heroic episode in the tradition of the country's long history of struggle to reassert Egyptian control over Egyptian affairs, and to return Egypt to its rightful place as a leader on the world stage.

INTERNAL CONSOLIDATION AND GROWING EXTERNAL CHALLENGES

During the first two years following the revolution, the domestic front had seen two power struggles: one between the Free Officers and elements of the *ancien régime*; and the second within the Free Officers group itself, which was settled with the sidelining of Naguib and his supporters and then the suppression of the Muslim Brotherhood. As Nasser consolidated his power, he scored a foreign policy victory in 1954 by securing an agreement on the complete evacuation of British troops from the country. During this period, foreign policy challenges took on increasingly dangerous proportions, which ultimately threatened the survival of the regime. These episodes were subsequently incorporated into the expanding narrative as examples of the revolution's fulfilling its promises, further reinforcing the leadership's legitimacy.

In early 1955, Britain launched a campaign to establish a pro-Western regional security alliance (ultimately called the Baghdad Pact) which Nasser rejected. These efforts, combined with the devastating Israeli military raid of 28 February on the Gaza Strip, which was under Egyptian military administration, left the Egyptian leadership exposed to both Israeli military superiority and internal criticism. Nasser's subsequent participation in the Bandung Afro-Asian Conference, which founded the nonaligned movement, aimed at establishing new external bases of political and diplomatic support, but he was also in need of military matériel. At the end of September, he secured an arms agreement from Czechoslovakia, a development that stunned and riled the United States and Britain because it represented the Soviet Union's first entrée into the region.

In January 1956, a new constitution was promulgated, putting an end to what in 1953 had been declared a three-year transitional period. The new populism promoted by the revolutionary regime was clear in the preamble, which began: "We, the people of Egypt," and was reinforced in article 2, which reaffirmed popular sovereignty. The preamble also adopted the revolutionary narrative's theme of continuous struggle for freedom against outside forces: "this constitution['s] . . . rules proceed from the heart of our struggle, and the dreams of the battle that our fathers and grandfathers waged generation after generation, from the sweetness of victory to the bitterness of defeat." The revolution of 23 July 1952 was portrayed as a major victory in this long battle, a new stage in which the people "have taken control of our affairs ourselves," "freed of fear, freed of need, freed of humiliation," thus again underlining the theme of independence and sovereignty, as well as the social revolution for justice. Indeed, the preamble emphasized "dignity and justice and equality as the roots of real freedom and peace." It also underlined the theme, spelled out in Nasser's *Falsafat al-thawrah*, of Egypt's special international role, locating it "at the meeting place of continents and oceans," and with an "historic mission in building civilization."

In terms of identity elements, the Constitution reinforced what was, in the regional political climate, a growing focus on Egypt's Arab identity and role in the Arab world: "We the Egyptian People: feel the interactive presence of the large Arab entity, and appreciate its responsibilities in the joint Arab struggle for the glory of the Arab people." The importance of the country's Arab identity was then reinforced by its inclusion in article 1: "Egypt is a sovereign independent Arab state, a democratic republic, and the Egyptian people are a part of the Arab *umma*." Not until article 3 was Islam stipulated as the religion of state (along with Arabic as the official language), although article 31 repeated previous constitutions' guarantees that there was no distinction among Egyptians according to sex, origin, language, religion, or belief.

Also new, and in keeping with the evolving narrative of the revolution and its goals, a section entitled "The Components of Egyptian Society" developed a new definition of national unity, referring to social solidarity, rather than an ethnic or religious component, as the basis of Egyptian society. The family is the foundation, resting on religion, morality, and nationalism/patriotism (*wataniyya*). In keeping with this emphasis, article 7 introduced the role of the national economy in overseeing the principles of social justice and raising the standard of living. It then elaborated on various forms of social justice that were to be ensured (a decent standard of living in terms of food, housing, health, and cultural services), along with facilitating women's work in both the home and the workplace. Articles 49 and 50 reaffirmed that education was the right of all Egyptians, and that the state was to supervise education and organize the law in matters of education.[47]

Thus in addition to the growing place of Arabism in the narrative, populist appeals, in the form of promises of expanded state services to address the needs of the less privileged, seemed aimed at consolidating support for the revolutionary regime. On 23 June 1956, both this constitution and Nasser as president were overwhelmingly approved by popular referenda, another instrument intended symbolically to accord the people a voice in building the country's future, but in practice to reinforce the regime's claim to legitimacy.[48]

Textbook Developments

In 1955, the Ministry of Education issued a broad directive entitled *Manahij al-thawra f-il-tarbiya w-al-ta'lim* (The Curriculum of the Revolution in Upbringing and Education), which listed the most important principles of the new educational policy. Education was to have an Arab nationalist (*qawmi*) orientation. New plans and curricula were put in place for all three levels—primary, preparatory, and secondary—and military education was added.[49]

While a growing emphasis on Egypt's role in the Arab world was promoted in both Nasser's foreign policy and the history curriculum, civics texts at this stage continued to focus primarily on Egypt. For example, the 1956 fifth-year primary school civics textbook *Al-Tarbiya al-wataniyya* opened with a series of pictures, the first of which portrayed a pharaonic tomb, a soldier, and a tank, with a mosque in the background. According to its caption, these symbols were intended to represent pharaonic, Islamic, and modern Egypt. Note that there was nothing Christian here, but also nothing Arab, unless Arab is defined as equivalent to Islamic. The Egypt the book presents seems timeless: all Egyptians, from the most ancient of times to the end of time, belong to it. It is the country that created civilization (*madaniyya*) for the world: when most of the peoples of the world were still living very basic lives, Egypt carried the flag of a civilization whose traces (*athar*) stretch from the Mediterranean to the heart of the Sudan (7). The text described Egyptians as "partners in a single heritage, with no difference among them between the small and the large, man or woman ... all children of a single *umma*." The Egyptian people are defined, not ethnically, but geographically and in terms of a cooperative existence: Egyptians are "the group of individuals who live in the cities and villages and in the fields and on the sea coast and in the valleys of the desert and the mountains, because they are all children [*abna'*] of Egypt who have inherited this great legacy and whose future depends on them. . . . This people is all of us together . . . whether we know one another or not, because without feeling it, we work together, and we live together and the life of each of us depends upon the other" (8).[50]

It then warned of the dangers of lack of unity: "We Egyptians must all join hands to ensure our freedom. . . . The Egyptian *umma* was always careful to defend its independence, and for several thousand years it was a free, independent country. But at one point, as a result of the population's failure to cooperate and unify, and their lack of concern for the general good, she lost her independence, and then the Egyptian people suffered greatly . . . then she struggled to make you and the children of this generation happy, so that we can live on free land, dignified and strong" (10). A series of pictures followed, illustrating foreign occupation, freedom in our homeland (*watan*), and past subservience to a corrupt foreign ruler, but the caption of the final one, a picture of Nasser, proclaimed "now our rulers are from among us." "Divisions threatened us, but we have strengthened our ranks with our unity and cohesion" (12–18). The text then asked the students if they knew who the creators of Egypt's glory today were. The answers it gave were all populist ones associated with work and contribution to community, and had no ethno-religious markers: the father who works for his family, the mother who looks after her children, the farmer who labors to produce a bountiful harvest, the teacher who undertakes his task with integrity, the doctor who treats people with care, the worker who perfects his job, the soldier who sacrifices his life for the homeland (24).

NATIONALIZING THE SUEZ CANAL COMPANY

The centerpiece of the revolutionary regime's development policy was the proposed new High Dam at Aswan, announced shortly after the coup, which was seen as the key to future economic growth. Not only would it help irrigate additional land, but the power it generated would provide electricity to Egyptian towns and villages. The details of the negotiations to obtain funding to build the High Dam are beyond the scope of this study. Suffice it to say that although agreement on external financing appeared to be within reach in mid-1956, by mid-July, first the United States, then Britain, and finally the World Bank had all withdrawn their offers. The rest of the story is well known. In response to what was seen as, not only an affront, but an attempt to obstruct Egypt's development in order to discipline the revolutionary regime, Nasser moved only days later to nationalize the Suez Canal Company.

The primary themes of Nasser's speech proclaiming the nationalization were the common struggle against imperialism to ensure Egypt's independence and the need for unity. As he usually did, he addressed his audience as "O Citizens" (*ayuha al-muwatinun*), suggesting a common civic identity. The focus on independence was already well integrated into the revolutionary narrative at this point, so the emphasis on imperialism (*isti'mar*) took center stage. Nasser began by focusing on elements reinforcing his and his regime's revolutionary legitimacy: the previous four years had been characterized by struggling to rid Egypt of the remnants of the odious past, of imperialism, and of foreign and internal exploitation that had oppressed Egypt for long centuries. He reasserted how difficult the task was, particularly given international plots and the greed of international actors. But Egypt had entered this battle to live free, with dignity and strength/pride (1). Much of the speech rehearsed the most recent attempts at remaining independent or asserting ultimate independence from the British. He then turned to the question of securing funding for the building of the High Dam, again using the frame of Egypt's long-standing struggle to end exploitation, achieve full independence from foreigners, and use its resources for its own development (3).

Throughout Nasser's account, it was the people of Egypt (*sha'b Misr*) who were the protagonists of the struggle; the enemy was imperialism and its supporters, including most prominently Israel. On several occasions, as part of this populism, he emphasized that there was no distinction between him and the Egyptian people. For example, he mocked U.S. Secretary of State John Foster Dulles's statement claiming that the decision not to fund the dam project did not indicate a change in the friendly relations between the Egyptian and American *peoples*: "so that everything that was said applies only to Gamal Abdel Nasser, it has nothing to do with the Egyptian people, and they speak directly to the Egyptian people. . . . We know these tricks" (23). Similarly, in discussing the Czech arms deal, he said he was able to stand up to Dulles, not with the power of Gamal Abdel Nasser although he would fight to the last drop of his blood, but "because I was certain that all of you, all the children of Egypt, would fight to the last drop of your blood, without discrimination, without partisanship, with no divisions like those they used in the past. We are one national bloc together, a united front behind the goals of the revolution" (14).

Egypt's Arabism was now central, as was its forward march: "Arab nationalism will progress, Arab nationalism will be victorious, Arab nationalism will continue its forward march" (3). Egypt's own growing power is also part of the emerging identity: "The world has begun to look at Egypt and take her into account . . . today the value of Egypt on the world stage has grown, along with the value of the Arabs, the Arab *umma*" (3). He further stressed the identity characteristic of self-reliance: Egypt had been successful because Egyptians had relied on themselves—on their products, their sweat, their power—and they had been able to raise national output (7). Similarly, Egypt's policies were independent, determined in Egypt, not in London or Washington. "No cooperation will be at the expense of our national identity, our Arabism, or our independence or dignity" (7).

"We are all working for the sake of these lofty principles of the revolution, [freedom, dignity, strength], we are all working for our national[ist] [*qawmi*] identity, we are all working for Arabism, we are all working to protect ourselves from imperialism and the supporters of imperialism, and Israel is a creation of imperialism. We will all struggle, we will all fight, we will all sacrifice our souls and blood for our homeland" (3). So this common struggle is the form that the presumption or construction of unity takes here. "We will go forward together, my brothers, united, one hand, one heart." Then, just before reading the daring and defiant nationalization decree, he said: "we will proclaim all of Egypt one front, one bloc, shoulder to shoulder, united, all of Egypt will fight to the last drop of its blood" (28).

The fight came, if several months later, when, on 29 October, Israeli forces invaded the Sinai, followed in short order by attacks by British and French forces. The fighting in the Canal area, particularly in Port Sa'id was particularly bloody, and the Israelis, when finally forced to withdraw, carried out a scorched earth policy in the Sinai. The opposition of the United States to the aggression and the threat of the Soviet Union to use force if necessary to bring about an end to hostilities forced the acceptance of a cease-fire on 7 November. Militarily, Egypt had lost the war, and under other circumstances, Nasser's leadership might have been significantly shaken, if not overthrown: that was certainly one goal of the authors of the war. However, thanks largely to the international politics of the time, Nasser was allowed to claim political victory. His daring, combined with his country's ability to withstand the attack of two colonial powers allied with one regional power, viewed as a beachhead of imperialism, catapulted him to larger-than-life heroic status in the Arab world and beyond. The destruction and losses were significant, but when the Canal finally reopened in April 1957, it, and the revenues it produced, belonged to Egypt.

Thus, rather than being shaken, the revolutionary regime was thereby able to add a new legitimizing episode to the discourse of struggle for sovereignty and independence. Following the war, to visually reinforce this, a number of postage stamps were issued that portrayed what had already been branded as a history replete with examples of aggression against Egypt. Some directly addressed the events of the war, as in one titled "Port Sa'id, November 1956," which shows an Egyptian man, woman, and soldier, with foreign parachutists in the background and a ship on fire in the canal. Both men hold guns, and the woman a grenade. There was also a series of stamps entitled "Egypt, the tomb of aggressors" which portrayed a series of much older, but also historic, battles: Avaris in 1580 BCE;[51] Hittin, where Saladin defeated the Crusaders in 1187 CE; Mansura, where Louis IX was defeated in the Seventh Crusade in 1250 CE; and 'Ayn Galut, where the Mamluks defeated the Mongols in 1260 CE.[52]

FROM THE SUEZ WAR TO UNITY WITH SYRIA

The textbooks produced in the wake of the Suez war both repeated and built on the legitimizing narrative elements already discussed. For example, the 1957 sixth-year primary school civics text *Al-Tarbiya al-wataniyya* reinforced the narrative of the causes of the revolution and the populist policies subsequently implemented by the regime. The story of the backdrop to the revolution was now well established: the corruption of the past, the hegemony of foreign interests; the king as oppressor and the parliament as false democracy; and the power of the large landowners, who controlled the votes of the peasants who worked their lands through various means of terrorism (*irhabiyya*) and threats (9–10).

The first chapter of this textbook stressed the advantage of a republic over the monarchy that the revolution had abolished. Basic again is the role of the people, which was repeatedly stressed. It is they who choose the president through elections and who can change the president if they are not satisfied with him; and he is equal to the people under the law (2). A republic also seeks to ensure the rights of individuals, to preserve their freedoms, which all enjoy fully (3). The text then elaborated on the social welfare projects in which the state was engaged, along with its efforts to protect workers and peasants from the exploitation of capitalists and feudalists (26–32). It reiterated the revolution's goals, as well as its many accomplishments: land reform, expanding schools, housing for the poor, the Aswan High Dam, and the nationalization of the Suez Canal Company, foreign companies and banks. Thus the results of the 1956 war were swiftly integrated into the expanding legitimizing revolutionary story.

Recall that the Aswan dam project had been proposed as part of the regime's proclaimed commitment to a qualitative leap in national development. To further reinforce that image, in 1958, a series of postage stamps depicting industrial development in Egypt appeared, each devoted to a different industrial sector: textiles; cement; iron and steel; petroleum; electricity and fertilizers; transportation and communication. Perhaps most notable for the narrative was a series commemorating the nationalization of the Suez Canal Company. These stamps also featured progress in the construction of the Aswan High Dam, however, as well as UNESCO's assistance in saving the antiquities at Abu Simbel, another high-profile projection of Egyptian identity both domestically and abroad.[53]

As for the evolving notion of identity as presented in textbooks, there were no dramatic departures at this stage, although the attention to developing the students' understanding of the concept of the people (*umma*) and its relationship to the homeland (*watan*) was likely an outgrowth of the increasing importance given to Egypt's supranational identity connection with other Arabs. The 1957 fourth-year preparatory civics text *Al-Tarbiya al-wataniyya* defined an *umma* as a group of people with the same origins who share customs, traditions, morality, interests, and dreams and goals to a large extent (23). But the members of an *umma* do not all have to be in the same homeland. Thus, the Arab *umma* is made up of numerous peoples (*shu'ub*) who have various homelands (*awtan*). The difference is that the homeland is a sovereign entity, whereas the people (*umma*) are not. The text then proceeds to frame Egyptian identity in the following terms: all are members of the Egyptian people (*sha'b*), speaking one language, respecting one tradition, sharing similar customs, tastes, and a single history, of which all are proud. "Our dreams are one, and we have shared common interests that revolve around expelling the imperialists, ending corruption, and developing the country" (28). Thus, unity is constructed in part in terms of support for the revolution's goals. The 1957 sixth-year elementary civics text *Al-Tarbiya al-wataniyya* stated that the British had tried to discriminate between Muslims and Christians in order to create conflict, but Egyptians had remained united and cohesive, because the health of the country depended upon unity, while "in divisions and discrimination are danger to our freedom and independence" (52). It also included a section on Egypt and the Arab League, which stressed the elements that had tied together parts of the Arab world since ancient times, as well as the importance of unity. The Arab League had been established because the Arabs realized that only through unity and solidarity would they be victorious against attempts by Western imperialists to control parts of the region (63).

Union with Syria

The Suez war led the Egyptian government to sequester and eventually nationalize all foreign economic establishments in the country. This turn to greater state control over or involvement in the economy could be seen as a direct consequence of the Anglo-French-Israeli aggression against Egypt, but also as an indication of a decision by the leadership that the demands of economic development required greater state participation. To that end, comprehensive planning was introduced in Egypt in January 1957. It aimed at achieving economic independence to complement political independence and implied a turn away from a Western and toward a Soviet model of development. If increasing state responsibility for capital formation was a hallmark of this period on the economic front, the appeal of and to Arab nationalism was its parallel on the political front. What had previously been constructed as a central identity component, shared by Arabs of different sovereign homelands, was now to be mobilized as the basis of a program aimed at formal political unity between or among those homelands. The preeminent regional role that earlier narratives had heralded was to be realized in the framework of a shared Arabism.

The daring Suez nationalization and Nasser's survival of it made him and Egypt the unmatched leaders of such a movement. As a result, when approached by leaders of a number of Syrian political groups worried about the growing power of communists in the country, Nasser came under enormous pressure (and temptation) to embrace the calls for unity between the two countries. In response, on 5 February 1958, he addressed the People's Assembly to announce a political union with Syria, a move that he undertook with some trepidation, but that marked the apex of his power and influence. In his address, he made it clear that there was no unity without strength and no strength without unity. Attempts at unity, he claimed, had been ongoing for four thousand years (2). The region had been unified by the sword, by prophets, by the power of belief under Islam, and by the adoption of Arabic.[54] There were times when Egypt's ties with the region had been cut, for example, after the French invasion and then under the rule of Mehmet Ali's family; but this, he claimed, was only on the surface. Authentic indicators affirmed that what God had brought together could not be divided (2). Unity was what was real, and everything but unity was artificial.

Textbook Developments

Aside from the name change, the Constitution of the new United Arab Republic, which formally joined Syria and Egypt, did not really introduce any new elements. Article 1 stated that the UAR was a sovereign, democratic, independent republic whose people were part of the Arab *umma*. The same type of equality before the law that was provided for in the 1956 Egyptian Constitution prevailed. There was to be no distinction among citizens based on sex, origin, language, religion, or belief. What the establishment of the UAR did trigger, however, was a new "unity curriculum," one that deepened the Arab nationalist (*qawmi*) orientation of education. Less than two months after Nasser's speech, ministerial decree 360 of 26 March 1958 charged a committee of experts with rewriting the texts on the history of the Arabs. The subject "Egyptian society" was to be changed to "Arab society." The texts produced during this period not only focused more on Arabism, but also included previously absent aspects of Syrian history.

A great deal of pedagogical writing at the time focused on training teachers, especially social studies and Arabic language teachers, in supporting the national(ist) guidance (*al-tawjih al-qawmi*) of the student.[55] History needed to be a record of the goals of the revolution and the struggle (*jihad*) of Arab nationalist heroes to put an end to elements of weakness and corruption. Arabic heritage instruction was to serve the nationalist (*qawmi*) orientation in the present, in part by anchoring it in the past. A summer program for school inspectors in August 1958 aimed at strengthening the Arab nationalist and unity orientation and making clear that the most powerful echo of this orientation should be directed toward the students: "we are people who have risen up against imperialism and oppression and we need to convey the hatred of imperialism to our students."[56]

To show the emerging differences in curricular orientation, Muhsin Khudr examined the 1959 version of *Ta'rikh Misr f-il-'asr al-hadith,* the 1954 history textbook reviewed above, which began with Egypt under the Ottomans. The modified 1959 title, *Ta'rikh al-'Arab al-hadith w-al-mu'asir* (The Modern and Contemporary History of the Arabs), signaled a series of other important changes. For example, it introduced the Arab world into the presentation from the beginning, so that the first chapter was changed from "Egypt in the Ottoman Period" to "The Arab World between Ottoman Rule and European Intervention in the Eighteenth Century." Another chapter title was changed from "Egypt's Economic Development in the Nineteenth Century" to "Building an Arab Empire in the Nineteenth Century." Beyond the title changes, however, new material was added on the Arab revolt, the Sykes-Picot agreement, the 1936 Arab revolt in Palestine, and so on.[57]

A 1960 history text for first-year preparatory students entitled *Al-Ta'rikh al-qadim l-il-Jumhuriyya al-'Arabiyya al-Muttahida w-al-'Alam al-'Arabi* (The Ancient History of the UAR and the Arab World) also examined by Khudr, illustrated another aspect of the unity curriculum: constructing even ancient history in nationalist (*qawmi*) terms. It treated Syria and Egypt together, beginning with a discussion of the unity of the Arab world, listing its elements as unity of history, geography, origin, language, religion (which included a discussion of both Islam and Christianity), economy, and hopes and dream. Chapter 2 was anachronistically entitled "Citizens [*Muwatinun*] of the Ancient Civilizations in the Arab World."[58]

Khudr also compared two pre-1958 civics books (from 1954 and 1956) and a third from 1959. He noted the transformation from the frame of the homeland (*watan*) in the first two to a nationalist (*qawmi*) affiliation to a single Arab nation in the third. Moreover, the 1954 and 1956 books were about Egypt and the goals of the revolution. While they did address the depths of bonds among the Arab peoples, they made no reference to a *qawmi* dimension in a political sense, and there was nothing about an Egyptian responsibility to achieve Arab unity.[59] On the other hand, the 1959 book, *Al-Qawmiyya al-'Arabiyya* (Arab Nationalism), dealt with the basis for and components of Arab unity and their impact on Arab development. The text listed the elements of Arab unity as shared land, unity of history and struggle, unity of language and culture, unity of interests, psychological unity and shared emotions, and unity of will and expression. Note in particular the absence of reference to religion. Thus, this book represented a new stage in national education, as part of the transformation from local citizenship to the broad understanding of belonging to the larger Arab nation (*qawm*).[60]

Other books of the period manifested similar themes. The 1961 second-year preparatory civics book *Al-Talmidh wa-watanuhu* (The Student and his Homeland) had a section on citizenship that emphasized the Arab homeland and its role in providing happiness to its children (*abna'*), while clarifying the students' rights and duties as Arab citizens of the UAR. In particular, UAR citizens had a duty to protect the homeland through various kinds of service: military, national (*qawmi*) mobilization, national guard, popular resistance, and cooperation with the army. The preface also mentioned other materials that participated in portraying this Arab citizenship: history and geography books, books produced by the Ministry of Culture and Guidance to enlighten Arab public opinion, the speeches of the president of the UAR (Nasser) and ministers and leaders of Free Arabs, and materials broadcast from Cairo, Damascus, and Alexandria.

Al-Talmidh wa-watanuhu went on to stress that the UAR was part of a larger homeland (*watan*) stretching from the Atlantic to the Arabian Gulf. "The people of this region live in one homeland even if there are many parts, and it is the large Arab homeland, and we are all Arab citizens . . . we are citizens of one country which we love and take pride in and sacrifice for" (10). Note that an earlier text had referred to the *watan* as having sovereignty, whereas the people (*umma*) did not. Now, however, the definitions of the terms have changed: *watan* here clearly refers to the entire Arab homeland, not an individual Arab state (61).

As for the goals of the UAR, the text listed the following: establishing a democratic republican system, working to awaken Arab consciousness and develop faith in Arab nationalism; working to raise the standard of living in the UAR, expanding the domain of various industries; expanding agriculture; increasing mining and local production rather than exporting just raw materials; achieving social justice; working to reduce class differences; raising citizens' level of income; providing work and educational opportunities to all; strengthening the army; working to liberate all Arab peoples from imperialism; and achieving independence (119–22). It thereby wove together the populist goals of the 1952 revolution, which had long been in the narrative, and Arab nationalism's political goals. The new entity would not only continue to strive to achieve social and economic justice, but would also now further strengthen the people (*umma*) through broader Arab political unity.

THE SOCIALIST DECREES, SYRIAN SECESSION, AND THE CHARTER

Despite the setback of Iraq's refusal to join the UAR following its revolution in July 1958, the unity held for the time being. Economic policies increasing the role of the state continued in both the southern (Egypt) and northern (Syria) regions of the UAR. Most notably, in July 1961, a series of laws that aimed at further extending and deepening the role of the state at the expense of the private sector, referred to collectively as the socialist laws or the socialist decrees, began to be promulgated. This new emphasis was underlined visually through a series of postage stamps issued in 1961 with legends such as "Planning increases national income," "Planning for the interest of the people," "Planning achieves social equality," "Planning for equality and welfare," and "Planning for higher production."[61]

In this context the gradual transformation that had taken place in the use of the word "revolution" (*thawra*) should be noted. In the early days, the Free Officers had insisted that their movement had carried out a revolution and not a mere coup (*inqilab*). Still, "revolution" tended to be used to refer to the changes immediately surrounding King Farouk's overthrow. As time went on, however, the goals of the new military rulers continued to be listed or touted, but the revolution itself was no longer restricted in meaning to a discrete period in 1952 or immediately thereafter. Rather, "the revolution" came to represent the ongoing changes that were reshaping the contours of Egyptian society and politics. The revolution became a dynamic and continuing process, with broad transformative goals, but with no foreseeable end point. The explicit turn to socialism, which was clear by 1961, and the way it was integrated into the narrative, must be understood in this context.

Nasser's Revolution Day speech in July 1961 came in the midst of the announcement of the socialist decrees/laws. In it, he mixed the themes of populism and unity, beginning with how 23 July would not have happened but for the call of the people; the revolution's real success was clear in the popular support it enjoyed. He made further reference to peasants, workers, intellectuals, and soldiers, sectors of society that thenceforth were regularly invoked in the narrative as the vanguard and basis of the revolution. Another key theme that began to be integrated into the founding narrative was that the revolution in Egypt had been bloodless, avoiding the civil war that so many other countries had seen: "With love and with patriotic unity we have achieved our goals." He reiterated the six goals of the revolution (3), and noted that while they had succeeded in ridding the country of imperialism and feudalism, social justice remained to be achieved. The socialist decrees were constructed in this way as another stage in the revolutionary march. "In the revolution, we did not seek reform. We seek complete societal change. We need to build a new state from all angles on the basis of justice and equal opportunity" (11). Nasser also constructed socialism as the natural next step toward Arab liberation and independence. Indeed the two were intertwined: Arab unity was inseparable from a call for socialism (15). In this way, the mission of the revolution was again broadened.

As for the themes of unity and identity, Nasser did refer to divisions in society, indicating sources of potential threat. One was social class. He again portrayed a society of two classes, a privileged minority, on the one hand, and the vast majority of the people, on the other. The revolution would work to solve the class struggle in the interests of the oppressed class, but, in keeping with Egypt's tradition, without bloodshed (5). He also mentioned *ta'ifiyya*, here in the sense of religious confessionalism, and criticized those who attempted to politicize religious identity.[62] "Political *ta'ifiyya* serves only the interests of reaction and feudalist and exploitative capitalism" (7).

In Egypt, as elsewhere, the fact that socialism was associated with the Soviet Union made it susceptible to charges that it was an alien, atheist ideology. While the Egyptian state had certainly dealt brutally with the Muslim Brotherhood, and came to stress Arabism rather than Islam as the primary basis of identity, the regime in no way suppressed or opposed religious practice. Quite the contrary; Nasser felt the need to further legitimize socialism by demonstrating its compatibility with Islam, indeed, the inevitable relationship between them. To that end, he argued in this speech that the Islamic state established by the Prophet Muhammad had been the first socialist state. It remained socialist under the first and second caliphs, Abu Bakr and 'Umar, who, he said, had "nationalized land and distributed it to all the peasants." More broadly, he insisted that all religions called for social justice; indeed, almsgiving (*zakat* in Islam) is one of the bases of socialism (13). He also stressed that the goal of the socialist decrees was neither to punish people nor to impoverish those who had resources, but to prevent exploitation "Our socialism is based on brotherhood, unity, and patriotism" (9–10).

Nasser could not have known as he gave this speech that the era of his successive political triumphs was soon to end. The socialist decrees may well have been the last straw for a Syrian commercial community chafing under the weight of imported Egyptian bureaucracy, but Nasser himself had known from the outset that this political project was fraught and underprepared. Still, the Syrian secession (*infisal*) was a huge blow to his and Egypt's regional political ambitions. His speech of 28 September 1961, after the coup makers in Damascus had announced the secession, but before the final outcome was clear, stressed Arab identity and unity. Nasser framed the coup using the theme of struggle that featured in the founding story. As noted above, by this time, that struggle had come to be defined in broader Arab and anti-imperialist terms than it had been earlier in his presidency. Nasser portrayed this unexpected blow as even more dangerous than the attack of 1956, because the Suez war had been launched by outsiders, whereas what had just happened had been the work of fellow Arabs. "Any division in national unity is far more dangerous that external aggression, for national unity was always a sacred demand and a beloved goal. National unity was always the preemptive deterrent of the UAR against its enemies" (1).

No doubt as an attempt to maintain the legitimacy of the foundering project and discredit the coup makers, Nasser repeated throughout the speech that he could not—meaning that he did not have the right to—announce the dissolution of the UAR, a republic that was the vanguard of Arab unity, the basis of Arab struggle, and the core of Arab unity and Arab nationalism (2). "This movement [of secessionists] is a great setback to our revolution which the entire people in all places have supported" (4). "This movement is a dagger aimed at the heart of Arab nationalism, and the back of Arab unity, Arab dignity and the Arab revolution" (4). In other words, it potentially undermined the foundations of Nasser's political project, certainly regionally, but even at home, since it meant the dissolution of what had been constructed as a natural extension of the Egyptian revolution.

Two weeks later, on 16 October 1961, in a speech presenting the way forward, Nasser again combined the themes of populism and unity. In the past few days, he reported, he had felt the reactions of the people everywhere, in villages and factories, universities and laboratories, on the front lines with soldiers, in small homes, and among peasants, workers, and intellectuals. After laying claim to inspiration from the people, he announced that, "in the name of God, this people [*umma*], its hopes, its highest examples, all the things we hold sacred, and all the battles we have waged," he had chosen to continue the path of the revolution (1). He then attempted to turn the setback into a reason for pride, arguing that it was the people's successes, the challenges that they had posed to imperialism, that had triggered the secession: "All the thrones not resting on popular will trembled, as the heavy shadow of imperialism began to retreat from the region" (2). It was imperialism itself that struck on 28 September 1961 through what he called the "reactionary assault in Syria."

He did admit that mistakes had been made: "we imagined that, whatever differences there were between us and the elements of reaction, we were the sons of the same homeland and partners in the same future, but experience showed us that we were wrong, we were dreaming." "While we thought that we could get rid of class contradictions peacefully in the context of national unity, reaction was moving in the opposite direction" (8). This is a striking admission of the limits of the previously highly touted common dreams and aspirations among the Arabs and of the bases of Arab unity. Arabism and unity would not disappear from the discourse going forward, but they would be more balanced with the language of socialism and economic development as the narrative was rescripted to deal with the fallout from the secession.

A broader initiative to rewrite history textbooks did not come until 1963, but some initial changes were introduced beginning in 1962, which appear intended to begin to reinforce Egypt's leadership and path in the wake of this setback. For example, the 1962 third-year secondary school textbook *Ta'rikh al-'Arab al-hadith w-al-mu'asir* (The Modern and Contemporary History of the Arabs) contained many of the same materials and headings as the 1954 textbook for the same level, *Ta'rikh Misr f-il-'asr al-hadith* (The History of Egypt in the Modern Period). Egypt had a central place in the text, and chapter titles from the earlier text were reused. The role of imperialism and resistance to it was the driving theme, and the narrative was familiar (1–6). New, however, was a section on the socialist decrees, which it referred to as the social revolution of July 1961. Recalling Nasser's distinction between the political and social revolutions, it argued that the political revolution had been launched in 1952, and it was now time to launch the social revolution, thereby underlining the place of the most recent reforms in the narrative of the revolution. "In this framework our new socialist society will be built. In it every citizen will enjoy real freedom, freedom that rests on liberation from poverty and want, and from fear and from social oppression. All of this is a basis of political liberation" (337)

This 1962 text also addressed the Syrian secession, framing it in a discourse of populist unity and identity. "Imperialism, Arab monarchical reaction, and monopolistic feudal reaction inside Syria" had allied to cause the coup of 28 September 1961 in Damascus, which was carried out "by some traitorous Arab officers, sons of Syrian feudal reactionaries, who sold out their Arabism for a few dirhams [cents]. This was followed by a serious struggle between them and authentic Syrians who believed in unity, Arabism, and socialism and appreciated the benefits that it had brought to all. Blood was shed all over Syria, but the six traitors managed temporarily to set up their reactionary government" (343). However, the student learns, Arabism depends not upon the rulers but the people; all the Arab peoples believe in Arab nationalism and want to see unity achieved. The fact that it was on the unity of the people that the Syrian-Egyptian union had been established indicated that. Further underlining the sins of the coup makers and vindicating Nasser, the text notes that on 28 March 1962, another coup overthrew the secessionists, and a temporary government was formed to look into steps to reestablish union with Egypt (348).

The Charter

Linguistically colorful propaganda and careful discourse framing aside, the end of the Syrian-Egyptian union was a huge blow to Nasser's power and prestige. While not giving up Egypt's regional ambitions, Nasser's next major policy initiative was domestically oriented, intended both to set the parameters of the next stage of socialist development and to reinforce the regime's legitimacy as it faced growing economic problems on the home front.

In May 1962, Nasser presented a document titled *Al-Mithaq al-watani* (The National Charter) to a national congress of elected representatives of a range of groups from across the occupational and communal spectrum.[63] Debated and subsequently accepted by the congress, it constituted the regime's post-secession political vision, as well as the definitive statement of the country's now crystallized socialist path. The Charter was taught in schools and universities as part of the curriculum, and for several generations more copies of it were printed than of the Quran.[64] Thus, widely distributed and studied, it was the most important text portraying regime mission and national identity since Nasser's *Falsafat al-thawra.* Hence an examination of its formulation of the three elements of the narrative upon which we have been focusing is central to understanding the regime's discursive response to the serious political blow inflicted by the Syrian secession.

The Founding Story Nasser began the Charter with the now familiar founding story: "The 23rd of July 1952 was the beginning of a new and glorious period in the history of continuous struggle of the Arab people of Egypt. On that day the people began a revolutionary experience in all spheres." It was carried out in difficult conditions, but the Egyptian people were honest and sincere in their vision and in their struggle, which was part of a broader struggle, "a contemporary continuation of the struggle of the free human being throughout history for a better life, freed of the bonds of exploitation and backwardness" (3). Theirs was a revolution with implications beyond Egypt, part of a broader path of human history. Indeed, one of the notable elements in this document is its increased focus on the extraregional impact of Egypt's struggles.

Nasser's recounting of earlier Egyptian history not only set the parameters of identity (see below) but also asserted Egypt's central role in the region and the importance of the struggle of the Egyptian people, who had been exploited but had never surrendered (24). The Charter then rehearsed the evils of the 1919–52 period, which had already become a well-established part of the narrative. It also touted the populist narrative of an "amazing revolutionary will among the Egyptian people." Indeed, the revolutionary leadership did not have a guide beyond the six principles of the revolution. Instead, "The great people wrote these six principles in the blood of their martyrs and in the light of hope for which they would give their lives. . . . That people then continued to deepen its struggle and broaden its content" (7). Just as important, natural historic conditions imposed upon Egypt's popular revolutionary leadership the responsibility for being the nucleus in demanding freedom, socialism, and unity for the entire Arab *umma* (11).

Identity The Charter is focused on the Egyptian and the "Egyptian Arab" people, who have an unshakeable faith in God, his Prophet, and his holy message (10), but it employs no other ethno-religious identity markers. Instead, again, Egypt's struggle and role in the region are presented as having implicitly shaped Egyptian identity, and there is a full chapter devoted to this theme (21). Cultural interaction was one hallmark: Egypt was never isolated from the surrounding region, it affected and was affected by it. Pharaonic history formed the first Egyptian and human civilization; and the Islamic conquests brought new thought and a new spiritual existence. In the framework of Islamic history, the Egyptian people undertook the greatest role defending human culture, whether against the Crusades or the Tatar (i.e., Mongol or Turkic) invasions. Egyptians also bore the moral responsibility for preserving Arab civilization, and they made Al-Azhar University a redoubt of moral and religious resistance to the weakness and social disintegration caused by the Ottoman Caliphate.[65]

Reprising a theme from the founding narrative, the Charter recalled the failure of the revolutionary leadership of 1919, but it did so to offer a new reason for it that related to the identity narrative: that leadership had been unable to extend its vision beyond Sinai. "It failed in defining Egyptian identity because it was not able to see through history that there was no conflict at all between Egyptian nationalism [*wataniyya*] and Arab nationalism [*qawmiyya*].

The leadership did not pay attention to the danger of the Balfour Declaration that established Israel . . . and with that failure . . . the imperialist forces were able to deal with a divided Arab *umma*" (28). Thus here and elsewhere, the Charter underlined the notion of Egypt's leading role in the Arab world as an inseparable part of its identity. "The UAR"—note that the name of the country had not been changed—was presented as "in the vanguard of the progressive Arab struggle and its fighting base and fortress. . . . The UAR in history in fact is the only Arab state in the current conditions that is able to shoulder the responsibility of building a national army that is a defensive [*rad*ʿ] force against Zionist, imperialist aggressive plans."

Unity Unlike earlier texts in which the boundaries of class conflict were left unspecified, the Charter not only identified the alliance that underpinned unity—the peasants, the workers, the soldiers, the intellectuals, and national capital(ists)—but also its enemies: the feudalists, the old classes who were "aligned with the imperialists" (8). The theme of domestic unity was implicit in socialism's goal of providing equal opportunity, melting away the differences among classes and ending class conflict (89). Putting an end to confrontation did not end the contradictions between the rest of the classes of the people, but it did open the way for the possibility for a peaceful solution (52).

The text also made numerous references to broader Arab unity, as "the natural state" of a "single Arab *umma*" (17–18). The Arab *umma* no longer needed to prove the real unity of its people (18). It insisted that coercion by any means worked against unity, while any partial unity in the Arab world that represented the will of two or more peoples of the Arab *umma* was a progressive step that brought closer the day of complete unity (110). Thus, in the wake of the setback of the Syrian succession, Nasser continued to stress the inevitable bases of Arab unity, while looking to more modest unifying projects as important steps along the way.

In terms of both language and themes, the temporary constitution promulgated two years later, in 1964, proceeded naturally from the presentation in the Charter. The country was still referred to as the UAR, but the text clearly took into account the socialist decrees. While the notion of "the revolution" had already evolved from that of a single or limited set of events to a longer process, the turn to socialism now implied an even more thoroughgoing and extended transformation. The Constitution reinforced the discourse of a long struggle toward achieving a better life, one of equality of opportunity and of the melting away of class distinctions, all part of the unity narrative. It also preserved the characteristics of the Egyptian people—article 1 stated that the Egyptian people (*sha'b*) was a part of the Arab *umma*—but, as in the Charter, national unity was defined in socialist terms as the alliance of popular forces represented by the working people: the peasants, the workers, the soldiers, the intellectuals, and national capital.

Historiography and Textbooks after the Charter

With the basic outlines set by the Charter, in June 1963, the Ministry of Culture announced a program to rewrite modern Egyptian history. It was to be overseen by a committee of twenty university professors, supervised by the minister and with financial support from the ministry. "It proposed to write modern Egyptian history 'along objective lines' and to purge it of 'all the impurities deliberately introduced into it under imperialism and feudalism.' In keeping with the evolving ideological orientation, it was to deal specifically with issues such as the history of feudalism, national and foreign capitalism, and the working class, which had been neglected by traditional histories."[66] The socialist orientation of this period also offered a new opening to the political Left. In 1965, after extended negotiations, the communist movement, which Nasser had earlier suppressed as fiercely as the Muslim Brotherhood, agreed to dissolve itself in exchange for a role for individual activists in the regime. At this point, to promote the leadership's vision of Arab socialism, leading communists and leftists were appointed as editors, writers, and publishers.[67]

Turning specifically to the educational sector, by 1966, the number of Egyptian children in school, and hence the size of the sector exposed to the national narrative through schooling, had risen to 3.448 million at the primary level, 678,000 in preparatory schools, and 244,000 in secondary schools.[68] A new fifth-year elementary text published in 1967, *Al-Mawwad al-ijtima'iyya, al-jiyughrafiya w-al-ta'rikh w-al-tarbiya al-wataniyya* (Social Studies, Geography, History, and Civics), included the official pre-1952 narrative (139–40), while reinforcing the goals of the socialist revolution (141) and the impact of the socialist decrees (148). Thus, the 1963 initiative does not seem to have had a major impact at this point on textbook content.

THE NAKSA: 1967

The period following the end of the union with Syria witnessed numerous critical developments related to the ongoing struggle over how Arab nationalism would shape regional politics. Beginning with the nationalist surge in the mid-

1950s, the anti-imperialist/anti-Western tone and content of Nasser's policies had led to a division in the region between those allied with him and those more conservative regimes whose stability he appeared to threaten. This division between the revolutionaries and reactionaries, or republicans and monarchs continued to shape Arab politics into the 1960s, although there were tensions within each of these two camps as well. Several attempts at unity among Egypt, Syria, and Iraq followed the breakup of the UAR, but also failed. In the meantime, a coup against Imam Muhammad al-Badr in Yemen opened the way to what became a proxy war between Egypt and Saudi Arabia, the leaders of the two rival camps. Israeli threats—in this case to divert the Jordan River waters—led to the beginning of Arab summitry and a modicum of cooperation, but Egyptian forces were increasingly bogged down in Yemen, putting even greater stress on an already severely strained economy.

The background to the June war of 1967 is a complex story, not only of Arab-Israeli conflict and Israeli territorial ambitions, but also of the tensions and competition between Arab states, above all, Syria and Egypt. The details are beyond the scope of this study. Suffice it here to say that rising regional tensions, initially between Damascus and Tel Aviv, were exacerbated by Nasser's request that UN troops withdraw from Egypt's border with Israel and his subsequent closing of the Straits of Tiran, between the Sinai and Arabian peninsulas. Israel then attacked Egypt on the morning of 5 June 1967. The results of the war, which lasted only six days, are well known: a humiliating military defeat for Egypt, Syria, and Jordan, near total destruction of their military and defensive capabilities, and the occupation of the Sinai, the Golan Heights, the Gaza Strip and the West Bank by Israel. The shock for the Arabs was all the greater because Egyptian broadcasts in the early hours of the war had been replete with lies about an imminent Arab victory.

The military, political, and economic disaster of June 1967 for Egypt, Jordan, Syria, and the Palestinians, and for Nasser's vision and leadership in particular, cannot be overstated. In the immediate aftermath of the war, on 9 June, the Egyptian president responded with a relatively short speech in which he began by admitting that the country had suffered a grave setback (*naksa*).[69] The Arabic word for disaster, *nakba*, had already come be used to refer to the Arabs' defeat in the 1948 Palestine War. Perhaps as a result, or perhaps to downplay the magnitude of the defeat, the word *naksa* was adopted. While it had been used in the past to refer to refer to the 1841 defeat of Ibrahim Pasha in the Syria campaign and to the 1961 Syrian secession, it subsequently became synonymous with the 1967 war.

Nasser addressed the theme of imperialism, and the role it had played in supporting the enemy. He also noted contributions of other Arabs in the wake of this setback (2) and insisted that despite what had happened, the Arab *umma* had the energy and strength to overcome "the results of the aggression." The situation required a united Arab stance. He then in effect accepted responsibility for the disaster by announcing his decision to step down. In so doing, he reprised his construction of his inseparability from the Arab nation: "The forces of imperialism imagine that Gamal Abdel Nasser is their enemy. I want to be clear before them: it is the entire Arab *umma* and not Gamal Abdel Nasser" (3). "The forces opposed to Arab nationalism try to portray it always as the Empire of Gamal Abdel Nasser, but that is not correct: the hope for Arab unity began before Gamal Abdel Nasser and it will continue after him. The *umma* remains, and the revolution is not limited to one generation of revolutionaries" (4). He closed by reaffirming his unlimited faith in the now familiar alliance of forces leading national work: peasants, and workers, and intellectuals, and national capital. "Their unity and coherence is capable of great miracles" (4). Given the extent of destruction and enemy occupation, the need to believe that a united people could achieve such miracles must have been overwhelming.

Major demonstrations followed on 9 and 10 June calling upon Nasser to rescind his decision to step down, and he did. Six weeks later, in his annual July Revolution Day speech, he addressed more fully what had happened prior to and during the war, as he linked the crisis of the day to the themes of past struggles and the revolutionary process. The Egyptian people had undertaken the 23 July revolution in the context of British occupation, they had fought the Suez war, constructed the Aswan High Dam, and built socialism.[70] "The crisis we are facing today is one of the most difficult we have faced in our revolutionary work (1) . . . surrender is out of the question, the only answer/solution is struggle" (6). "Our goal must not just be putting an end to the aggression, but also supporting the revolutionary system, deepening the revolutionary system, and supporting the Arab revolutionary movement" (8). "If we can protect the social revolution in Egypt and support the comprehensive Arab revolution, then we shall be able to liberate the occupied lands" (9).

However, the people expected more than words in response to the defeat. Nasser acknowledged their shock and outrage, again drawing on revolutionary and populist themes: "the people are calling for revolutionary cleansing and purification, and I am calling for that along with the people" (11). In this way, having offered his resignation and having had it rejected, he positioned himself, using traditional formulae, to lead the call for institutionally addressing what came to be referred to as "the footprints of the aggression." The steps that followed aimed at relegitimizing and reconsolidating Nasser's leadership. In the months that followed, a number of high-ranking officers, were arrested and put on trial, including his longtime personal friend ʻAbd al-Hakim ʻAmir, who was charged with leading a conspiratorial cabal. ʻAmir reportedly committed suicide shortly thereafter. Others were sent to jail, but the leniency of the sentences triggered riots in February 1968. While students were prominent in these protests, other long-suppressed forces such as the Muslim Brotherhood also began to stir.[71] To further assuage popular discontent, Nasser shuffled the composition of his cabinet, moving out some members of the military and replacing them with university-trained civilians.[72]

Then, on 30 March, he issued a manifesto, called a "Mandate for Change,"[73] intended to be a formal statement of the lessons of the war and a road map for moving forward. Without specifying the notion of unity, he insisted that it was the demonstrations of the people on 9 and 10 June calling upon him not to leave the presidency that had made it possible for Egypt once again to find solid ground (179). In terms of the narrative going forward, he introduced a new term, "centers of power" (*marakiz al-quwa*), a pejorative intended to refer to unnamed individuals and groups whose mistakes had purportedly led to the *naksa*, or who "stood in the way of the process of correction, out of fear either of losing their power or of revelations about hidden aspects of their behavior" (180). After listing a series of transformations since the war that the people had forged to enable Egypt to pull back from the edge of disaster and look to the future, Nasser proclaimed: "we have succeeded in eliminating the centers of power that had appeared." What was needed was now a defined plan of action, one that "we have studied together and decided upon together" (181).

Indeed, unity among Egyptians had perhaps never been more important than at this point, and the president specified two parts to the work ahead: (182) "bringing all of our military economic and intellectual forces together to the battle lines with the enemy to liberate the land and achieve victory; and mobilizing all the masses' capabilities and energies toward the duties of liberation and victory." He also noted the importance of working with brother Arabs, whether through Arab summits or direct bilateral cooperation, and with all the popular Arab forces to resist the enemy militarily and otherwise (182). Finally, he drew again on the country's identity of successful struggle as inspiration for the challenges ahead: "Our people's struggle has changed the map of the Middle East and put an end to the control of old imperialist empires. It has repelled new attempts at imperialism, shouldered the responsibilities of Arab unity in peace and in war, opened the era of social revolution, built the greatest of dams, conquered the desert, and established the first Arab base of advanced industry. This people has the ability and the experience to overcome a broad defeat. . . . We shall achieve as we have achieved in the past, we shall be victorious as we were in the past, and the will of what is right will prevail above any other will, because it is part of God's will" (188).

In keeping with the 30 March "Mandate for Change" manifesto, law 68 of 1968 stipulated that education in Egypt should produce socialist citizens aware of their responsibilities toward God, family, homeland, and all of humanity, and prepared to undertake responsibilities in keeping with their abilities, so that they could be productive members of their society.[74] The now standard third-year secondary school text *Ta'rikh al-'Arab al-hadith w-al-mu'asir* (The Modern and Contemporary History of the Arabs) was reprinted in 1969 with only marginal revisions from the 1962 version: some updating of statistics, the excision of the story of the Syrian secession, reference to the 1962 revolution in Yemen, and discussion of new unity attempts, but nothing about the 1967 war and its aftermath. Given the decimation of the Egyptian military and the occupation of the Sinai, there were apparently greater exigencies at the time than rewriting history texts. And in any case, with textbooks already stressing Egyptians' unity, their past travails, and their historical ability ultimately to prevail against powerful enemies, it is difficult to imagine any further narrative change that could have helped to reinforce the domestic front.

Most pressing was Egypt's need of Soviet assistance to rebuild its decimated military. At the same time, on the Arab front, if he was to secure financial assistance to alleviate the now further exacerbated domestic economic crisis, Nasser had to reach a modus vivendi with the "reactionary monarchies" he had long pilloried. In the meantime, the standoff between Egypt and Israel, now separated by a closed Suez Canal, morphed into periodic attacks across the canal and ultimately a war of attrition. Concerned about further escalation, the United States responded with a settlement proposal at the end of 1969, dubbed the Rogers Plan, after U.S. Secretary of State William Rogers. As Nasser made clear in his Revolution Day speech in 1970, his acceptance of Rogers's proposal owed to the fact its elements were all things that Egypt had already agreed to in UN resolution 242 in 1967. However, he remained skeptical of American intentions and insisted that Egypt would continue to rebuild, militarily and otherwise. Despite the occasion, there was no narrative of revolution at all. Indeed, both this speech and that of Revolution Day in 1969 focused almost exclusively on the importance of the masses and of steadfastness in rebuilding national strength for the struggle to secure an Israeli withdrawal.

Outside Egypt, the response from the Palestinians and other members of the so-called Arab radical camp, was a rejection of Nasser's and Jordan's King Husein's acceptance of the American initiative. Jordan's stability was the most immediately affected, since the growing strength of the Palestinian resistance organizations that had taken the kingdom as a base ultimately triggered bloody confrontations with the Jordanian army. It was Nasser who led the negotiations aimed at ending what came to be known as Black September, securing a cease-fire on 27 September. It was his last act. He had long suffered from a heart condition, and he died of a heart attack the following day.

CONCLUSIONS

The overthrow of King Farouk in 1952 brought to power a military leadership and ended a dynasty. Over the course of the next eighteen years, the regime, which shortly after the revolution came to be headed by Colonel Gamal Abdel Nasser, faced a number of serious challenges to its position. The preceding discussion has attempted to show how several key elements constitutive of the official national narrative subsequently changed, or were changed, suggesting the leadership's use of discursive tools as one means of securing its position.

The first was the initial need to establish legitimacy in the wake of the coup. The malaise and growing instability that had characterized Egyptian politics in the early 1950s may have made the status quo increasingly untenable, but the Free Officers still needed to legitimize overthrowing the king and terminating the monarchy. On a discursive level, establishing a new founding story was a necessary first step. To that end, a story that began as a limited set of grievances justifying the removal of the king quickly evolved to include a robust set of reasons for his overthrow. The events of 23 July 1952, the centerpiece of the emerging official narrative, were quickly portrayed as a revolution, not a coup, to underline its authors' commitment to broad social and political change. To further underline its legitimacy, the Free Officers' narrative of the revolution was situated historically as the successful culmination of a centuries-long struggle that had produced such nationalist leaders as Ahmad 'Urabi and Mustafa Kamil. Its legitimacy was therefore scripted as deriving, not only from its carrying the torch of these heroes, but from finally achieving the goals of independence and sovereignty that they, too, had espoused.

As for national identity, from the early post-1952 period on, the basis of national belonging was in the first instance territorial, meaning being a "son of this land." The implication of such a characterization was that there was also a shared history, an important part of which involved successive heroic struggles against a series of invaders. The pharaonic past was regularly acknowledged as proof of Egypt's proud past,[75] and on numerous occasions Nasser rehearsed the many civilizations and peoples who had left their mark on the country. As for national ethno-religious components, Nasser's *Falsafat al-thawra* specified three circles of which Egyptian identity was a part: Arab, African, and Islamic, in that order. Although there were few references to Egypt's Coptic identity, past or present, in the narrative throughout this period, there was no focus on Islam either.[76] At no point did the narrative imply subnational bases of possible dissention from national unity. Indeed, to the extent that the narrative acknowledged anything other than popular unity behind the revolution, it did so on the basis of class, vilifying feudalists or wealthy corrupt politicians.

The Suez war was the next great challenge. Nasser's survival in this test owed more to the role of the United States in opposing the British, French, and Israeli invasion than to any strategy of his own. However, the resulting dramatic rise in his prestige led to increased assertions, through both discourse and active policy, of Egypt's natural leadership role in the region, and of Arab nationalism as a basis and program for action. Changes in the textbooks produced during this period illustrate the discursive development of these themes. Immediately following the revolution, narrative rescripting had already rendered the Arab world, rather than Europe, the broader frame of historical reference for Egyptian students. In the wake of the establishment of the UAR, the emphasis moved further in the direction of Arabism, as witnessed by the shift in the titles of and chapter headings in textbooks.

The third major challenge came with the Syrian secession. The early 1960s had seen mounting economic troubles, to which the leadership had responded by nationalizing growing numbers of economic establishments to augment the state's capital resources. However, it was the socialist decrees of 1961 that first explicitly embodied the discursive and policy turn toward socialism. Following the termination of the Egyptian-Syrian union, an additional narrative innovation was introduced, certainly to legitimize the socialist path but also likely to reinforce Nasser's position. To reduce the damage to Nasser's power and prestige, the Syrian secessionists had to be fully discredited. The narrative therefore portrayed them, not just as political opponents, but as political and economic counterrevolutionaries, traitors aligned with capitalism, imperialism, and Arab reactionaries. The most important document of the period, the Charter, echoed these themes. It not only further explained socialism, but also constructed it as a key part of the broader Arab revolution, which was itself implicitly portrayed as an extension of the 1952 founding story.

The textbooks of the late 1950s and early 1960s were swift to respond to these dramatic events. First, they quickly incorporated the narrative of political unity and framed earlier historical events as precursors to the UAR. Then, following the secession, they introduced stinging critiques of those responsible for the coup. For his part, of course, Nasser never gave up the language of Arab political unity or of its inevitability, but, badly stung by the experience with Syria, his vision of what constituted steps in the direction of such political unity became decidedly more modest.

The Suez war could well have led to Nasser's ouster, and Syrian secession from the UAR was a serious blow, but beyond the initial need to consolidate power in 1952, the regime probably faced no challenge greater than surviving the defeat of 1967. Nasser's decision to step down, the most dramatic offer of responsibility and contrition possible, was probably instrumental in his political survival, since the massive demonstrations demanding his return to the presidency implied a renewed popular mandate. Several new terms were introduced at this time as part of the relegitimation strategy. "Centers of power" were cracked down on as part of a purification process termed "revolutionary," no doubt to draw on the population's reserves of faith in the movement begun in 1952. The theme in the established identity and unity narratives of Egypt's having many times overcome great trials, all the while maintaining national cohesion, took on heightened importance in the narrative post-1967. The insistence upon steadfastness in order to rebuild expressed a basic, wrenching need after the destruction wrought by the war. However, it also aimed at doing discursive battle both with political forces long suppressed, which now saw an opening to resurface, and with those whose outrage had been triggered by the defeat and by what they viewed as insufficient accountability.

The way forward, Nasser insisted, required a continued focus on the goals of the revolution; but the 1967 disaster had drained his socialism and revolutionary Arab nationalism of much of their motive force. The goal of rebuilding, not simply to recover from the destruction, but also in order to liberate occupied Egyptian territory from Israeli occupation, was a daunting task that overwhelmed any and all other political considerations. It was not to be accomplished in his lifetime.

3 EGYPT UNDER SADAT AND MUBARAK

Rescripting Revolution, Redefining Legitimacy

THE DEATH OF GAMAL ABDEL NASSER came as a shock to the Egyptian and broader Arab publics. Anwar al-Sadat, one of the original Free Officers, whom Nasser had appointed vice president in December 1969, immediately assumed the presidency, and the transition was orderly. Nevertheless, Sadat was a largely unknown quantity. He did enjoy some historical legitimacy for his participation in the 1952 revolution, but not the deep respect enjoyed by his predecessor. The military's rule itself seemed secure, however, if factionalized, and many of its key members expected the former vice president to be a transitory figure. In the event, Sadat proved far shrewder than most had anticipated. Within nine months of Nasser's death, he had marginalized or imprisoned his opponents, thus closing the book on the succession question.

The presentation that follows employs the same approach as in the previous chapter. It focuses on several episodes from the presidencies of Sadat and his successor, Husni Mubarak, as potentially representing challenges to the leadership's power or legitimacy. Against that backdrop, speeches, policy documents, school textbooks, and several other sources that contributed to constructing the official narrative are carefully analyzed to discern what changes were introduced, if any, and how they may have served the ends of power consolidation or legitimation.

For the period of Sadat's rule, we begin by exploring the narrative responses to the challenges of the transition from Nasser. The discussion then moves on to consider the discursive changes that accompanied or followed the other key challenges of Sadat's decade in power: the impact of the continuing Israeli occupation of Egyptian territory; a growing economic crisis that triggered a reassessment of the revolution's goals of social equity; a dramatic peace initiative that confirmed a broader regional and international realignment; and mounting sectarian conflict. The second half of the chapter turns to discursive changes under Mubarak. The transition following Sadat's assassination is the first episode considered, followed by the 1986 conscript riots, the Islamist insurgency of the 1990s, the impact of neoliberalism, and finally the question of succession. Narrative developments since February 2011 are taken up in the Epilogue.

SUCCESSION AND RECONSOLIDATION

Sadat did not definitively emerge from Nasser's shadow until the 1973 war, but he consolidated his rule between 1970 and 1972. His first step was the so-called corrective movement of May 1971. This was followed by the promulgation of a new constitution. Then, finally, Egypt's Soviet military advisors were expelled. The language Sadat used in making each of these moves aimed at setting and legitimating a new course. In addition to reconstructing the meaning of "revolution," "centers of power," and "legitimacy," he gradually introduced religion into the discourse and rebalanced the weight of Arab versus Egyptian in the national identity.

The Corrective Movement, May 1971

Although not resigned to accepting his rule long-term, the more powerful members of the Egyptian ruling group initially allowed Sadat's constitutionally mandated succession to take place, because they believed he would preserve the existing power hierarchy.[1] Indeed, Sadat's early pronouncements all suggested continuity. For example, on 7 October 1970, when his candidacy for the presidency was placed before the ruling Arab Socialist Union (ASU), he stated: "I came to you along the path of Gamal Abdel Nasser," and "I consider the decision to nominate me as a directive for me to pursue Nasser's path." He referred to the 30 March 1968 manifesto as "the last comprehensive program given by Nasser to his nation" and accepted it as critical to the country's desperate need for national unity. As if reaffirming his commitment to the path of his predecessor, and perhaps trying to draw legitimacy from it, on 25 March 1971, Sadat issued an order that a picture of Nasser comparable in size to his own be placed to the left of his in all government offices.[2]

In the meantime, the stage was set for a showdown, which took on ideological overtones, but was at base about who would rule Egypt.[3] In this context, Sadat no doubt saw value in reinforcing his position by symbolically continuing the march of Arab unity initiated by Nasser. Indeed, the 1970-73 period saw a number of unity experiments between Egypt and other Arab countries, the first of which was the Federation of Arab Republics (Egypt, Libya, and Syria) of 17 April 1971. Less than a month later, a group of left-leaning officers and political figures, led by Vice President 'Ali Sabri, a Free Officer and former head of the ASU, attempted to mobilize popular support against the new president and his allies, a "more diffuse conservative faction."[4] Manifesting political acumen that his opponents had not anticipated, Sadat moved first and decisively: he had them arrested and subsequently purged other officers who showed political ambitions.

Sadat's 14 May 1971 speech in response to the Sabri plot and its defeat set a new tone for a presidency that would gradually reverse or abandon significant parts of Nasser's legacy. First, rather than addressing Egyptians as citizens or brother citizens, as Nasser almost always had, he began with "Bismillah" (In the name of God) and addressed his audience as "brothers and sisters," later also referring to "my sons" on the battlefront.[5] Although common in religious discourse, such framing of Egyptian identity in terms of a family, with Sadat as the father, had none of the progressive or civic connotations of "fellow citizens." Moreover, Sadat declared himself to be responsible first and foremost to God and the people—a formula that, while still populist, marked a departure from Nasser's construction of the Egyptian people as sovereign and citizens (8).

Sadat's reference in this speech to "centers of power" (*marakiz quwa*) was also significant. As we saw in the previous chapter, this term was introduced into official discourse to refer to those deemed responsible for the 1967 defeat. Sadat reappropriated it at this stage as part of his discursive battle to secure his position against his enemies. It echoed the implication of responsibility for the 1967 disaster and served to negatively frame those who were opposed to "what the people wanted." Of course, his use of the term in effect admitted the presence of discord or disunity, but in a way that automatically discredited or delegitimized his opponents: "I will not allow the establishment of a center of power in this country; indeed . . . I will deal in the most severe of ways with anyone who tries to divide the home front" (14). Allowing the emergence of centers of power could lead to the collapse of the internal front, and "stab our troops in the back" (analogously, like what had happened in both 1967 and1948) (19). Then, in a seeming departure from his earlier lionizing of Nasser, Sadat argued that Egypt was full of capable men. "The giant Abdel Nasser, whom none of us could ever imagine losing . . . we lost him, and the people were able to continue" (17). By implication, Sadat was capable of running Egypt's affairs, even if he was not Nasser.

The 1971 Constitution

Nasser had promised in 1969 to work on a new permanent constitution, but had failed to oversee its introduction before he died. Sadat now used the promulgation of such a document to further consolidate his victory over his enemies. The new constitution included critical continuities, but also several key innovations, the most obvious of which was the change in the name of the country from United Arab Republic to Egyptian Arab Republic. At the time, this could have been read simply as an overdue recognition of the end of the 1958 Syrian-Egyptian union, but subsequent developments led to its being interpreted as an indication of Sadat's intention to set the country on a more Egypt- rather than Arab nationalist–focused path.

Egypt was defined in article 1 of the new constitution as "a state whose system is democratic and socialist, based on the alliance of popular working forces. The Egyptian people are a part of the Arab people, which works to achieve comprehensive unity." Nothing here represented a departure from the Nasserist path, nor are its elements of sovereignty or social solidarity modified. Article 40 reiterated that all citizens were equal before the law, without distinction, although this stipulation appears much later in this constitution than in its predecessors.

On the other hand, article 2 now stipulated that Islam was the state religion and Arabic the official language. This presentation might have been regarded as nothing more than a reinforcement of two basic national identity components had it not been for the addition of the phrase "and the principles of Islamic *shari'a* are a primary source of legislation." Article 12 further developed what was a new emphasis on morals and religion: "Society must oversee morals and protect them and enable authentic Egyptian traditions." Article 19 then stipulated the introduction of religious education as a basic subject in the public school curriculum, meaning that for the first time, grades in religion would figure into students' final exam scores. Since such a provision could easily have been introduced though a ministerial decision, its inclusion in the constitution appears to have reflected the balance between the secular and religious forces who participated in writing the constitution, as well as the president's own preferences. These discursive changes were all indicative of a central element of Sadat's legitimation strategy: the need to cultivate the religious Right in order to cut the power of what he saw as a more threatening Left committed to the memory and policies of his predecessor.[6] True, 'Ali Sabri and his allies had been defeated, but Nasser's legacy had to be contained and superseded, otherwise it would continue to impair Sadat's ability to consolidate power in his own right.

Expulsion of the Soviet Advisors, July 1972

On 23 July 1972, the twentieth anniversary of the revolution, Sadat addressed the opening of the general conference of the ASU. As had become his wont, the speech was directed to "brothers and sisters." He began by evoking the memory of Nasser and of the 23 July Revolution, insisting upon its historic contribution and role. "This country has known no real revolution but the 23 July revolution. . . . Indeed, anyone who is honest knows that this Arab *umma* knows only one basic revolution, the mother revolution of all the deep changes that the Arab *umma* has known."[7] The basic narrative of the revolution that he presented was unchanged (2, 4), and he saluted its key documents: Nasser's *Falsafat al-thawra* (Philosophy of the Revolution), the Charter (4), and the manifesto of 30 March 1968 (6). He invoked the people and their role in the revolution, but recalled "the struggle against centers of power that tried to take control of the people's capabilities." He then justified his 1971 "corrective movement" by locating its goals in the Charter: democracy is political freedom and socialism is social freedom and you cannot divide the two (25). It was a theme he continued to develop.

This was Sadat's first speech following his surprise expulsion of some 20,000 Soviet advisors. As noted in the previous chapter, from the time of the Czech arms deal in 1955, Egypt had gradually developed stronger and stronger ties with the Soviet Union. The military embrace was dramatically strengthened after the 1967 war left Egypt's defenses in ruins. Soviet support in the form of matériel and advisors (even pilots who flew missions during the war of attrition with Israel) attested to the importance of the relationship. Consequently, Sadat's decision to dismiss such a large and critical contingent of foreign personnel took Egyptians and other observers by surprise. The president discursively justified his move in terms of one of the most basic principles of the revolution: Egypt's sovereignty. "I don't want a Soviet soldier to fight my battle for me. Give me weapons and leave me to act, it's not your business" (41).

As for the question of unity, in a situation of no war and no peace, which he described as draining Egyptian blood drop by drop, national unity was essential. Now more than at any time in the past, he claimed in this same speech, the domestic front was of greatest importance because Egyptian nationalism (*al-wataniyya al-misriyya*)—the first time this term had appeared in official discourse in decades—would be the principle instrument of liberation (43). This striking contention further suggested that what may have triggered changing the name of the country the previous year was a resetting of the respective weight of Egyptian versus Arab in both regional policy and the national identity narrative. He went on to explain: "We were by ourselves [i.e., on our own] when we made the revolution, when we repelled imperialism, when we brought down the Baghdad pact, most of the time during the Suez War, and in the face of the economic siege and psychological war, and thanks to God, we were victorious" (44). However, he proceeded to refer to Egypt's membership in the Federation of Arab Republics, claiming "the Arab *umma* is with us in our destiny. And Syria and Libya are with us in the battle" (44). Thus, the language suggests a shift in emphasis rather than a dramatic departure. Under Nasser, Egypt had never been completely subsumed by Arabism, and under Sadat, despite a greater emphasis on Egypt and Egyptian identity, the country and its people's place in the Arab world continued to be a central constituent of identity.

He then introduced two other themes—renewal and correction—that became increasingly important as he concretized his new course, all the while careful to keep them within the discursive frame of "the revolution." "The revolution continually renews itself in the shadows of the *naksa*; it renewed itself with the masses of 9 and 10 June [when the people called for Nasser's return to power], and it renewed itself with the announcement of 30 March 1968 and in the correction of 14 May 1971" (45). He did insist that Nasserism remained the program of the revolution, but added, tellingly: "Correcting mistakes and excesses committed by some who then tried unfairly to attribute them to Nasserism cannot be called a pulling away from Nasserism" (45).

One final element in this critical speech related to national unity, but not as under Nasser, when class conflict was openly addressed and feudalists or exploitative capitalists were vilified. Rather, under Sadat, the first specific references to sectarian tensions and sedition (*fitna*) appeared. Recall that under Nasser there was neither a suppression of Islam (as distinguished from suppression of the Muslim Brotherhood) nor were there significant references to Egypt's Coptic heritage or community in the narrative. However, in this speech, in citing the need to continue to hew to Nasser's program, Sadat explicitly rejected those who called into question national unity between Muslims and

Copts (45), even though his "religious turn" on both the discursive and policy levels had clear elements of Islamization.

In a 28 December 1972 speech, Sadat again focused on the domestic front, saying that the enemy knew that victory and defeat began *within* any society.[8] He used this opportunity to stress the *umma*'s preeminent need for unity as a prerequisite for this stage in which the presumption was that war would be necessary to confront the Israeli occupation. "There is no war without national unity and no peace without it" (3). This speech was also significant for its introduction of the concept of a "state of institutions" (*dawlat mu'assasat*) (5), which Sadat framed within the discourse of revolution, arguing that it would fulfill the Free Officers' promise of establishing "correct democratic practice." Ultimately, this term evolved to become what he called "constitutional legitimacy" (*al-shar'iyya al-dusturiyya*). He utilized it to provide discursive legitimation for significant departures from what he labeled the "revolutionary legitimacy" (*al-shar'iyyah al-thawriyya*) that had operated under Nasser.

FROM THE 1973 CROSSING OF THE SUEZ CANAL TO A NEW ERA

Since 1967, the need to end the Israeli occupation of the Sinai had preoccupied the Egyptian leadership. Casting its shadow well beyond the military realm, the demands of this critical national security challenge informed the regime's approach to all aspects of national development. The lack of progress in securing an Israeli withdrawal contributed to Egypt's financial woes, significant even before 1967, by depriving Cairo of revenues from the Sinai oil fields and Suez Canal transit.

Frustrated by the lack of movement toward a political solution, Sadat made plans for war. The attack was launched on 6 October 1973, which coincided that year with the tenth day of Ramadan, the Muslim holy month of fasting. It began with a dramatic assault on the Bar Lev line, a defensive installation on the eastern bank of the Canal that the Israelis had touted as impenetrable. It was, in the event, the first high-profile casualty of the war, and its dramatic destruction enabled Egyptian forces not only to drive the Israelis from their positions, but to push onward. Sadat's refusal to push ahead and the U.S. decision to resupply Israel in the face of Egyptian advances ultimately allowed the Jewish state to retake this territory and move beyond, crossing and penetrating more than a hundred kilometers onto the *West* Bank of the Canal. Still, the initial dramatic crossing served as the basis of an heroic narrative of a war that, as the phrase insisted, "destroyed the myth of Israeli invincibility" spawned by the 1967 defeat. In 1956, Nasser had extracted a political victory from the mouth of military defeat. In 1973, even though Egypt was by no means victorious, the bold attack and its initial success provided Sadat his own legitimacy narrative deriving from politico-military daring.

In a speech delivered ten days into the war, Sadat described the crossing of the Canal and the destruction of the Bar Lev line as one of the greatest and most glorious episodes of Egypt's history. Clearly, this crossing had both physical and symbolic referents: it was not just the crossing of the waterway, but also a crossing "by the heroes of our people and our *umma*" from despair (referring to the results of the 1967 war) to hope.[9] The mixture of Arab and Egyptian nationalism discerned in the July 1972 speech was repeated here: liberating the national (*watani*) and nationalist (*qawmi*) land was the first task (1), and the enemy was the enemy of the entire *umma* (5). The speech also exemplified the growing religious references in the regime's narrative. First and foremost, the war had been launched during the symbolically important holy month of Ramadan. Noting the importance of the people's faith, Sadat added, describing his launching of the war: "I tried to be faithful to what I promised God and what I promised you" (2).

The "victory of October" finally enabled Sadat to close the book on consolidating his rule. "For a decisive two to three years, he was virtually free from challenges; the beleaguered, insecure Sadat of the pre-war period was transformed into a President radiating confidence and determined to get his way," Raymond Hinnebusch writes.[10] In early 1974, Sadat had Nasser's picture removed from government offices and, in keeping with the growing religiosity of state discourse, he started adding Muhammad to his name—thereby calling himself Muhammad Anwar al-Sadat—and began to be referred to as *al-ra'is al-mu'min*, the faithful/believing president. In his speeches and policy statements, he continued to develop the narrative lines that he had utilized as part of his early struggle to secure the presidency. However, he also manifested much greater freedom in introducing policies that departed significantly from those of the Nasser period, all the while scripting his initiatives within the discursive framework of "the revolution."

The October Paper, April 1974

In April 1974, in this changed political atmosphere, Sadat issued the "October Paper," the first expansive exposition of *his* vision of the country's mission and future, one that included increasing criticisms of "the revolution." Not surprisingly, the October victory was the centerpiece. "The Egypt of October is the Egypt of the future," it was asserted, and what came to be referred to simply as "the crossing" was "the culmination of national action whose lessons we must take as a model."[11] Sadat attributed the victory to several factors.

The first two were related to identity, and they underscored the increasingly important juxtaposition of Egyptian *and* Arab nationalism by Sadat. Regarding Egyptian patriotism/nationalism, the president repeated the traditional refrain about Egypt's 7,000-year history, into which he wove the theme of unity: since the dawn of history, Egyptians had been united, and as a result their history had been free of any regional, tribal, or sectarian wars. Egypt "is open to the world, assimilating all that is new and useful . . . remodeling and reshaping it and adding to it its own Egyptian character." When there were invasions, they did not obliterate Egyptian civilization or its personality. Instead, the invaders were either absorbed or expelled. Now, "the October battle has unified the ranks of the people in an unprecedented way" (51). In this formulation, unity was essential for moving ahead with economic development, which became the new battlefront.

The second reason for the victory was Arab nationalism: Egyptians believed deeply in their affiliation with the Arab nation. "They know their historic destiny is to bear the major burden, however brutal the invasion to which the great Arab nation is exposed," whether in the face of the Tatars (i.e., Mongols), the Crusaders, or the Zionists. This theme of Egypt's being the centerpiece was certainly clear in the Nasser period, but Sadat emphasized it even further. "Egypt's geographic position, human potential, civilizational heritage, and national bonds place it in the vanguard of the world's people who are struggling for freedom, progress, peace, and prosperity" (3). The October war "released Arab potentials" and established a new dignity: "the Arab world is no longer booty over which the powerful quarrel, nor an area whose destiny is drawn up in remote capitals" (24–25). That said, while there was a continual emphasis on Arab identity and cooperation, there was no program for furthering Arab *political unity* in this document.[12]

The third element was the achievements of the July Revolution. Sadat did not repeat them all, but he did rehearse the traditional narrative of the background to the revolution while stressing a new theme, that fundamental changes had taken place peacefully (12–13): "The revolution saved the country from civil war." More important, he now arrogated to himself the right to criticize the revolution. As "a partner in responsibility for what has happened in Egypt since July 23, 1952 . . . I exercise self-criticism of the experiment with satisfaction, because of my deep faith that the outcome of the experiment is utterly positive" (37). "Whatever mistakes were made can be forgiven." These negatives had to be acknowledged because they justified his "corrective" or "rectification" movement.

In fact, Sadat cited the rectification movement as a fourth reason for the October victory. It had not only eliminated the "centers of power," but also aimed at asserting the rule of law (*siyadat al-qanun*) and respect for the judiciary; establishing a state of institutions (*dawlat al-mu'assasat*); and placing safeguards so that a citizen could know his rights and duties. These claims were all part of the growing narrative of the institutional legitimacy (*shar'iyya mu'assasatiyya*)—which he claimed to initiate—that was needed to complete the revolution (36). Adopting the duality first proposed by Nasser, Sadat argued that with the goals of the social revolution achieved, his role was now to move Egypt toward fulfilling the promise of the second revolution, the political one, and he noted various measures taken up to that point, including lifting press censorship (39). Even as far back as the 14 May 1971 address, he had begun to note his closure of political detention camps as a major sign of his departure from what had come before him. He never blamed Nasser, at least not explicitly, for the existence of these camps, but he used their closure as evidence of his commitment to greater political freedoms.

A final theme concerned modernization. While it was not directly related to the foundational narrative, or definitions of unity and identity, it became increasingly important as a basis for setting a new economic path. Indeed, it is for its proposed change in economic course that the October Paper is best known. After more than a decade of commitment to socialism, the narrative regarding the private sector began to change. Sadat noted the importance of Arab capital in particular: "the interrelation of economic interests consolidates the organic ties between the Arab countries and, consequently, strengthens their national identity" (62). The president denied that he was abandoning socialism, and he challenged those who insisted he was. The fact remained that law 47 of 1974, which introduced the policy of the open door, or *infitah*, represented a fundamental reversal of Nasser's economic policy: it opened the economy to foreign investment and imports, sought to reduce the state's intervention in the economy, and downgraded the role of the public sector.[13]

External Political Realignment

In the meantime, the results of the political impact of the 1973 war had produced a reinvigorated U.S. role in trying to secure Arab-Israeli peace. U.S. Secretary of State Henry Kissinger's shuttle diplomacy led to two disengagement agreements, the first between Israel and Egypt and Syria in 1974, the second between Egypt and Israel alone in 1975, prompting scathing criticisms that Sadat was embarking on a unilateral rather than a coordinated Arab course. Sadat regularly proclaimed in his speeches that the United States held "99 percent of the cards" when it came to regional peacemaking, and seemed to move increasingly in a direction of a separate, bilateral peace with Israel. Nevertheless, his discourse continued to intertwine elements of both Egyptian and Arab identities. For example, in his speech reopening the Suez Canal on 5 June 1975, he combined Arab nationalist and Egyptian nationalist as well as religious themes, framed by his 1973 victory, which now generally supplemented, when it did not supplant, the founding narrative. Opening with his now standard "Bismillah," he announced in the name of God and with His support, that the canal had been completely cleansed of the Israeli aggression thanks to "the glorious crossing on 6 October 1973." He referred to the Egyptian population as the "Arab people in Egypt" and insisted that Egypt was "determined to carry out its sacred duty toward its land, toward the pure Arab land that was still occupied by the enemy in the Golan, Sinai, and Palestine, and toward usurped Arab rights."

In his speech for Revolution Day that same year (1975) he referenced the traditional narrative, but included his now familiar innovation that some, understandable mistakes had been made along the way.[14] In discussing the revolution, he also took on those who had been criticizing him: "We are today witnessing some pretenders to Nasserism in the Arab world who do not understand the difference between the essence of the revolution and its extraordinary measures. They imagine that the extraordinary measures are the revolution and consider the termination of these measures to be the termination of the revolution, while actually, the elimination of these measures is, as I have often said, proof that the revolution has arrived at the shores of safety and stability." He then reviewed the many times that Nasser, too, had been attacked, yet continued to be supported by the vast masses of the Arab nation (D6).

Perhaps because of these attacks, he also sought to reinforce his position on both domestic and foreign policy by invoking Nasser's name and record and, in so doing, redefining Nasserism as embracing his policies. For example, regarding the criticisms of the disengagement agreements with Israel, he claimed:

> I realize, as did Abdel Nasser, that the duty of the leadership here in Cairo is to shoulder its responsibilities, to take arrows in its chest and, if necessary, stabs

> in the back, as long as our movement is motivated by concern for the highest Arab interests and as long as we represent the opinion of the overwhelming majority, and do not forfeit Arab rights. . . . This is Nasserism, or what Abdel Nasser called and we called our national Egyptian experiment. . . . I promised that our role would be that of one seeking to unify and not to divide. . . . As for those who are sick at heart and motivated by deep-rooted rancor. . . . Time will teach them that Egypt is the elder brother, the guarantee and the axis for moving forward. . . . We have had to bear with the campaigns . . . of those who, because they have been holding the microphone for so long, are no longer able to handle a rifle or a gun to fight with. They have set up what they termed the rejection front. (D7, 12)

As we saw in the previous chapter, Nasser had periodically alluded to Egypt's leadership in the region, but under Sadat, such references were more frequent and, no doubt because of the criticism he received, they assumed an increasingly arrogant or patronizing air.

Sadat reiterated the goal of what was no longer the corrective *movement* of 1971, but the corrective *revolution*: political freedoms, which had been sacrificed, needed to be restored fully to the people "to correct the course of the revolution and to restore it to its origin, principles, and intrinsic ability to develop" (D9). It was also launched to restore unity to the nation. That unity required a guaranteed degree of social justice, as well as political institutions. After outlining the changes that he had introduced along those lines, with the closure of political detention camps again at the top of the list (D10), he asserted the new banner theme of regime legitimacy: "We are now moving from revolutionary to constitutional legitimacy" (D19).

It was during this period when Sadat was asserting a new economic and foreign policy course, both of which triggered significant criticism, that he set up a committee to write the history of the July Revolution.[15] As part of this initiative, he issued two presidential decrees: one which restricted writing about the 1952 revolution to this specially constituted committee and another that made it difficult for historians to use documents less than fifty years old. He was, no doubt, seeking to control how historians would portray him. Members of the special committee were announced in the press in October 1975 and collected a great deal of documentation, but in the end published very little.[16]

Sadat's subsequent speeches continued to feature the same basic themes. The relationship with Arabism, however, became increasingly problematic the further he departed from Nasser's path. To address the growing dissonance, in a 14 March 1976 speech, he introduced a new story line of Egypt's sacrifices and sufferings for Arab causes. "Since the 1950s, Egypt has been subjected to many economic pressures, which have resulted in its present economic position. It suffices to note the four wars waged by Egypt to protect Arab rights and the rights of the Palestinian people. They required a huge increase in general military expenditures, which resulted in an inability to renew and strengthen the fundamental utilities in line with the population increase."[17] "The October battle would not have been possible had I not worked for two years to make the Arab nation one family again." "The decision for the crossing was Egyptian-Arab; the solidarity was Egyptian-Arab; the surge forward was Egyptian-Arab. Thus from being disunited, we became united; instead of acting against each other, we developed an understanding." In this way, Sadat portrayed himself as a new kind of hero of Arab unity, one not dependent on "empty slogans" (D20). Taking a swipe at the attempts at Arab unification under Nasser, he asserted that Egypt believed in Arab unity, but not in the unity of "constitutional forms, which were created artificially and have collapsed" (D19).

In short, there was no lack of Arabism in these speeches, but it was no longer a revolutionary Arabism. Discussions of Arab political unity gave way to calls for Arab economic cooperation. Thus, rather than characterizing his discourse as shifting away from Egypt's Arab identity, it would be more accurate to say that Sadat reconstructed the goals of inter-Arab initiatives and changed his set of Arab allies—from the soldiers to the monarchs, especially the oil-wealthy ones. It was a shift that was needed to help close the door on Arab unity as a political project—a hallmark of Nasser's legacy—and open the way to the arrival of the Arab investment Sadat felt was critical to solving Egypt's economic problems in order to ensure domestic stability.

ECONOMIC CRISIS AND SADAT'S VISIT TO JERUSALEM IN 1977

Despite the economic opening of the *infitah*, the Egyptian economy continued to suffer. In the absence of peace, external investors remained wary, while domestically, those Egyptians with some capital sought out sectors such as construction and importing that offered quick gains and contributed little to longer-term development goals. The inflation that accompanied the resultant state borrowing was further fueled by remittances from the large numbers of Egyptians who had migrated to the Gulf oil states since the early 1970s.

Thus, rather than seeing their economic lot improve, most Egyptians saw a reopening of the class and income disparities whose closing had been a hallmark of the 1952 revolutionary program. Sadat ultimately had to seek assistance from the International Monetary Fund to address the deficit. In exchange, Egypt was required to cut some of the long-standing price supports on basic commodities. When he announced the reduction of some subsidies and the cancellation of others in mid-January 1977, popular anger exploded into two days of rioting. The violence was so severe that Sadat was forced to rescind the reductions. Only two weeks earlier, he had authorized the creation of new political parties. In the wake of the riots, however, as Jason Brownlee notes, "Sadat seemed to cling to power more tightly than ever, preserving the dominance of his own party behind the fresh façade of multipartyism."[18] The popularity he had secured through the 1973 War and other reforms in the direction of a proclaimed commitment to institutional legitimacy appeared badly shaken.

In his 29 January 1977 speech immediately thereafter, Sadat's anger over this direct challenge to his rule was palpable. He claimed that in the context of demonstrations in 1971, 1972, and 1973 he had been tolerant; "but it is impossible to be tolerant about this—never." Such a departure from unity was not to be allowed. Thenceforth the dates 18 and 19 January were associated with sedition and sabotage, a direct and unacceptable challenge to the rule of law and to unity, which he defined as the proper frameworks within which to solve problems: "Through legal channels, everything is permissible. But there will be no strikes, sit-ins or demonstrations. . . . We have the supremacy of law and a sound democracy that must be implemented soundly" (D13). "We believe in the family, solidarity, collaboration and support. . . . We are overcoming our difficulties with the spirit of one family, with all members assuming their burden" (D14).[19]

Sadat's desire to end to the conflict with Israel, so that domestic resources could be reallocated and more foreign investment attracted, was made all the more urgent by the explosion of January 1977. To that end, in a move that shocked the Arab world, Sadat announced his willingness to go to Jerusalem to make peace. Before most had fully absorbed the implications of such a trip, Sadat had traveled to the Jewish state and, on 20 November, addressed the Israeli Knesset. His speech was replete with Arab, Egyptian-Arab, and religious themes, all mixed with his own sense of importance and heroism: "No one would have expected that the president of the largest Arab state, which bears the heaviest burden and the highest responsibility regarding the issues of war and peace in the Middle East, would declare his readiness to go to the land of the enemy."[20] Yet, he saw as part of his responsibility "to exhaust all and every means in a bid to save my Egyptian Arab people and the entire Arab nation [from] the horrors of new, shocking and destructive wars" (3). He even claimed that he had the same responsibility toward everyone, including the Israeli people (4). He drew further on religious symbolism, seemingly comparing himself to Abraham, inasmuch as his speech coincided with 'Eid al-Adha (5), the Islamic feast that ends the month in which the pilgrimage, which also commemorates Abraham's willingness to sacrifice his son, takes place. He also rehearsed the identity trope that fanaticism was not a part of the Egyptian tradition, that Egypt's sons, "Muslims, Christians, and Jews, live together in a spirit of cordiality, love and tolerance" (12).

He followed up the Knesset speech with an address in Cairo on 8 December 1977. Having already been broadly criticized in the Arab world for the Jerusalem trip, Sadat struck back with a strong dose of Egyptian superiority or patronizing nationalism, punctuated by verses from the Quran. He made the 1973 crossing a centerpiece saying that "the entire Arab nation crossed with us. It crossed the barrier of humiliation, defeat and division. . . . We have been faithful and remain faithful. We are still carrying the dwarfs on our shoulders, but this is the fate of Egypt, and this is Egypt's big heart. We fought in war and triumphed, and the Arab nation triumphed through us . . . we shall make peace and our Arab nation will also triumph through us."[21] "Egypt will rise above these wounds that they want to inflict on us today out of a sense of envy, ignorance and stupidity." He closed with a phrase he had used before: "I will bow to no one but the people of Egypt, and I will kneel only to God" (D24).

Thus, by traveling to Jerusalem in a period in which the legitimacy he had secured through the 1973 war had been shaken by the most extensive rioting since prior to the 1952 revolution, Sadat undertook yet another initiative of a completely different order. The narrative he used to accompany this trip drew heavily on the religious references that he had introduced early in his presidency. He also continued to shift the mix of (now at times haughty) Egyptianism and Arabism in his construction of the ethnic identity narrative, no doubt to tap into Egyptians' sense of national pride in the face of the barrage of attacks on their president from elsewhere in the Arab world. Yet there was another new element as well. Sadat began to present himself as the larger-than-life figure that once only Nasser had been. No longer just the daring hero of the 1973 crossing of the Canal, he now saw and presented himself as a visionary unparalleled in his country's history.

THE ROAD TO CAMP DAVID AND THE PEACE TREATY

If Sadat had expected an easy road ahead after his dramatic trip, he underestimated the intransigence of the Israeli government under Prime Minister Menachem Begin. In the meantime, however, with the exception of relatively small circles of leftists and Muslim extremists, his peace initiative enjoyed broad approval at home, although the country's economic woes continued to generate dissatisfaction. The president did not hesitate to move against his domestic critics, but in his speeches he also drew on long-standing tropes to reinforce support for his policies. For example, to legitimize was what seen by his critics as a traitorous departure from the Arab fold, Sadat utilized a populist theme that had been part of both the founding and identity narratives of Egyptians' struggle against aggressors, stressing the country's many sacrifices in Arab-Israeli wars over the years. What then ultimately developed into a separate peace was scripted, not as a breaking of Arab ranks or a betrayal of Arab causes such as Palestine, but rather as a move that demonstrated Egypt's *sovereign* rights, as well as Sadat's wisdom in being able to recover territory that was a key part of its identity.

In a 14 May 1978 speech on the anniversary of the corrective revolution, Sadat first appealed to populism, asserting that this day marked a shift from the coercion of the "centers of power" to the supremacy of the will of the masses; from the threat to security and livelihood of the citizens to their freedom to enjoy all the political and social rights. He also appealed to the identity theme of independence, insisting that Egypt was capable of charting its own course, making its own decisions and defeating all the forces of oppression and aggression."[22] He touted the achievements of the October war and briefly paid homage to the results of the revolution (D2 and D4).

He then drew on the narrative of the revolution, but in a new way, intended to counter his domestic opposition. He claimed that Egypt was in fact returning to the problems of the pre-1952 period (D13), as chaos was beginning to spread in the labor unions and in the political parties (D14). Just as such instability had been a threat prior to the revolution, so it was now, and he sought to justify his approach to quashing it. Reaffirming his patriarchal approach, which he tried to present as a form of kindness, he insisted: "I want every president of this country to be the head of the family, not a president who rules with an iron fist" (D13). Nonetheless, to rein in what he viewed as excesses, including charges of corruption circulating against prominent businessmen associated with the ruling group, he called on the People's Assembly to formulate a "law of shame" (*qanun al-'ayb*), which in fact sought to suppress public expressions of opposition (D12). Despite a growing challenge coming from the religious Right, he instead singled out his traditional nemesis, the political Left, for purportedly undermining national unity: "It must not be said that the country is becoming capitalist, that some are getting rich and the rest of the people are being deprived" (D15).

Two months later, in July 1978, Sadat founded the National Democratic Party, a reinvention of the ASU.[23] He claimed that just as in the past, the majority had been guided by the principles of the 23 July revolution, and then those of the 15 May revolution, so now a majority of the people had joined this new party. In other words, regardless of the growing chorus of criticism of his domestic and foreign policy, in the name of the revolution and his subsequent series of legitimizing policies, he claimed majority support for the path he had chosen for Egypt.

Regardless of his populist appeals and claims, Sadat had often stated that he was responsible first before God, and only then to the people. In the May 1978 speech referred to above, he seemed to go a step further, perhaps in an attempt to shore up support among religious conservatives, but certainly distancing him from the notion of popular sovereignty: "I am responsible for this trust first before Almighty God, not you."[24] Then, building on his morality discourse, he stipulated, "there will be no leadership or information post or any other post affecting the masses in Egypt for anyone who does not believe in the laws of God" (D16). He addressed the same themes in his speech of 23 November 1978, following the conclusion of the Camp David Accords, when he referred to the "law of shame," which was intended to cleanse political life of "those who wanted to smash the values and virtues of religion by casting doubt and propagating anarchy" (D4).

The Camp David Accords ultimately evolved into the first peace treaty between Israel and an Arab state. To respond to his critics, Sadat initially employed traditional identity elements to legitimate his signing of the treaty. For example, in his speech on 29 March 1979, he claimed that not only had Egypt entered "a new chapter that is worthy of our spiritual values and our civilization," but these steps would also serve vital Arab interests.[25] His proclamations notwithstanding, the conclusion of the treaty only further galvanized a majority of Arab states against him and Egypt. Many severed formal diplomatic ties, while Egypt's membership in the Arab League was frozen and its headquarters were transferred from Cairo, its home since its founding, to Tunis. In his speech a few days later, on 5 April 1979, after rehearsing the traditional narrative of the revolution with his additions, as well as the now common and basic national identity elements,[26] he launched a full-scale discursive assault. He mocked Arab solidarity by talking about the crimes committed daily in its name (D6). He also reminded his audience that the Arabs had attacked Nasser in 1970 in the context of the Rogers Plan, forcing him to back down to be "courteous" to them: "How long will courtesy be maintained at the expense of the interests of the nation and the interests of our peoples?" (D7).

He also vented his full rage against the Palestinians, insisting that those Palestinian leaders who vilified Egypt needed to be taught a lesson in ethics (D13–17). He vehemently rejected the contention that what Egypt had achieved was a "separate solution" (D18), or that Egypt would now become a U.S. gendarme, in effect surrendering its hard-won, highly prized independence. "I shall work for no one," he insisted, reminding the audience that it was he who had expelled the Soviet advisors (D23). Finally, he constructed the peace treaty as one of the long line of heroic episodes in Egyptian history: "We just need to prove to ourselves before we prove to the whole world that the heroes of 6 October 1973 and the heroes of 26 March 1979—the heroes of war and the heroes of peace—are also the vanguards of the heroes in the hardest battle of our existence, the struggle of the soul" (D25). Thus, Sadat made the case justifying Egypt's path, following its interests instead of sacrificing them because of Arab opposition. That said, he did not ever imply that Egypt was not concerned with or had abandoned broader Arab interests. It was the Arabs who opposed his decisions who were the ones in the wrong.

Vice President Husni Mubarak delivered the Revolution Day speech on 22 July 1979. He began with a short summary of the traditional narrative of the reasons for the revolution, then situated what Egypt had achieved through the peace treaty in the framework of its long history of struggles, most specifically those to liberate its territory, but also regarding identity. With the peace treaty, Egypt had taken a huge step on the road to liberation, Mubarak said, because it had recovered a part of its valuable national soil, "which is one of the basic components of the Egyptian identity." [27] No doubt as part of the continuing attempts to legitimate the peace treaty, he repeated Sadat's anecdote about Nasser in 1970: Nasser had emerged on 23 July at the head of a faithful group of sons of this county (a group of which Sadat was also a part, of course) seeking to end the British occupation; however, in 1970, when Nasser sought to end the Israeli occupation, he was criticized, even charged with treason, for accepting the Rogers Plan (3). In a seeming direct response to the freezing of Egypt's membership in the Arab League, Mubarak defended Egypt against charges of abandoning Palestine and asserted that Egypt was the beating heart of the large Arab nation: "no one is allowed to doubt our belonging to it."

Curricular Developments and the Narrative

By 1976, the number of children in Egyptian schools had risen to 4.152 million at the primary level, 1.436 million in preparatory schools, and 393,000 in secondary schools. Still, the numbers attending remained well below what the compulsory nature of the system suggested, and illiteracy remained high.[28] Until the mid-1970s, when a new curriculum began to be drafted, textbooks were largely carried over from the Nasser period. Thus throughout the first half of Sadat's presidency, the narrative as presented in school textbooks went unchanged.

The effect of the new curriculum was apparent, however, in the 1977 version of *Ta'rikh al-'Arab al-hadith w-al-mu'asir* (The Modern and Contemporary History of the Arabs). Although the broad Arab nationalist frame (with numerous anachronisms) remained,[29] this edition did devote more space to Egypt. For example, it included a significant section on post-1952 history, with a great deal of historical detail on Egypt and the rest of the Arab world. Sadat's seven years in office were given as much coverage as Nasser's sixteen, including notable attention to the October war, although the long-standing narrative of the revolution was unchanged. The corrective revolution was mentioned, as was the 1971 constitution as part of what was described as a continuation of support for democracy in the country. There was no discursive turn away from Egypt's long-standing commitment to Arabism or its role in the Arab world.

The title of the 1980 first-year preparatory textbook *Al-Hadara al-Misriyya al-qadima wa 'ulaqatuha bi-haradat al-watan al-'Arabi* (Ancient Egyptian Civilization and Its Relations with Civilizations of the Arab World) may well have been intended as part of a new kind of intertwining of Egyptian and Arab identity narratives, although it, too, maintained a strong Arab nationalist orientation. For example, it called Egyptian resistance to the Hyksos the first *Arab unity* in history, included a map of the *Arab world* in the age of Thutmose III (1479–1425 BCE), and the sections on Syria and Iraq asserted their *qawmi* nature going back to ancient times. Any of these claims would have easily conformed to the national narrative in the Nasser period.[30]

What appear to be conflicting currents in the ongoing struggle between Egyptian nationalism and Arabism for identity priority also appear in the 1978 version of the third-year preparatory civics textbook *Al-Tarbiya al-qawmiyya*,[31] which was given a new subtitle that translates as "The Egyptian Arab Republic and the Contemporary World." Nevertheless, the introduction indicated that the curriculum sought to highlight the importance of Arab nationalism and Arab unity (2), and the chapter outline largely followed that of its predecessor, although instead of referring to "Egypt" as the 1971 book did, it often substituted "the Egyptian Arab Republic," the country's new name following the promulgation of the 1971 constitution. In terms of content, this book had more coverage of Egypt and its external relations than its predecessor, including a new chapter on Egypt and the Islamic world. It also contained updated material on Egypt (and the international community) and the Palestine question. "Without the steadfastness of Egypt, Palestinian rights would have been lost," it insisted (49). The 1980 version of the book followed suit, adding more than six pages on the Palestinian issue, largely focused on Sadat's peace initiative. It seemed intended as a defense of Egypt's position, insisting that there had been no retreat from its principles or its nationalist (*qawmi*) commitments despite the treaty with Israel (64–70). Also notable is that the introduction began with "Bismillah." While this religious invocation soon became commonplace in such works, it had not been characteristic of earlier textbooks.

Sadat's last year in office saw the promulgation of law 139, which provided for the first comprehensive educational reform since the 1940s. It was also the first reform since the 1940s in which multiple sectors participated.[32] The law stipulated that pre-university education should aim at developing the student culturally, scientifically, and *qawmiyyan* (with regard to the Arab nation), with the goal of preparing the Egyptian as a believer in his Lord (*rabbihi*), his homeland, and good values. In this way, Sadat's emphasis on values and religion were combined with national identity. The law also referred to the development of "society" rather than a larger Arab political entity. Just as critical, and emblematic of the shift away from the revolution's commitment to social justice through the state provision of education, the law referred to the growing number of private schools as a form of assistance (*mu'awina*) to the state schools.[33]

THE INCREASING THREAT OF SEDITION

In May 1980, a number of amendments were made to the constitution, which illustrate basic changes being introduced into regime and societal identity. The first was in the description of the country's political system, which was no longer "democratic socialist" but "socialist democratic." The altered language participated in the ongoing policy of abandoning the socialism of the past and replacing it with democracy à la Sadat. As a key corollary to restructuring the role and responsibility of the state toward its citizens that such a transformation involved, in article 4, the phrase "removing class differences" was replaced with "and leading to the rapprochement of differences in income, protecting legitimate gains, and ensuring justice in distributing the costs and burdens." Also striking was the rewording of article 2 such that *shari'a* became "the" rather than "a" primary source of legislation.[34] The timing was particularly sensitive, since March 1980 had seen a series of bombings by Muslims of Coptic properties throughout the country, to which the Coptic patriarch, Anba Shenouda, had responded by canceling all Easter celebrations. When emigrant Copts in the United States and Canada demonstrated against him during a May visit to North America, Sadat accused Pope Shenouda of conspiring to establish a separatist Coptic state.

The overwhelmingly successful popular referendum that had been held on the peace treaty in spring 1979 had also included a segment on preserving national unity, and the 22 July 1979 speech discussed above had insisted that unlike other societies which had been torn apart by sectarian conflicts, "our society is cohesive, tolerant, pluralistic" (13). Yet, developments on the ground indicated otherwise. Hence, Sadat's speech on the anniversary of the corrective revolution in 1980 focused on the threat of sedition (*fitna*).[35] He began by presenting his narrative of the many successes of his presidency, citing a major accomplishment for each year: the corrective revolution (1971); expelling the Soviet advisors (1972); the Ramadan war (1973); the open-door economic policy (*infitah*) (1974); the reopening of the Suez Canal (1975); the cancellation of the Soviet friendship treaty (1976); the peace initiative (1977); the Camp David Accords (1978); and the peace treaty with Israel (1979). He then announced the termination of martial law as his historic decision for 1980. With this step, "we complete a march that began 100 years ago" (D5). With the cancellation of martial law (D7), the last of the negatives of the past had, he contended, been corrected.

He then turned to sectarian sedition. While he underlined that Egypt was not Lebanon, and insisted upon the unity of the Egyptian people regardless of religion, his decision to focus on *fitna* underlined the severity of the problem. He first turned to the Copts and insisted that they were indivisible from the national community in terms of both identity and politics: "The Copts are Egypt's origin. . . . A Copt means an Egyptian. . . . If we go back to the origins, we will see that many Coptic families adopted Islam long ago, at the time of the conquest. This is why this homeland belongs to us all, before Christianity and before Islam" (D21). "The Copts are an indivisible part of both our Egyptian nation and of Egypt's national history. Under no circumstances could they be—as certain religious leaders would have it—a foreign community or subject to clerical command" (D25).

As for the Copts' concerns about article 2 of the constitution regarding the role of *shari'a*, Sadat responded with a striking formulation of his (and Egypt's) central position in relation to Islam, and the responsibilities toward Christians that it implied: "Since I assumed power in Egypt, I have been ruling as a Muslim president of an Islamic state. Egypt is an Islamic state, and not an ordinary Islamic state. It occupies a leading position in the Islamic world, a pioneering position" (D20). "In my capacity as a Muslim ruler of a Muslim state, I assume religious and temporal responsibilities. I am responsible for protecting religion and secular politics for all the people, Muslim and Copts. . . . I derive my help from God Almighty and from the confidence of my people, Copts and Muslims alike. My responsibility makes it incumbent upon me to care for the Christians exactly as I care for the Muslims" (D24). "The real security for Christianity in Egypt is Islam itself" (D21).

Although he increasingly injected religion into the public sphere, Sadat denied others the same right: "I say there is no religion in politics and no politics in religion, although Islam combines religion and state. Yet there is a great difference between Islam's being a religion and state, and utilizing Islam for attacking the state. Islam does not say this" (D26). "I say to those frenzied fanatics, both the Copts and the Muslims, shame on you" (D11). "The sedition must end today" (D26). "Brothers and sisters . . . your strength lies in your unity and your unity lies in your security and safety" (D35). He then closed with a prayer.

In a speech on 1 October 1980, he reprised and amended the old narrative of revolutionary legitimacy—even though for several years he had been stressing the move under his presidency to constitutional or institutional legitimacy—to justify his approach to religion and politics: "It is a basic line of the 23 July and 15 May revolutions that religion should not be exploited for politics—absolutely not." "If a man of religion wants to deal with politics, he must quit his Islamic or Christian role and go to the parties to work there."[36] "Egypt is proud that it is the cradle of the three religions. . . . We condemn anything that is against the three religions" (D5). Then, in a reconfiguration of the priority of national identity components he stated: "Clearly and frankly, Islam comes first and then Arabism—clearly" (D6). He even justified his commitment to giving military facilities to the United States—something for which he had also come under severe criticism—on the grounds that they would be used to assist Arab or Islamic nations. "I did this on the basis of Egypt's historic responsibility to the Arab nation and the Islamic world" (D7).

These rescriptings in which the president sought to undermine his enemies and reinforce his position were innovative, but they failed to produce the intended effect. Criticism continued to mount, as did religious tensions, economic crisis and corruption, while Sadat and Vice President Mubarak made numerous trips to Europe and the United States in search of economic and military assistance. In June 1981, an apparent misunderstanding between Muslim and Christian neighbors in the Zawiya al-Hamra district in Cairo escalated into armed clashes. On 3 September, Sadat moved decisively against his political opponents on both the religious Right and the Left, ordering the arrest of more than 1,500 people, including activists, journalists, and other professionals. Two days later, in his last major speech before his assassination, he again focused on the question of *fitna* and the incidents in the Zawiya al-Hamra neighborhood, but he insisted that there was a broad and genuine popular base which insisted upon national unity.[37] He blamed the Coptic Church, even though he admitted that the Islamic groups' response had been 100 times greater than that of the Christians (6). "We need a radical solution (17), he insisted: "Beginning from this night there is nothing called "the two components of the people [*umma*]"; "there is one *umma* and one component" (26), and he repeated his order that there was to be no politics in religion and no religion in politics (28).

As for the opposition he had imprisoned, Sadat claimed that it counted only about 1,500 people, of whom 250 were criminals (18). At stake, he argued, were the safety, reputation, and unity of Egypt (22). He then announced a list of measures to be taken against those people and groups whom he contended had engaged in work that threatened national unity or social peace (28). Perhaps most provocatively, he dismissed the Coptic patriarch, Anba Shenouda, and replaced him with his own choice for the position (30). His campaign of repression continued: he dissolved a number of religious organizations, outlawed the Muslim Brotherhood, which he himself had allowed to reenter the political field only a few years earlier, and authorized the Ministry of Religious Endowments (Awqaf) to take over sixty-five mosques belonging to disbanded religious groups.[38] The president who had long trumpeted his policies as aimed at reintroducing pluralism and greater freedoms into political life had had his fill of oppositional expressions. Unfortunately for him and for Egypt, the genie unleashed by his decade of economic and political realignments, growing indebtedness and corruption, and support for a re-Islamization of the public sphere would not go easily back into its bottle.

SADAT'S ASSASSINATION AND THE TRANSITION

Sadat had deliberately introduced into the official narrative a discourse of Islam and morality in order to marginalize his opponents on the political Left and court the religious Right. It was therefore at least ironic—although some would say deserved—that he was killed by gunmen from Islamic Jihad, one of the extremist groups that had emerged in the climate created by the "believing president." Symbolically, the gunmen chose a military review commemorating Sadat's great achievement, the Suez Canal crossing of October 6, 1973, to assassinate the man who had become a symbol of corruption and peace with the enemy. In the context of a concern with the construction of identity elements, it is worth remembering that when he fired at Sadat, the lead assassin, Khalid Islambuli, reportedly shouted, "Death to Pharaoh!" This was clearly not the "radical solution" Sadat had had in mind in his 5 September speech.

Despite the violent end to Sadat's rule, the succession took place without incident. In terms of public personae, however, Sadat, with his flair for the dramatic, and the low-key, uncharismatic Mubarak could not have been more different. Yet, after a decade of the jarring contradictions of war and peace, the unexpected economic right turn to *infitah*, and the menace of growing sectarian tensions, the Egyptian people were more than ready for a steady, rather than daring, hand to guide the country through its difficulties. Mubarak had been Sadat's vice president since April 1975 and a key figure in the National Democratic Party (NDP) since its founding in 1978. More important for his assertion of authority over the institutions of state was the fact that he had had a long and distinguished career in the military, an institution that Sadat had depoliticized and professionalized since surviving the 1971 coup attempt. Mubarak had commanded the air force during the 1973 war, and his generation led or controlled much of the officer corps.[39] Finally, given that Sadat had been assassinated in a climate of growing opposition, Mubarak did not face the challenge Sadat had had in filling the shoes of a larger-than-life predecessor. In other words, neither the legitimacy of Mubarak's rule nor his ability to rise to the task of governing was broadly questioned.

The intent here is not to examine in detail the many domestic and foreign policy developments that took place during Mubarak's nearly thirty-year rule.

Rather, in considering the evolution of the narrative during these three decades, the discussion will explore how the first president who had not been a member of the Free Officers engaged the founding story and the questions of identity and unity in the context of four very different challenges: his initial assumption of the presidency; the conscripts riots of 1986; the Islamic insurgency of the 1990s; and the question of political development and succession in the 2000s.

REGIME CONSOLIDATION

Mubarak was nominated for the presidency by the People's Assembly the day after Sadat's assassination, and was formally elected president on 13 October 1981. Even before his election, however, bloody clashes had erupted between Islamists and security forces in Upper Egypt, leading to a wave of arrests of religious militants. Subsequent dismissals in the army, from which Sadat's assassins had come, suggested that organized opposition in the security forces had been extensive. It was in in this climate that in a speech to the People's Assembly on 8 November 1981, Mubarak had his first opportunity to begin to set the discursive frames of his presidency. As was now common, he opened his speech with "Bismillah," but he mixed his forms of address, sometimes using the more traditional "brothers and sisters" and at others, the "brother citizens" that had been common currency under Nasser. He began by paying tribute to Sadat's great leadership, his concern for the interests of his country, and his "absolute belief in God," the people, and "the one Egyptian family."[40] Given that Sadat had been assassinated in a climate of increasing religious tension, it is not surprising that Mubarak focused on national unity. He first insisted that Egyptians needed to "stay away from wrangling, whims, and self-interests" (1). "Egypt is for all. . . . it is not the society of [a] distinguished minority that monopolizes wealth and influence, nor is it the society of [a self-]chosen elite that rises above the people and imposes its tutelage on them, nor is it [a] society of class dictatorship or sectarianism that seeks to humiliate the people and their honor. Egypt must be for all its sons" (1).

He then moved on to a direct rejection of terrorism. Bloody, barbaric, abhorrent, and evil, terrorism "intruded upon religion and faith and was an enemy of knowledge and development." He noted what he termed "the terrible symbolism" of "the hero of mankind and peace falling victim on 6 October, one of the most immortal days in Egypt's history" (2). He insisted, however, that "every citizen and lover of Egypt can be reassured that the internal front is completely sound" (2), and he singled out the security services for special praise (3). He underlined that the destruction of terrorism was the responsibility of all, but attributed particular responsibility to the role of education and religion. Young people needed to be acquainted with "the true meanings of the religious mission and its legal and subjective rules." "Terrorism represents a criminal deviation. The responsibility begins at school and should be present at all stages of education; it should also be shouldered by those spreading the call of religion" (2). In this way, while the stage had been set under Sadat, Mubarak's discourse more thoroughly securitized the construction of religious and national identity.

The rest of Mubarak's speech engaged long-standing themes. Echoing the goals of the revolution, he insisted that basic needs had to be provided, although he also stressed that the success of Egypt's forward march would depend upon its ability to face economic challenges firmly and effectively. He continued the departure from the Nasserist path that was already clear under Sadat—that the citizens must all maintain a spirit of initiative—a code word for a retreat in the role of the state in the economy. "We are all citizens and not subjects. We are all equal in our rights and duties. We all share responsibility" (4).

Turning to the October war, Mubarak praised the armed forces and underlined the war's achievements: The victory was not limited to the restoration of Arab dignity, and the removal of fragmentation and the sense of loss. It was the key to comprehensive and just peace, and to building prosperity (5). He then repeated the trope of Egypt's leading regional role, and touched on Nasser's three circles of identity: "Egypt shoulders a major responsibility that goes beyond its geographical boundaries, because of its unique position in the heart of the Arab nation" (5). Egypt is an Arab African state, but Egypt will not revolve in the orbit of any state. . . . Egypt, which God has honored with Arabism and Islam, is a firm stronghold of freedom and honor in this age, and will remain so forever" (7). He concluded with a reaffirmation of Egypt's commitment to the Palestinians, and its relations with African and nonaligned states (6).

Although Mubarak reimposed emergency law as soon as he took office—Sadat had lifted it just a few months before his death—on other fronts he offered an easing of state repression. In addition to releasing political prisoners, he countenanced greater press freedom, allowed NGOs to proliferate and political parties to grow, and permitted various professional unions to have additional fora to demand political and civil rights. These liberalizing moves all gradually came to an end; nevertheless, initiating them at the beginning of his presidency served to close the chapter of the Sadat era by establishing a different tenor for Mubarak's rule and suggesting that even more significant openings lay ahead.

July 1982 marked the thirtieth anniversary of the revolution, and in his Revolution Day Speech to the NDP, Mubarak repeated the narrative of the revolution, led by Nasser, as one of the most important events in the Third World in the second half of the twentieth century and one of the Egyptian people's greatest achievements. Through it, they proved their "creative renovation and their enlightened invention," as well as their spiritual values, their tradition of civilization achieved over many thousands of years, their rejection of blind imitation.[41] Moreover, they had done this without bloodshed, fanaticism, or isolationism. He stressed Sadat's innovation regarding the revolution's openness to change or flexibility, but to reinforce the legitimacy of this claim, he invoked Nasser, under whom, he contended, every stage had witnessed a renewal and improvement in harmony with the changing situation, but without abandoning the revolution's principles. He also repeated Sadat's refrain that the revolution had had its retreats and failures, but the real test was whether it could survive debacles and correct mistakes (3).

In referring to Sadat, he praised a list of his achievements: putting in place a permanent constitution; making progress toward democracy, the rule of law, and respect for the citizen; reopening the Suez Canal; reconstructing the canal cities; and implementing the open-door policy and the peace initiative (4). Nasser, on the other hand, was described in more nostalgic and populist terms: "The genius of Abdel Nasser was part of the genius of the people. His revolutionary call could not have achieved this overwhelming success had it not reflected a driving power with civilizational roots." "It is Egypt that created Abdel Nasser and his glories, and it is Egypt that protects his heritage and accomplishments and produces his peers in every age for mankind. If it is possible to say that Egypt has become great because of Abdel Nasser, it is also necessary to say that Abdel Nasser was great because of Egypt" (5).

Having recounted the successes of his predecessors as a way of situating himself as a worthy successor, Mubarak then framed his own stage, separate from that of Nasser and Sadat. "There is no difference between the 23 July generation, the 15 May generation, and the 6 October generation," he insisted, reinforcing and building on the notion that the revolution was a "continuous thread." In such a formulation, of course, Sadat was implicitly the leader of the "15 May generation," thus rendering Mubarak the leader of the 6 October generation. He thereby appropriated as the centerpiece of his *own* legacy an accomplishment that had for the previous nine years been described as Egypt's most glorious battle, of which *Sadat* was the heroic author. Note that earlier in his speech he did not mention the October war as one of Sadat's achievements. The fact that Mubarak had been the commander of the air force during the 1973 war allowed or emboldened him gradually to reconstruct this war as his own signature and heroic contribution.

He then linked the solidity of the home front with unity and stability: "We have learned from our successive experiences in the various stages of our national struggle . . . that the strength of the state and its place politically and diplomatically depend to a great extent on the solidity of its internal front, the strength of its national economy . . . the homogeneity of its social structure" (11). Radicalism was totally alien to Egypt's spiritual and social values (12). The Egyptian people had rejected the calls for extremism, and any attempt to undermine a stable internal front was a breach from which only Egypt's enemies could benefit (11). Setting out what became key themes in his regime's narrative, he defined his objectives: "Maintaining security and stability, developing our defensive capabilities in accordance with the latest systems, and strengthening and solidifying the economic structure" (11).

This speech was given following the final stage of Israel's evacuation of the Sinai, as specified in the 1979 peace treaty, but also during the Israeli siege of Beirut, a development that could not have taken place had the peace treaty not shielded Israel from the possibility of a future two-front war. Hence there were long sections in the speech regarding the concern of the "Arab people of Egypt"—note the formulation—for the Lebanese and the Palestinians, and Mubarak listed many of the contacts Egypt had had with Arab parties and the United States to try to end the war (8). In fact, Egypt's contacts during the war constituted an important first step in Mubarak's campaign to return Egypt to the Arab fold. However objectionable growing numbers of Egyptians and large numbers of Arabs found the peace treaty, it was not Mubarak's legacy, and they did not hold him responsible for the policies of his predecessor. The treaty constrained Egypt's room for maneuver regionally, but did not harm the new president's legitimacy. In fact, commercial and political ties between Egypt and other Arab states had not been completely severed, and reestablishing more robust relations was critical to both addressing Egypt's economic problems and distancing the country from key, negative aspects of Sadat's legacy. Mubarak's statements demonstrated that his vision of Egypt's Arab role differed from Sadat's. During his presidency, as Mubarak sought to reprise a central regional role for Egypt, the mix between Egyptian identity and Arabism in the narrative shifted again.

THE CONSCRIPT RIOTS

Externally, the new president's efforts to restore ties with the Arab world were facilitated by the Iran-Iraq war (1980–88), in which Egypt became a key supplier of military matériel to Iraq. Domestically, the atmosphere of greater opening seemed to be confirmed by relatively free parliamentary elections in 1984. Thereafter, however, the margins of political expression began to narrow, while economic policy reinforced the status quo rather than driving more thoroughgoing reform. The benefits of the open door had created a new class whose socioeconomic distance from the rest of society continued to grow, accompanied by increasing corruption. The narrative of lesser state involvement and more personal responsibility simply sought to normalize and legitimize the growing inequality.

The month of February 1986 began with labor unrest in textile factories, but it was rioting by the Central Security Forces (al-Amn al-Markazi) on 25–26 February that, at least briefly, shook the regime. The violence, by poor conscripts, came in response to rumors that their three-year term of service (for which they were paid less than $2 a month) was being extended by a year. Their barracks, located south of Cairo near the Pyramids, were close to a host of luxury hotels, nightclubs and casinos, all symbols of an Egypt both foreign to their experience and in stark contrast to their poverty. These establishments served as the target of their anger, which left scores dead, and hundreds wounded, not to mention millions in property damage. Other units also rioted in areas around the capital—Hilwan, Shubra, and Heliopolis—and broke into the Tura prison south of the capital, releasing inmates. The state responded by imposing a curfew, which was not lifted until 8 March.[42]

Not surprisingly, Mubarak's 26 February 1986 speech focused on security as related to unity. He referred to a "deviationist minority that has carried out acts of violence, chaos, arson, and destruction.[43] "These criminal actions threaten the security of the homeland and its citizens and menace the safety of the internal front, which is the foundation of all social and economic stability and the indispensable support for the success of the process of national work (3). He then reassured people that "regardless of their intensity, such incidents cannot create a gap in the cohesion of our domestic front." He ended with "May God protect dear Egypt and keep its heroic people from the evil of sedition and intrigue" (4).

However surprised the regime may have been by the riots, it recovered quickly and imposed order. In April, a number of army officers and civilians were arrested on charges of plotting to overthrow the government. They were indicted later in the year.[44] In the regime's narrative of the events, there were no legitimate claims, and hence no need to address concerns about social equity or justice. By employing a security narrative that classified the rioting conscripts as seditious deviants, the state criminalized and thus depoliticized their actions.

The NDP nominated Mubarak for a second term the following year. In his 6 July 1987 acceptance speech, he constructed his role in the 1973 war and in the presidency in populist terms: "More has been accomplished in six years than had been done in decades. In this respect, I am not practicing one-upmanship against anyone, but I am merely putting all the people's efforts on record."[45] He described the party's nomination of him "as a pledge . . . by every Egyptian citizen to fully share with me the assumption of the responsibility and the carrying out of the trust. None of us will hesitate to fully perform his role in working for Egypt" (3). "Listen to the call of duty . . . and we shall complete traversing the road together . . . then we shall enrich our national unity together" (4–5).

Narrative Developments in Textbooks

The 1986 version of *Ta'rikh al-'Arab al-hadith w-al-mu'asir* (The Modern and Contemporary History of the Arabs), which we have been following, contained only a few new sections. One concerned Egypt's efforts to end the Arab-Israeli conflict, with very short descriptions of Sadat's 1977 trip to Jerusalem, the Camp David Accords, and the peace treaty of 1979 (176–77). It concluded with a paragraph on the echoes of the treaty, which is a stinging critique of other Arab states typical of the late Sadat period: the civilized/advanced nations of the world welcomed the peace treaty, but the Arab countries were unable to understand the changes in the world and in the balance of power, and hence did not welcome it (177). More interesting were points listed at the end of the chapter, which the student was supposed to remember, one of the more shocking of which for an official Arab text was the assertion that the Arab rejection of the partition of Palestine in 1947 had been short-sighted (178). This edition also had a new section on Egypt and the Sudan and the efforts to achieve greater unity between them, an important part of Mubarak's work toward "Arab unity" (183). Page 185 also included a paragraph that underlined the commitment by Mubarak's Egypt to a comprehensive solution to the Arab-Israeli conflict, especially focusing on the Palestinians.

The title of the 1987–88 civics textbook (Part I) had been changed to *Al-Tarbiya al-wataniyya* from the previous *Al-Tarbiya al-qawmiyya*, thus underlining a move away from a more Arab nationalist orientation. Intended for the first grade of secondary school, it was subtitled "The State of Knowledge and Development." According to the preface, it was one of a series aimed at developing in the student an understanding of *al-dawla al-ʿasriyya*—the modern or contemporary state. The intent was to show the government's efforts to promote an Egyptian society that would build a modern state, which the text admitted had not been completely achieved (5). There was only a short paragraph on the 1952 revolution, but it did claim that with the abolition of the monarchy and the establishment of a republic, the revolution had begun to build a modern state, taking an interest in industry, agriculture, education, culture, health, and a range of social services. There was also a short paragraph on the 1971 corrective revolution, but only to note that it had righted the path of the revolution (22). The text had no significant Arab nationalist content. On the other hand, Part II of this 1987–88 text, subtitled "The State of Social Justice and the Law," stressed the social justice that the 23 July revolution had insisted upon throughout. Indeed, the topics all seemed to have been taken from the Nasserist narrative: agricultural reform, nationalization, limiting high salaries and raising low ones, and so on. There was no discussion of *infitah* or neoliberal economic policies. However, when the text turned to the characteristics of democracy and the law, the narrative of political democracy and freedoms from the Sadat era reappeared. Democratic socialism, which had entered the discourse under Sadat, was mentioned (45), but the text was not consistent in its usage.

These various elements suggest a narrative that was not stable or not completely agreed upon. Mubarak's dismissal of four prime ministers in less than five years meant that four different men held the position of minister of education in the 1982–86 period, which seems to have contributed to contradictory decisions being taken at different levels of the ministry.[46] After Dr. Ahmed Fathi Surur was named minister in 1986 (a position he held until 1990) a national conference for developing education was held in July 1987. Amal Andrawus terms it a turning point in the making of educational policy, for it involved a variety of groups, including political parties and both official and unofficial institutions. In the context of serious economic and social problems in Egypt, and the continued threat of extremism, the conference concluded that "educational policy needed to go in the direction of building the Egyptian personality without fanaticism or bigotry [*taʿassub*]."[47] As we saw above, like Sadat before him, Mubarak insisted on the existence of an essentialized Egyptian character or identity that shunned extremism. Nonetheless, domestic political developments indicated that simply repeatedly asserting the deviance of fanaticism was not sufficient to effectively combat it.

The 1988–89 civics textbook for the first year of secondary school, *Al-Tarbiya al-wataniyya* (whose subtitle translates as "The Development [*tanmiya*] of Egyptian Society"), was part of the resultant curricular changes. What is most striking about this text is that it seems to represent a new hybrid identity narrative, one combining growing religious influences with a continued emphasis on Egypt's Arab identity. For example, it included reading selections that, in promoting *qawmiyya* and railing against imperialism, could easily have come from the Nasser period. With regard to the Arab-Israeli conflict, it repeated the refrain common under Sadat that Egypt had shouldered the largest share of the burden against Zionism and imperialism because of its obligation to Arabism (67). It also claimed that although attempts to achieve Arab unity had not succeeded, Egypt continued to fight for cooperation and integration between Arab countries in various fields (70).

As for the influence of religion, the preface begins not just with "Bismillah," which had been increasingly used in texts produced in the late 1970s, but with the longer formula "*Bismillah, al-hamdu l-illah, wa-salat wa salam 'ala sayyidna Muhammad al-nabi al-amin*."[48] Relatedly, the preface states that the development of Egyptian society is to be based on combining contemporary civilizational and scientific accomplishment, on the one hand, with Arab authenticity (*asala*), on the other. This language of *asala*, which is common in Islamist discourse, is new in these texts. The book also contained numerous reading selections dealing with religion or replete with verses from the Quran, including one on Islam and equality, which said that Islam insists upon equality among all believers and that God's preferences are based on belief/faith, not on social situation (63). In other countries, such as Turkey, countering the language of class conflict by appealing to religion has been part of state approaches to implementing neoliberal economic policies,[49] so the intent here may well have been the same. There is a selection on Egypt and the Islamic world, which outlines Egypt's contributions, focusing on al-Azhar, the victory over the Crusaders, participation in Islamic summit meetings, and extending support to Islamic countries in their liberation struggles and revolutions (71). Egypt's cooperation with other Islamic countries to put in place a plan to protect Islamic peoples and countries from external dangers and internal sedition (*fitna*) is also highlighted (73). With this as background, it is notable that in 1988, a group of Coptic religious figures reportedly complained to the minister of education, Ahmed Fathi Surur, that the Arabic language books contained many Quranic verses and asked that Quranic selections be limited to religious education textbooks.[50]

In short, it appears that there was a lag in time between the growing influence of religion in society and the public sphere promoted by Sadat and its incorporation into educational materials. That said, the language in these materials related to religion seems aimed at defusing socioeconomic tensions, cultivating tolerance, and reinforcing the notion of national unity. This emphasis was clearly specified as part of education's role as part of a broader domestic policy introduced under Mubarak that aimed at reinforcing national security.

ISLAMIST INSURGENCY

Clashes with religious opponents of the regime punctuated Mubarak's presidency from its beginnings, and the Ministry of the Interior had therefore begun monitoring schools for signs of Islamist political tendencies early on. However, not until 1991, when the People's Assembly voted to extend the state of emergency, did a new minister of education, Husayn Kamal Baha' al-Din (1991–2004), turn the public spotlight on the issue of the ideological control of schools. In his view, schools and universities were slipping "out of the state's control and into the hands of Islamist extremists, thereby posing a threat to the country's national security." He emphasized that instilling national pride and patriotism had to be central objectives of education.[51] Indeed, it was he who popularized the notion of the relationship between education and national security.[52] As we have seen, Mubarak had already incorporated a focus on internal security against the threat of Islamist extremists into the unity and identity themes in his own discourse. Baha' al-Din placed education "on a par with the military, and by so doing abandoned decades-old socialist era rhetoric of education being a service of the state, like health care or infrastructure development."[53]

In 1992, clashes between Islamic radicals and government security forces increased, heralding a period of intensified struggle. Some attacks targeted policemen and minor government officials; others were aimed at cabinet ministers, leading intellectuals, and even the president himself. Perhaps most devastating for the Egyptian economy were a number of high-profile attacks on foreign visitors and historical sites, which sought to disrupt Egypt's revenues from the extremely lucrative tourism industry. In response, the state launched a brutal anti-insurgency campaign that involved massive sweeps and arrests of militants, their sympathizers, and even family members in neighborhoods in Cairo as well as in many towns and villages throughout Upper Egypt. Human rights violations became commonplace as the state sought to intimidate, jail, and torture the opposition into submission.

Education in the Service of National Security

Baha' al-Din's efforts to reassert control over state educational institutions and obstruct the further growth of militancy among the youth involved direct use of the security forces. He pursued a strategy that included intensifying the screening and surveillance of students in teacher-training colleges, and purging Islamist teachers, administrators, and materials from schools. Between 1993 and 1995, some one thousand educators were transferred out of schools to other government jobs, and the minister expressed a willingness to eliminate ten thousand if necessary.[54] The concerns covered private Islamic schools as well, which had begun to open in the 1970s.[55]

Two major debates can be discerned in policy papers on education in the 1990s. The first related to the continuing provision of free education by the state, part of the legacy of the revolution, in the context of the growing impact of neoliberalism. The second revolved around "the challenges of globalization to Egyptian national and religious identity and the long-running conflict of religious versus secular education."[56] Islamists, Arab nationalists and pro-Western secularists struggled to control educational content, while the ministry sought to avoid rejecting the socialist legacy of the Egyptian state, but also tried to appease the Islamists.[57]

For example, a 1992 Ministry of Education document, "Mubarak and Education: a Look to the Future," included Baha' al-Din's construction of education as a matter of national security with three axes. The first was democracy and social peace, which were considered the basis of internal security and a natural product of a good education; the second was the relationship between education and an individual citizen's ability to be productive in society; and the third involved the military, treating knowledge metaphorically as the weapon of the future.[58] A second document, the curriculum development section of the education reform plan of 1995, listed the following as its top objectives: deepening children's affiliation to their homeland, its history, and civilization; upholding national loyalty; affirming faith, religion, divine and social values, and respecting others' needs, rites, and holy places.[59]

A final example is a 1993 document from the Public Information Authority entitled "Mubarak and the Egyptian National [*qawmi*] Program" (1993). It argued that unity and solidarity, complementarity, and integration of the social fabric were conditions for Egyptian revival. All patriotic (*watani*) forces needed to unify around higher national (*qawmi*) goals so that a view of society would prevail which would reject conflict and choose solidarity and unity as a path in life.[60] Strengthening the roots of peace was among the priorities listed. In the realm of culture, the national (here *watani*) cultural awakening had to center on values contributed by Islam: equality, consultation, freedom, justice, brotherhood, and peace. Equality, it stated, meant regarding human beings as if they all had come from one father—note the familial rather than a civic form of belonging—without distinction according to race, color, or class. The path of real revival was the path of an *umma* that was united and cohesive.[61] National unity was thus the first goal of the national community (*al-jama'a al-wataniyya*).

At the beginning of this period, a new history textbook for the third year of high school entitled *Ta'rikh Misr w-al-'Arab al-hadith* (The Modern History of Egypt and the Arabs) was introduced for the 1991-92 school year. In the preface, the authors made the case for focusing on Egypt because of its centrality to understanding the larger context of what they called the "Arabo-Ottoman" world. They also noted that this book looked, not only at political leaders, but also at the people as the builders of culture/civilization, an approach that, as we saw in the previous chapter, had been introduced immediately following the 1952 revolution (4). The text included the traditional story of the historical backdrop to the revolution, although it had no section devoted to the revolution itself. More significant, this book contained pictures of Naguib, who had long been absent from the narrative of the revolution, and even of King Farouk, as well as of Nasser (152–53). There was also a picture of Sadat, whom the text credited with putting an end to Arab differences and unifying Arab ranks in the lead-up to the 1973 war. The anti-Israeli (and anti-imperialist) language remained strong, and the text repeated the traditional claim that the 1973 war had ended the myth of Israeli invincibility. Not surprisingly, it included a picture of Mubarak, who was identified as a commander of the air campaign in 1973 (191).

As for other subjects, according to a study conducted in the mid-1990s, social studies books in the lower grades emphasized tolerance (*tasamuh*) as one of the characteristics of piety and faith.[62] Along these lines, a fifth-grade Arabic language textbook insisted that "unity is the most important manifestation of the life of the residents of this country." "The Muslim is the brother of the Christian; both of them make the homeland holy and religion is the concern of the creator."[63]

Mubarak's Security Narrative

During this period of internal threats, Mubarak focused on the identity elements of tolerance and faith, and the importance of national unity in confronting the country's problems, all the while maintaining a largely unchanged narrative of the revolution. For example, his 1993 Police Day (25 January) speech referred to an Egypt "of civilization, of tolerance and faith, of thought and culture, and of the enlightenment that rejects rigidness and backwardness."[64] Later that year, in a 30 August speech, he repeated the theme of Islam's tolerance in order to reject the violence of regime opponents by delegitimizing their claims to be pious Muslims: "We are not bound by these alien concepts that some, falsely and slanderously, claim are religion."[65] "In many parts of our Arab nation, we see things that are unacceptable to those who care about Arabism and the Arab nation's interest. . . . They distort our image as Arabs and Muslims " (3) He then affirmed these two identity elements, calling the country "the heart of Arabism and the shield of Islam" (4).

Mubarak used the same approach in his 1996 Police Day speech, when he linked terrorism to a perversion of religion, and used the fight against it to strike a populist chord regarding the people's unity and faith: "The people rejected . . . these groups' false affiliation with Islam and regarded them as groups of sedition and darkness, harming religion and distorting its image."[66] "The wave of terrorism will break against the solid rock of this homeland" (4). Indeed, Mubarak anchored unity in religion. For example in his 30 August 1993 speech on the Prophet Muhammad's birthday, he contended: "At its core, Islam is based on the cohesion and unified ranks of the sons of the nation. The Prophet Muhammad . . . moved society from scattered tribes to a large unified Islamic family" (1). "The call for unity was evident in many Quranic verses. . . . In this Islamic spirit that urges cohesion and solidarity, Arabs . . . became united brothers after being scattered enemies" (2).

As for the founding story, in a 21 July 1994 speech, Mubarak repeated the now long-standing narrative of the revolution. Its enemies had launched unjust campaigns against it, but it had survived, as a bright spot in the history of national struggle.[67] As Sadat had before him and as he had already done on numerous occasions, Mubarak reasserted that the revolution refused to be trapped within a rigid doctrinal framework. In so doing, however, he broadened its message for this period of domestic insurgency, presenting it as primarily one of peace. He contended that the revolution had come as "an historic response to the requirements of a new age. . . . it came to advocate relations between nations on more equal and just bases and to herald a world that allows peaceful coexistence among all nations" (1). He reiterated the theme of change and flexibility, saying: "Any fair patriot who respects the truth can easily understand the great difference between the revolution's constants and its variables, between the fundamental principles that are the revolution's core values and the phased objectives that might require flexibility and freedom of action" (2). "The constants are: liberation of the national will; doing away with foreign control of the country; seeking social justice for the sake of society's cohesiveness; and siding with the overwhelming masses of the people. This is at the national level. In the larger arena, the revolution's constants included Arab unity"—something that had been incorporated well after 1952—"founded upon a unified objective and destiny" (2). So, although he called for openness to change, the principles he cited were certainly ones with which Nasser would have been comfortable.

By the end of the 1990s, the state's draconian measures had put an end to the insurgency in Cairo, if not entirely in the south, but the effects of the repression lingered. Any manifestations of opposition to regime policy were seen through a national security lens. At the same time, in order to chip away at the support base of the religious Right, and especially the Muslim Brotherhood, the regime sought to coopt basic parts of its program. Indeed, a working paper submitted to NDP leaders in advance of the party's July 1998 congress urged the revision of a number of laws in accordance with *shari'a*. Thus, under the guise of a secular regime, the ruling elite increasingly introduced religion into the national discourse and into policy, an approach initiated by Sadat.

NARRATING NEOLIBERALISM: STASIS AND THE SHADOW OF SUCCESSION

Whatever advantages Egyptians may have seen when Mubarak brought a more staid, less flamboyant ruling style to the presidency in 1981 dissipated over time. Economic and political reforms were promised, but there was little effective follow-through. A new group of businessmen exploited openings and connections to amass fortunes, but significant domestic forces prevented benefits from reaching the majority. Corruption was as rampant as its practitioners were unapologetic. Gross electoral fraud had become business as usual as any earlier inclination to offer freer expression or more democratic political participation had dissipated. In the foreign policy realm, the leadership's close relationship with the United States had gradually diminished its room—and perhaps its desire—to maneuver. Egypt became more a paid enforcer of American and Israeli interests than a regional force to be reckoned with. Meanwhile, Mubarak grew older, and the question of who would succeed this man who refused to appoint a vice president was raised with greater and greater frequency. As time passed, it appeared that the president was considering what for much of the Egyptian population, including—most critically—the military, was the unthinkable: succession by his younger son, Gamal: the hereditary transfer of power, commonly refered to in Arabic as *tawrith*. This final section examines how the narrative was shaped to address the gathering crises of unequal economic development and lack of meaningful political reform.

The primary vehicle through which Gamal Mubarak rose as a political force was the NDP, and hence the party became increasingly important in this period in setting the official narrative. The themes of its September 2000 national program were modernization of the state and deepening the role of institutions, but there was no historical preamble or framework for this. The language was that of the neoliberal policy reforms promoted by international financial institutions such as the IMF. The NDP accomplishments it highlighted typify the program's contents: rebuilding basic services (infrastructure), neutralizing the negative impact of economic reform on the neediest sectors of society, financial and currency reform, widening the base of private ownership, strengthening the role of the private sector in development, making the investment climate more attractive, and developing the legal and organizational infrastructure to regulate the process of economic transformation (3). On the political front, the language was that of pluralism, rule of law, and adherence to international conventions on human rights (5 and 9). The democracy promoted bore no relationship to the social democracy or economic justice that had been among the goals of the revolution.

In September 2002, a number of cases of corruption among high-ranking party members came to light, and there was speculation that the NDP might address this at its upcoming congress. Instead, the concern with corruption was eclipsed by the introduction of Mubarak's "new thinking" (*al-fikr al-jadid*) as the theme. The party issued a twenty-nine-point paper explaining its adherence to what it called a "centrist ideology," calling for "moderation, rationality, and liberalization," that would strike a balance between the interests of the people and those of the state. One key element was the NDP's contention that the state's free provision of basic services had led to a deterioration in their quality; its proposed solution was to open up the health and education sectors to private investment. To try to dispel any notion that this meant the end of state concern for the less fortunate, the program stressed that giving the private sector a greater role did not mean leaving citizens with limited incomes "prey to the ravages of market economics." These classes should be cushioned from the negative effects of liberalization, it argued, although it offered no formal program for doing so.[68] The party thereby formally buried any remnants of the revolution's commitment to economic justice. In addition, as part of the party's and the state's attempt to undercut the popular base of the Muslim Brotherhood, the program affirmed the NDP's belief that Islam should be the basic source of legislation in Egypt, although it insisted that this was not intended undermine citizens' equality before the law or their enjoyment of equal public rights and duties, without discrimination.[69]

It was at this conference that Gamal Mubarak asserted control over the newly founded Policy Secretariat (PS) (al-Amana al-Siyasiya), a body that soon became the most important institution outside the presidency for policy making.[70] The PS was responsible for managing most of the party conferences and planning its electoral strategy. It also had a Higher Policies Council charged with assisting in policy discussions and proposing reforms. Debate within the council was open, but the circle of economic and political interests centered around Gamal also ensured that its recommendations remained largely irrelevant.[71]

Curricular Narrative Breakdown?

Concerns continued to be expressed about inconsistent or conflicting narrative lines in textbooks, particularly regarding elements of national identity. Writing in 2001, and referring to the curriculum's failure to include Coptic history, Fayiz Murad Mina argued that, contrary to its proclaimed goals about reinforcing unity, textbook content could instead weaken those bonds.[72] He and others pointed out that Muslim identity, on the other hand, continued to be strongly stressed. Linda Herrera, for example, observed:

> Implicit in the upbringing component of schooling is the attempt—by planners and educators—to transmit to students, regardless of their religious affiliation, a sense of belonging to a Muslim society with a culture and history embedded in Islam. Islamic messages and symbols are formally incorporated into the daily life of schools through, among other means, rituals, religious passages in

> textbooks, religious signs and posters displayed throughout the schools and the emphasis by teachers on an "Islamic disposition."[73]

Sa'id Isma'il 'Ali, on the other hand, claimed that textbooks for the earliest grades, before history was taught as a separate subject, promoted yet another message, that of pharaonic identity.[74]

To contextualize the criticisms of curriculum content, two interrelated issues must be noted. The first concerns finances: since, salaries represented 95 percent of the Ministry of Education's annual budget by the 2000s, any improvement in educational facilities depended upon foreign aid.[75] That then related to the second issue: the possibilities of foreign influence in the curriculum, particularly on national religious and cultural identity in the history, Arabic language, and religious education curricula. Those who expressed this concern saw, not undue Islamic influence, but the opposite trend: a deliberate attempt by the ministry to rewrite history in order to marginalize the role of Islamic civilization, the period surrounding the 1952 revolution period, and the 1967 Arab-Israeli war. "The MOE is accused of sacrificing Egypt's Arab and Islamic identity in favor of its pharaonic one, thus diminishing national and cultural identity in favor of the neocolonial project," Fatema Sayed writes.[76] "The critics' objections to the Arabic and Islamic religious curricula are that they are condensed, their grades are reduced (reflecting a lower priority [in the final grade]), and that their content is lacking in religious values and a clear position on the Arab-Israeli conflict."[77] As a result, many parents decided to send their children to one of the growing number of private Islamic schools.[78]

In contrast to popular perceptions, Sayed's study of the role of external funders found no evidence of attempts to undermine Egypt's identity. In fact, most foreign educational aid had been channeled to higher or technical education, not materials related to religion, civics, or identity instruction at the pre-university level. That said, the involvement of USAID has always been sensitive. Its funding of the establishment of the Center of Curriculum and Instructional Materials Development (CCIMD) in the Ministry of Education has given rise to all sorts of conspiracy theories, generally by leftists and Islamists, that an "international orientation" of the curricula is being enforced at the expense of national, Arab, and Islamic identity. Sayed contended that the criticisms of the CCIMD were actually the result of insufficient consultation with Egyptian experts and the fact that the center was superimposed on existing ministry units already performing the same function: the Curriculum Development Unit and the National Center for Educational Research and Development (NCERD). The bureaucratic competition or overlap then triggered controversy when a series of new texts developed by CCID staff in the 1990s were leaked to the press and presented as if they had been drafted by Americans. A firestorm ensued, with writers who had never read the books nonetheless harshly criticizing them. The opposition to the history textbooks led the ministry to admit that the history curriculum was inaccurate and incomplete. In the end, the books were never used and a plan to rewrite them was announced in 1999.[79]

A review of the social studies texts in use at the preparatory level in 2008–10, *Al-Dirasat al-ijtima'iyya, zawahir tabi'iyya wa-hadara Misriyya* (Social Studies, Natural Phenomena and Egyptian Civilization), in fact reveals continuity on basic themes. In the historical discussions, there was much less of an Arab or Arab nationalist framework than had been the case in some earlier texts—the title mentions only Egyptian civilization—yet the units dealing with nature or the environment are entitled "Our Arab Homeland." There seems to be relatively balanced attention in the books for all three preparatory school levels to the pharaonic period, Islamic history, and modern Egyptian history, and there was no noticeable change in key narrative elements relating to identity or unity. The language on imperialism had been significantly toned down, although not completely eliminated, as exemplified in the discussions of Palestine and the 1956 war. The language of socialism, on the other hand, was completely gone. Most notable in terms of differences or innovations was a separate chapter on Christianity in Egypt in the second-semester first-year preparatory book, and a chapter on women in politics in the second-semester third-year book. Two of the books discussed the bases of solid citizenship, and referred to rights and obligations, but the "education as national security" narrative that had been promoted in the 1990s had disappeared.

Stagnation to the End

Mubarak's speeches and the party's sloganeering embodied the malaise and apparent lack of vision among the elite regarding anything beyond reinforcing the bases of the neoliberal police state kleptocracy that had come to pass for government. The September 2004 NDP Second Annual Conference program did focus on the principle of citizenship as the basis of the complete equality of Egyptians, but little else that was notable. Mubarak stressed citizenship as a major element in the party's framework of ten bases of reform, which also included achieving economic growth without compromising the responsibility of the state toward the poor, and encouraging individual initiative and competition. However, this new emphasis on citizenship and civic identity was in no small measure intended to do battle with the more identity-focused program of the Muslim Brotherhood, the only political group with a significant base and presence among the population outside the NDP and the state.

Tellingly, the constitutional amendments of the following year (25 May 2005) had nothing to do with citizenship; rather, they involved provisions apparently aimed at ensuring that Gamal Mubarak would be his father's successor. Similarly, the constitutional amendments of 29 March 2007 sought to change the competencies of the judiciary vis-à-vis elections to ensure the elder Mubarak's reelection in the next round of presidential balloting, then scheduled for fall 2011. In terms of the narrative, the one significant change was the removal of the words "socialist" and "socialism" (*ishtiraki* and *ishtirakiyya*) from the document,[80] which was long overdue, since, as we have seen, they had ceased to figure in state policy well before Mubarak came to power.

The Revolution Day speech for 2006 was quite short, as was increasingly the case under Mubarak, whose legitimacy in any case had little to do with the 1952 narrative. Much had changed in fifty-four years, he acknowledged, but "what did not and will not change is the commitment to maintain Egypt's security and stability and to preserve its sovereignty and independence of its national will" (2). The party convention that year boasted the slogan "a second leap toward the future," inevitably begging questions about when the first leap had occurred.[81] The ninth annual Party Congress, in November 2007, offered repetitions of previous themes. Its slogan, "our country is moving forward with us" further exemplified how intellectually vacuous the NDP's "new thinking" was. To the extent that any creativity was at work, it was channeled in a more visual direction: "The previous lackluster NDP emblem was given a fresh look in TV ads with creative video editing emphasizing the emblem's component elements: the white stars, crescent and schematized lotus flower."[82]

In what was his last Revolution Day speech, in July 2010, Mubarak used the occasion to "recall the many memories before and after the revolution and the remarkable events in Egypt's contemporary history."[83] He praised the Egyptian people, citing faith, mettle, and solidarity as some of their basic identity elements. Against all evidence, he insisted: "We adhere to the sovereignty of law and hold it high . . . away from nepotism . . . against corruption. . . . We never accept any violation of Egyptian rights and dignity. Our foreign action is governed by Egyptian interests and [the] causes of our Arab region" (2). He did not know at the time that in less than seven months, the faith, mettle, and solidarity of the Egyptian people would, in a dramatic reappropriation of popular sovereignty and dignity, put an end to his rule of nepotism, police brutality, corruption, and foreign policy that had long since ceased to serve the interests of anyone in Egypt besides the ruling clique.

CONCLUSIONS

Egypt had traveled a long and difficult road since the Free Officers had overthrown the king in 1952. When Sadat stepped in after Nasser's untimely death, the fact that he, too, had been one of the original revolutionaries, provided him with a certain legitimacy, even as he faced the impossible task of measuring up to the legacy of his larger-than-life predecessor. Initially, then, and unsurprisingly, Sadat continued to stress the traditional elements in the founding narrative. However, after confronting and triumphing over his enemies in May 1971, he gradually scripted his own acts into a continuation of the revolution by using the trope of the revolution's ability recover from mistakes and right itself. As time passed, this "corrective movement," took on tones of additional grandeur. It, too, came to be called a revolution. Another aspect of this proclaimed flexibility of the revolution involved the need to complete it. To that end, Sadat added to his own credentials by moving away from the revolutionary legitimacy that he said had characterized Nasser's approach, toward a new form of legitimacy—constitutional legitimacy—or a state of institutions, of which he was the sole author.

The emphasis on the revolution's flexibility and previous mistakes also provided the discursive space for Sadat to chart a new economic course. He would not dismiss socialism formally, indeed he would continue to stress the regime's commitment to many of its principles, but at the same time, he gradually pushed for a different economic orientation, that of the open door. Throughout his presidency, he invoked Nasser's name to deflect criticism and to frame his policies as in keeping with the goals of his predecessor. In a particularly inventive twist, when domestic criticism mounted following his Jerusalem trip, he used the frame of the revolution to suggest that the forms of opposition were reminiscent of the pre-1952 period. In other words, those who opposed him were moving Egypt back to the prerevolutionary period—in effect, going against the revolution. He also drew on the legitimacy of the revolution to justify his approach to religion and politics, proclaiming: "It is a basic line of the 23 July and 15 May revolutions that religion should not be exploited for politics—absolutely not."[84]

On the question of identity, there were two clear shifts during the Sadat decade: one regarding the use of religious language and symbols; and the other concerning the mix of Egyptianism and Arabism. While the change in the country's name in 1971 from United Arab Republic to Egyptian Arab Republic may have been an early indication that Sadat would seek to reconfigure the country's identity, the new emphasis on religion was clearer, and it was sustained throughout his presidency. The form of address he used in his speeches, the regular references to morality and values, the introduction into the 1971 constitution of *shari'a* as a primary source of legislation and of religious education as a basic subject in school, prefixing his name with Muhammad, and the emphasis on the religious symbolism of the 1973 Ramadan war: all helped establish a frame for national identity quite different than Nasser's discourse of Arabism and the citizen.

As for the mix between Arabism and a narrower Egyptian identity, the picture is much more complicated than has often been presented by analysts' stylized summaries of the Sadat era. In the context of preparation for war and the need for unity on the home front, Sadat did begin talking about an Egyptian nationalism/patriotism (*wataniyya misriyya*), along with periodic references to Egypt's self-reliance or singular contributions. At the same time, however, he continued to refer to Arab unity and the Arab people (the *umma*) being with Egypt. Just as important, the narrative that students were consuming in textbooks also continued to stress Egypt's Arabism, Arab commitments, and leadership role.

That said, as opposition grew following the second disengagement agreement with Israel (Sinai II), Sadat's tone shifted. He increasingly scolded or patronized other Arabs: Egypt was the "elder brother" that had to bear the campaigns of those who criticized it. He also developed a narrative of Egypt's role in the Arab world that, instead of just proclaiming heroic defense, stressed how much the country had sacrificed and suffered for Arab causes, as if there had been no Egyptian national interests involved at all in the 1948, 1956, 1967, or 1973 wars. So, there is no lack of Arabism in these speeches; indeed, the peace treaty was justified in part as serving Arab interests. However, it is no longer a revolutionary Arabism or an Arabism with a political project. Instead, the calls for political unity gave way to calls for Arab economic cooperation, usually with the wealthy oil producers, who were now viewed as supporters rather than an enemy Arab camp, as they had been prior to 1967. Even after the peace treaty, and even after Sadat's anti-Arab tirades, the discourse continued to portray Egypt as the beating heart of the Arab nation.

Regarding religious identity, by the mid-1970s, as intercommunal tensions openly manifested themselves, Sadat had begun to emphasize how religious, forgiving, and tolerant the Egyptian people were. Fanaticism was not part of their character. He also made numerous direct references to Muslims and Copts in discussing national unity, something that had been completely absent from the national discourse under Nasser. After his trip to Jerusalem, Sadat ratcheted up the religio-moral discourse: the signing of the peace treaty was justified in terms of Egypt's spiritual values and civilization; constitutional amendments in 1980 made *shari'a* the primary basis for legislation, and Sadat called himself the Muslim president of a Muslim state. Later that year, he gave a speech in which he even insisted that Islamic identity preceded Arabism in importance. Thus, if there was a shift in relative weight among identity terms under Sadat, it was not just or primarily between Egyptian and Arab identity, but between civic and religious bases of national belonging.

Finally, on the question of definitions of unity, Sadat's early confrontation of a coup attempt gave him the opportunity to draw on language Nasser had used to identify those who were responsible for errors and discord. He used the term *marakiz quwa* to great effect as he sought to reinforce his power in the critical consolidation period.[85] Soon thereafter, however, his attention turned to the occupation of Egyptian territory. He regularly spoke of a coming battle, and the consequent need for unity on the home front. The subsequent October "victory" was scripted as having unified the ranks of the people (and the Arabs) in an unprecedented way. This unity was then to be mobilized to wage a new war, this time against economic "backwardness."

The two disengagement agreements came shortly after the announcement of the so-called open door policy in the *October Paper*. In the context of the new economic orientation, the frank references to class struggle that we saw under Nasser disappeared, as did proclamations of the heroic alliance of progressive forces. In the context of the attacks he encountered as a result of Sinai II, Sadat reasserted the narrative of historic national unity, the long history of cohesion and lack of divisions among Egyptians. To the extent that lack of unity was mentioned, it was now constructed as sedition, *fitna*, the growing sectarian tensions of the period, all against the background of claims that Egypt had always been free of rancor and bigotry. In this way, whatever extremism or sectarianism arose, it was by implication defined as counter to true religion and to the age-old Egyptian character. After the January 1977 riots, Sadat talked about the importance of family solidarity to overcome difficulties, but thereafter, popular discontent manifested in both economic and religious terms led to increasing repression. He continued to construct the perpetrators as a seditious minority of criminals, but claims of national unity were more and more difficult to sustain.

Before turning to the Mubarak record, one additional element must be noted: the evidence of what could be called a fracturing of the narrative, the gap between the message that the president was sending through his speeches and what students were studying in textbooks, or even between or among textbooks at any given time. In particular, the relationship between Egyptian and Arab identities remained unclear, as was the message about the economy in the context of the shift from socialism to *infitah*. The lack of consistency seems to have resulted from the intersection of several factors. One was simply bureaucratic malaise and failure to regularly review and update the curriculum. Competing political/ideological factions, each of which had an interest in making sure that its message was included, also seem to have played an important role. Finally, the political system under Sadat was, at least at certain points, more open that that under Nasser. While the exact dynamics involved here are not clear, it would seem that such a difference in regime type also opened up the possibility of some divergence from a single, united narrative.

As for Mubarak, he certainly lacked the charisma or the flare for the dramatic of his predecessor, but he also faced less of a challenge to his assumption of the presidency than had Sadat. There were no major factions seeking his ouster, and hence he was not forced to confront elite opposition as he consolidated the legitimacy of his presidency. Nor, however, was he of the 1952 generation. He did not seek to replace the founding narrative; he simply adopted it as he had inherited it from Sadat, who had already introduced the extremely valuable story line of "flexibility and change." During the insurgency of the 1990s Mubarak used this flexibility to broaden the message of the revolution to include peace, but as time went on, his Revolution Day speeches grew shorter, as did references to the revolution itself. He placed himself in the "revolutionary line" of Sadat and Nasser, but constructed himself as the leader of the October generation, appropriating that position from Sadat and thereby laying claim to the glory and prestige of having been a commander in the 1973 war.

In terms of identity, two of Mubarak's most important achievements were his shepherding of Egypt back into the Arab fold after the 1979 peace treaty with Israel and reasserting Egypt's regional role, both in support of the Palestinians and in helping to resupply Iraq in the 1980s. He often invoked Egypt's African,

Arab, and Islamic identities. He also reintroduced the use of the word "citizen" (*muwatin*) into his speeches, so that forms of address were no longer always those of "family" relations (brothers and sisters, sons and daughters), as had been the case under Sadat. Later in his presidency, in the 2000s, the language of citizenship (if not its content) became a major focus of the NDP, chosen precisely because it constituted a striking contrast to the Muslim Brotherhood's religio-communal identity politics.

When he assumed the presidency, Mubarak inherited a home front more dangerously mobilized along sectarian lines than had ever been the case in the past. Like his predecessor, he insisted that radicalism was totally alien to Egypt's spiritual and social values, but in the 1990s that radicalism constituted the most important domestic challenge to his regime. In response, official discourse and policy thoroughly securitized religion and national identity. One example of this was the approach of Education Minister Baha' al-Din, who defined education as a national security issue. In order to fight religious extremists, national pride and patriotism had to be central objectives of education. Texts were to emphasize tolerance as a characteristic of piety and faith, and reject Islamic extremism as satanic.

Finally, on the question of unity, Mubarak initially stressed Egypt's economic and political bases. He referred to the importance of domestic solidarity, by which he meant a strong economy and a homogeneous social structure. After the conscripts' riot, instead of acknowledging the underlying economic malaise, the discourse criminalized those who had engaged in violence and insisted that such incidents could not damage the cohesion of the domestic front. However, in the 1990s, the Islamic insurgency created a need for unifying around higher national goals on other bases, and he then began to refer to the unity and cohesion that were implicit in Islam. The path of real revival was the path of a people (*umma*) that was united and cohesive. "The wave of terrorism will break against the solid rock of this homeland," he insisted.

Whether terrorism broke on the rock of a discursively asserted national unity or, more likely, security force repression, the regime survived the challenge. It could have taken from the experience the lesson that the country's mounting socioeconomic problems required broad structural reform, including reducing corruption. Instead, Mubarak and his colleagues continued to pursue economic policies and political maneuvers intended to benefit the ruling group centered around the upper echelons of the NDP, while the majority of the population had to deal with growing economic difficulties, declining state services, the gutting of the rule of law, and increasing repression. Despite the presence of some who were hailed as the best and the brightest in Gamal Mubarak's discussion circles, state discourse about the country's path was reduced to the hollow *langue du bois* of neoliberalism and the younger Mubarak's vapid "new thinking." Perhaps, feeling secure in their power (in no small measure underpinned by their relationship with the United States and Israel) and so well practiced in appropriating phenomenal rents, the political elite felt no need to offer a more creative narrative to justify or reconstruct their corruption. In the end, whether uninterested or unable, neither of the Mubaraks nor the host of sycophantic NDP members and fellow travelers succeeded in formulating a vision for the future capable of legitimating their rule or addressing Egypt's massive problems. Their fall from power did not come as soon as many would have hoped, but it did, eventually and most deservedly, come.

4 ALGERIA FROM THE LIBERATION STRUGGLE THROUGH BOUMEDIENNE

Historic to Revolutionary Legitimacy

THE MODERN ALGERIAN STATE emerged from the ashes of a 132-year French colonial enterprise brought to an end by a brutal eight-year war of national liberation. The armed revolutionary struggle launched in 1954 by the Front de libération nationale (FLN) rallied many Algerians to its side, but also resorted to coercion (and worse) to enforce its claim to sole leadership of the national movement. During the war, the FLN attracted supporters from a range of backgrounds and political tendencies, and the group that came to power following independence similarly reflected an uneasy coalition of factions from various societal sectors and parts of the country.

Once the colonial power had withdrawn, the political differences between regions and factions that had grown during the course of the war surfaced with a vengeance.[1] Scholarly and other informed depictions of the postindependence political history of the country have therefore focused on the struggles among these factions as they were backed by or allied with the army, the state bureaucracy, the FLN (the sole legal party after independence), workers, or peasants to secure power. In addition to shifting sectoral alliances, control of the emerging state also involved different *projets de société*: experiments with development strategies and cultural visions underpinned by divergent models of how the economy and society should be organized. Unable to secure a sufficiently strong base of support in any one sector of the population, the government was "obliged to temporize with a wide range of social forces and interests and propose changes rather than impose them."[2]

In this discussion of the state-promulgated post-independence narrative, official documents will be the primary sources for considering the same three components examined in the Egyptian case. As with Egypt, the founding story is also called a revolution, but in Algeria, it could never have been mistaken for a coup. Launched on 1 November 1954 and ending with the Evian Accords and the vote for independence from France on 5 July 1962, what transpired in Algeria was a war of national liberation. A bloody saga that convulsed both the nation and the metropole, this struggle and the FLN that led it subsequently acquired near mythic proportions.

As for the questions of identity and unity, the Algerian case involves a broader range of factors than does that of Egypt. In the wake of independence, the people and the leadership were caught up in complex battles—economic, political and sociocultural—that the exigencies of the liberation struggle and the broad "Front" nature of the party that had led it had largely sidelined or suppressed.[3] Questions of ethnicity (Arab or one of the population groups generically identified as Berber),[4] language and education (Arabic and traditional, French and European), and religious identity (Muslim, but of what degree of religiosity and nature of practice), crosscut or intersected with differences of region, tribe, ideology, and class. The post-revolutionary leadership addressed these complex forces by imposing a one-party state, perhaps as much a product of the ideological inclinations of the first generation of leaders who had internalized the colonizers' Jacobin tendencies as it was of the deeply ingrained secrecy needed to prosecute a violent independence struggle and then confront the daunting challenges of state building that French settler colonialism left in its wake.

In surveying the history since 1962, several critical stages or developments suggest themselves as possible junctures that may have triggered a restructuring of the official narrative. The first is that of the immediate post-independence period, which witnessed Algerian internecine fighting after the French departure, followed by the first attempts at state building and regime consolidation under Ahmed Ben Bella, one of the historic leaders of the revolution and Algeria's first post-independence president. This "first republic" was overthrown only three years later and replaced by the government of Ben Bella's erstwhile ally Houari Boumedienne, who during the war had led the armed forces in Wilaya V[5] and become chief of staff of the Armée de libération nationale (ALN: National Liberation Army), in command of Algerian forces in Tunisia and Morocco. This coup was a second critical juncture. The departures from Boumedienne's governing coalition, beginning in the early 1970s during the planning and implementation of the agrarian revolution, constitute a third. (Chapter 5 addresses the period since Boumedienne's death in 1979.)

As in the Egyptian case, in order to set the stage for examining narrative (re)scripting after independence, we need first to explore the narrative's evolution and the forces involved in its production in the preindependence period. The discussion therefore begins with a brief examination of the pre-1954 traditions in Algerian historiography. It then explores several key documents produced during the revolution, before turning to the construction of the official postindependence narrative.

THE COLONIAL PARADIGM AND THE ALGERIAN FOUNDING STORY

Given the fabrication and distortion that characterized the French colonial narrative about Algeria and Algerians, it is not surprising that members of the indigenous elite sought to provide their own version of their history.[6] It is also not surprising that what they produced was an account constructed around negating the French myths rather than a story with new bases or problematiques.[7] The main lines of the French narrative either contributed to a divide-and-rule strategy or attempted to justify colonization. Algeria was home to a diverse (and fluid) set of tribal, economic, ethnic, linguistic, and religious groupings, yet Paris sought to reconstruct Algerian society as falling into two groups: Arabs and Berbers.[8] The French portrayed the Arabs as violent, untamable nomads, descendants of the forces that had swept across North Africa in the "Islamic conquests" of the eighth century CE. Devout, even fanatical Muslims, they were responsible for destruction and were opposed to the many benefits and development that, the French argued, colonial involvement could bring them. Berbers, on the other hand, were defined as the original inhabitants of North Africa who had been overrun by the Arabs.[9] True, they had converted to Islam, but in the French narrative, their conversions had been under duress and were in most cases superficial. Just below the surface were Christian or Jewish pre-Islamic inclinations, the bases of a cultural affinity that rendered them natural allies—although still inferior. Indeed, some French tried to make the case that the Berbers—a designation, by the way, that was not at the time used by the population to which the French referred—had originated in Europe. In any case, the goal was clearly to "cultivate"—certainly a relative term—one group in order to facilitate domination of the whole.

The second goal of the French narrative was to legitimate France's colonial presence. To that end, multiple story lines were devised. One was the classic *mission civilisatrice*: the French had come to bring the benefits of their more advanced culture and society to backward North Africans who neither constituted a recognizable people nor were governed by a state-like authority prior to their arrival. The French narrative turned to the Roman presence in North Africa, a period of imperial flourishing under an earlier European presence, and located in it a logical predecessor. Since then, or certainly since the Arab invasions, so the narrative ran, there had been only chaos and deterioration.[10]

The two earliest Algerian authors who sought to counter the French narrative were members of the reformist (*islahi*, sometimes also referred to as *salafi*)[11] Jam'iyyat al-'Ulama'al-Muslimin al-Jaza'iriyyin[12] (AUMA: Association of Algerian Muslim 'Ulama),[13] Tawfiq al-Madani[14] and Mubarak al-Mili. Unfortunately for post-independence politics, Madani accepted the colonial construction of distinct Arab and Berber identities, although he countered the French contention that they were opposing forces. Instead, he argued, Berber resistance to the Arabs had initially arisen because they were unknown invaders, like the Romans. However, they soon realized that, unlike the Romans, the Arabs brought a liberating message, that of Islam, a new civilization that destroyed oppression and offered the Berbers equality.[15] Mili, on the other hand, argued that the Berbers were in fact of the same eastern (*mashriqi*) origin as the Phoenicians and the Arabs, and that their distinguishing characteristics—love of freedom[16] and independence, hard work, admiration of knowledge, and resistance to integration—had continued to be part of the Algerian people. Indeed, he looked for a golden era of the Berbers, which he found in the period of what, in an attempt to insist on historical continuity from classical times, he called the "national" (*watani*) kingdoms: those of Masinissa and Jugurtha.[17]

Countering the French claim that Algeria had never been a real nation (as if that somehow justified plundering it), the *islahi*s argued that Algeria had been a nation since ancient times, with its population and borders well established before the arrival of the Arabs. What the Arabs had brought was a basis of national cultural unity through the cement of Islam. While the French sought a basis for making Algeria French by stressing the Roman past, the *islahi*s accepted the comparison between France and Rome, but called them both colonial occupiers and oppressors, responsible for the decline of civilization. The French made the Romans the builders and the Arabs the destroyers, while the *islahi*s argued exactly the opposite.[18]

There was also an Arab nationalist narrative, which shared the *islahi* tendency to negate colonial theses, but differed from the predominant narrative in key ways. For example, instead of Islamicizing or Semitizing North Africa, they Arabized it. Thus, Berbers were not just Semites, but rather were also of

Arab origin, and had, like the Arabs who arrived in the seventh century bringing Islam, originated in the Arabian Peninsula. Islam had been adopted—the Arabists did not use the word "conquest" to refer to the process by which Islam was introduced—by both groups because it was an Arab idea.[19]

In order to argue that an Algerian people had existed since ancient times, historians and other nationalists insisted upon a set of stable identity elements that characterized "the Algerian." For most, Arabo-Islamic civilization was the basic characteristic, although many also added characteristics like love of liberty and freedom as a nod to the country's pre-Arabo-Islamic past. But there was no attempt to interrogate these presumed characteristics regarding origins, fluctuations, and transformations. The insistence upon an unchanging national personality, born largely of the need to counter the colonial narrative, led to a desire to identify with an idealized past[20] and to assert or emphasize elements of a purported national "authenticity."[21]

Before concluding this section it is critical to point out that a Berber mythology[22] also grew out of the French narrative, but then subverted it. The Berber narrative accepted the differences or dichotomy between an indigenous people and Arab invaders who had sought to suppress or replace indigenous culture with their own so-called Arabo-Islamic one. However, these Berbers, whom the French had actively constructed as a separate and distinct ethnic group and then sought to Frenchify, were well aware of the limits of assimilation and the nature of the colonial administration into which they were disproportionately drawn as part of the colonial divide-and-rule strategy. Indeed, large numbers of them (mostly Kabyles)[23] joined the national movement, both at home and in France,[24] where they represented an even larger relative percentage of the Algerian immigrant population. They may have been willing to call the arrival of the Arabs a conquest, but they saw the French in a similar light: they understood quite well that the colonial goal was to coopt them, not to defend their culture.[25]

Important as the various narrative strains about the presence of national Berber kingdoms or the arrival of the Arabs were in asserting the existence of an Algerian people and polity of long-standing, when the country secured independence, the founding story was to be found elsewhere: in the anti-colonial struggle, specifically, the National Liberation War launched on 1 November 1954. Indeed, it soon became the principle reference for anything called nationalist or patriotic, anything characterized as resistance or jihad, dwarfing the national political movements that had preceded it.[26]

The tradition of national heroic struggle in the broader narrative is traced to the emir 'Abd al-Qadir (1807–83), the leader of the earliest resistance against the French. A statue of him on horseback stands in an eponymous square in central Algiers, and an obelisk has his face on all four sides in a main square in Oran. Other symbols of the resistance narrative are to be found in the names of streets, squares, and schools throughout the country. Districts and squares as well as major streets in both major cities and small towns are named for martyrs (*shuhada'*) or FLN fighters (*mujahidin*). Among the most common are Didouche Mourad, Hassiba Ben Bouali, and Larbi ben M'hidi, along with 'Abd al-Qadir and a handful of other resistance leaders from the prerevolutionary period. Cities and towns all have their 1 November square or avenues commemorating the launching of the revolution; and elementary, middle, and high schools are often named after nationalist or revolutionary heroes. In addition, plaques commemorating events during the revolution punctuate walls in town centers as daily reminders to citizens of revolutionary heroism. Last but not least, museums, not only in the capital but across the provinces, focus exclusively or in part on the revolution or on local martyrs, and the organ of the FLN, which was long the only newspaper in the country, is named *El Moudjahid*.[27]

The discussion that follows of the initial emergence of the revolution as the founding story will focus on three key themes. The first is how the national political movements that preceded the FLN are treated. Second is if or how conflicts among the various participants or factions in the anti-French struggle are presented.[28] Finally, we shall explore the extent to which individual political actors, as opposed to simply "the people," are included.[29]

OFFICIAL REVOLUTIONARY DOCUMENTS

The official documents of the revolutionary movement participate in the construction of what later became the narrative of the Algerian revolution, although they do not include much historical coverage. Their authors could not have foreseen it at the time, but because the FLN succeeded in forcing the French departure, its members' visions and portrayals of the course of the war were key to later official constructions of the narrative of this period.

The Declaration of 1 November 1954, which announced the launching of the revolution, is *the* foundational document for the narration of the founding story.[30] It calls its struggle a North African one, although it is clearly directed to "all the Algerian people" and all "purely Algerian parties and movements." It states that its political program aims at: (1) the *re*establishment (note the implicit affirmation of a *prior* Algerian state) of the sovereign, democratic, and social Algerian state in the framework of Islamic principles; and respect for all fundamental freedoms without distinction regarding race or confession. In this way, in terms of identity components, a role for religion is affirmed, but so is ethnic and religious tolerance.

This is a short document, but three remarks are in order concerning subsequent constructions of the founding story. The first is that the declaration was directed to all the Algerian people, regardless of religion or origins. Thus it was open and inclusive, with no other identity markers. Second, it insisted that those behind it were "independent of the two clans that are disputing power," thus referring to preexisting dissension in the ranks of the nationalist political parties and placing the FLN above or beyond that fray.[31] The third is that, although the narrative that later emerged insisted that by 1954 it had become clear that violence was the only way forward, in this document, the FLN proposed a political program for discussion with the French and talked about limiting bloodshed.

The second document was the Platform of La Soummam,[32] drawn up at a meeting of the internal leadership of the FLN in August 1956. Although FLN militants based outside Algeria did not attend this gathering—a development that created intra-FLN dissension, which continued to grow—Soummam was historic for its affirmation of collective decision-making and the primacy of the political over the military. Further, it is credited with institutionalizing the revolution and reaffirming its legitimacy by establishing the Conseil national de la révolution algérienne (CNRA: National Council of the Algerian Revolution), the equivalent of a parliament, and the Comité de coordination et d'exécution (CCE: Committee of Coordination and Enforcement) to run FLN affairs on a daily basis.

In terms of the evolution of the narrative, however, Soummam's importance was somewhat different. First, it initiated a story of the unity of the revolutionary forces, a unity whose importance carried over into the postrevolutionary period. For example, it asserted that the Armée de libération nationale (ALN) fully enjoyed "the love of the Algerian people, its enthusiastic support, its active solidarity, moral and material, total and unfailing." It has also led to "a psycho-political union of all Algerians, a national unanimity which feeds the armed struggle and renders the victory of freedom inevitable." It further claimed that in a very short period of time, the FLN had succeeded in supplanting all the political parties that had been around for years. "The union of the people is achieved through struggle against the common enemy. The FLN affirms that the liberation of Algeria will be the work of all Algerians and not just a fraction, regardless of their importance." It was also the beginning of a story line that downplayed or ignored those Algerians who continued to fight alongside the French. It claimed that, despite the gross imbalance of forces, there had been mass defections of officers and regular (Algerian Muslim) soldiers from the French army: France could no longer count on the loyalty of Algerian troops. In reality, ALN numbers never reached those of the Algerians who fought on the side of the French.[33]

Also critical to this emerging narrative of unity and the founding story was the reference to the routing of the most serious challenger to the FLN, Messali Hadj (1898–1974), a figure who was subsequently banished from the narrative,[34] and his followers. The FLN was determined to destroy the influence of Hadj's Mouvement national algérien (MNA: Algerian National Movement), particularly among the politically important community of Algerian workers in France. The result was an internecine struggle and many of the atrocities that characterized the war.[35] In a formulation that set the stage for subsequent references to those who opposed the FLN or deviated from its orthodoxy, Messali's partisans were referred to as counterrevolutionaries who trafficked in "gangsterism, confusion, and lies." It claimed that his remaining supporters were "precisely those journalists and intellectuals who are close to the French presidency"—a deadly charge.[36] Finally, Soummam delegitimized any claim Messali had to fathering Algerian nationalism, thus also setting the stage for his disappearance from the narrative: "the nationalism for which Messali shamelessly claims the initiative is a phenomenon of universal character, the result of a natural evolution followed by all people emerging from their lethargy."

Soummam hailed the 1955 strike on the anniversary of 1 November as proof that the FLN had taken charge of all sectors of the population. Unity was also an underlying theme in Soummam's story line regarding the key societal groups in the revolution, in particular the peasants (who are noted as the majority of the *mujahidin*), the workers, the youth, the intellectuals, and women. Again, as part of the growing insistence upon unity, the platform insisted that the Union générale des syndicats algériens (UGSA: General Union of Algerian Labor Unions), which had emerged in 1954 out of the French Confédération générale du travail (CGT: General Labor Confederation), had to dissolve itself and give way to the Union générale des travailleurs algériens (UGTA: General Union of Algerian Workers), "the authentic national and *sole* union that groups Algerian workers without distinction" (my emphasis).

The document claimed that the peasants had already defeated the old fantasy of the French administration that "artificially divided Algerians into Berbers and hostile Arabs." A subsequent section, regarding Algeria's Jewish population, insisted that the Arab-Israeli conflict did not have grave consequences in Algeria; proofs existed of religious tolerance, of cooperation at the highest levels of the state, and of sincere coexistence. Moreover, "the Algerian Revolution has demonstrated by its acts that it deserves the confidence of the Jewish minority to guarantee it its part in the prosperity of an independent Algeria." The platform noted the systematic repression of Arabic, which it called "the national language of the immense majority," by the French. "The Islamic religion is scorned, its personnel have been cowed, chosen and paid by the colonial administration," it asserted. "The dividing line in Algeria is not between religious communities, but between the partisans of liberty, justice, and human dignity, on the one hand, and the colonialists, on the other."

Diversity—ideological, political, cultural, social, religious—was in fact inherent in the kind of organization that the FLN—a broad nationalist front—aspired to be. Indeed, the 1 November Declaration had stated, "we are calling it the FLN, thus . . . offering the possibility for all Algerian patriots, from all social backgrounds . . . to join in the liberation struggle, without any other consideration." Still, given the tremendous challenge that achieving independence posed, it was essential to limit dissent. Hence, it should not be surprising that these early documents downplayed, delegitimized, or dismissed the most serious internal threats facing the FLN. Instead, they stressed the basic unity of the Algerian people forged through their resistance to the French (or, in some texts, predating it), while at the same time occasionally hinting at forms of deviation characterized, depending upon the source, as being in league with the French or other, unnamed outside forces, or as a manifestation of a counterrevolutionary ideology.

Nevertheless, the potentially fragmenting effects of the absence of a broadly accepted ideology were subsequently compounded by other developments. First was the arrest in 1956 of five of the top FLN leaders (Ahmed Ben Bella, Mohamed Khider, Mohamed Boudiaf, Mostefa Lacheraf, and Hocine Aït Ahmed), followed by the flight into exile of other top leaders after the February 1957 Battle of Algiers. The result was a serious divide between the internal leadership (to which Soummam had given precedence) and that outside the country. An additional divide, which came to the fore in 1960–61, evolved between the political leadership (which Soummam had also favored) and the military leadership. The military itself was then further split between the more formal forces based in Morocco and Tunisia and those fighting in the country. These problems of inside versus outside and military versus political led to divergent strategies and priorities, as well as different alliances, personal and professional, cultural (*arabisant* or *francisant*)[37] and ethnic (Arab, Kabyle, etc.).

The last major preindependence document, the June 1962 Tripoli declaration,[38] an outline of the political, social, and economic ideas of the Algerian elite, represented an attempt to preserve some semblance of unity within FLN ranks and to work out internal differences without resorting to the use of force. Its primary authors were four leftist intellectuals: Redha Malek, Mohammed Ben Yahia, Mostefa Lacheraf, and Mohammed Harbi. The Tripoli declaration is notable for its critique of the failings of the FLN during the war—the most important of which was the distance between the leadership and the masses—and its proposals for the future.

This is the first foundational document to mention 'Abd al-Qadir, the figure who would come to symbolize historical Algerian resistance and be cited as evidence that there had been an Algerian state prior to the French conquest. In addition, with the war now over, an accounting of the terrible losses and destruction—human and material—would come to figure more prominently in the official narration of the revolution. In its construction of the historical narrative, the Tripoli declaration repeated the theme of a colonial war of extermination led by the French against the Algerian people, villainized "feudalists," who, it said, had thrown their lot in with the French at the time of the invasion, and then moved on to the all-important theme of unity, which it intertwined with the founding story:

> It was in direct action against colonialism that the Algerian people recovered and then consolidated their national unity. They then banished from their ranks the old sectarianism of the parties and the clans and overcame the divisions that the French occupation had established as a political system. It is in the unity of combat that the nation, oppressed by colonialism, rediscovered itself as an organic entity and demonstrated its full dynamism. . . . The unity of the people, national rebirth/resurrection, perspectives of a radical transformation of society—these are the principle results of the years of armed struggle.

Unfortunately for the country going forward, it was a narrative that bore little resemblance to reality.

THE TRIUMPH AND CRISIS OF INDEPENDENCE

At independence, the Algerian political elite were divided by their varying experiences during the war and by their differing visions and aspirations for the future. On the one side were the interior *wilayas* (two, three, and four), angry with the inferior levels of supplies the État-Major (the external military leadership) had supplied them during the war, the Fédération de France du FLN (FFFLN: FLN Federation of France)[39] and much of the Gouvernement provisoire de la République algérienne (GPRA: Provisional Government of the Algerian Republic).[40] On the other side were the État-Major, which the GPRA had attempted to dissolve, along with *wilayas* one, five, and six, Ben Bella, and Khider.[41] These alliances were in part based on wartime experiences, but were also shaped by personal feuds and clan competition.[42] With no governmental institutions in place to resolve the competition, the contest for power was ultimately decided in Ben Bella's favor by armed conflict. As the head of the État-Major, Houari Boumedienne marched on Algiers with his better-armed and -organized troops in September 1962. "The Algerian people . . . played virtually no part in these events, except when mobilized by the UGTA to intervene between the two warring Algerian factions while crying 'Seven years is enough,'" William Quandt records.[43] That said, much disorder continued in the countryside, where guerrilla leaders had established personal fiefdoms; indeed, in Kabylia, opposition continued to be rallied by one of the historic leaders of the revolution, Hocine Aït Ahmed.

Ben Bella in Power

The question of the power relationship between and among key institutions was still to be determined at independence. Of particular importance was the relationship between the FLN and the state,[44] and between the FLN and the army. Ben Bella ultimately asserted control of the state over the party by assuming the role of FLN secretary-general himself. With the so-called March (1963) decrees, which nationalized French lands and legalized the system of *autogestion*,[45] Ben Bella won the support of the UGTA and other leftists. That still left the question of the army, but with the help of Boumedienne the internal *wilayas* were largely integrated into what was now called the Armée nationale populaire (ANP: National People's Army).[46] Thus, Ben Bella had consolidated his position, at least temporarily;[47] but with the exception of Boumedienne, who led the army, none of those who supported him had significant constituencies. To enhance his standing, Ben Bella "resorted more and more to a politics of gestures designed to win over constituencies such as workers and peasants who perceived benefit from those gestures."[48]

According to Hugh Roberts, at least for the first decade following independence, personal loyalties were more significant than ideology in determining alliances.[49] Nevertheless, the revolutionary socialism espoused by the leadership was not a comfortable fit for much of Algerian society. Despite its emphasis on development and equality, a wide gap existed between the small, largely francophone national leadership, many of whom had been influenced by European ideologies, and the largely un(der)educated and generally socially and religiously conservative rural population. As a result, as we shall see below, under Ben Bella, the reformist *islahi* narrative of Algerian history, with its appeal precisely to those sectors, began to be adopted by the state.

The Emerging Narrative

The Constitution of 1963, ratified by popular referendum on 8 September 1963, enunciated for the first time the theme of a 100-year armed, moral and political struggle by the Algerian people against the French invasion and occupation of the country. It also contained the first reference to the "million martyrs," (which later becomes 1.5 million) as summary shorthand for the brutality of the liberation struggle. The people were largely excluded from the political battles during this period of attempted regime consolidation, except to be signaled as sources of legitimacy or to be mobilized to carry out economic policy. Yet in the preamble to the constitution, it is precisely the Algerian people who are the protagonists. The FLN and ALN have their roles, but in the emerging narrative, if not in reality, *le peuple algérien* is always central. Moreover, the beginnings of the process of sacralization of the revolution can be seen in the oath of office specified for the president (article 40), which begins "Faithful to the principles of the revolution and to the souls of the martyrs, I swear. . . ."[50] Further reinforcing the role of the revolution in the official narrative, two political holidays associated with it were established: 5 July, as Independence and FLN Day; and 1 November, as Revolution Day.

Six months later, the first post-independence FLN party congress issued a more detailed historical statement and political map in the form of the 1964 Charte d'Alger (Algiers Charter),[51] the first of a series of charters, each seeking to define a new era. Organized by Ben Bella and Ben Alla,[52] the congress was dominated by the president's men, two of the most leftist of whom, Mohammed Harbi and Abdalaziz Zerdani, wrote most of the document.[53] Its content represented doctrinal compromises between these Marxist intellectuals, on the one hand, and the army, which was supported by some of the more religious elements in the political elite, on the other.[54] In terms of the emerging national narrative, three elements are notable. First, it incorporated the most important elements of the *islahi* historical narrative. Second, it repeatedly insisted upon the unity of the people, most likely to delegitimize dissent and to reinforce the leadership's claim to power in the aftermath of the ugly intra-ALN violence from which the country had just emerged. Third, it initiated what became a preoccupation, regardless of leadership, with establishing and controlling historical "truth."

This concern is apparent from the beginning, as the text starts by claiming that an objective knowledge of Algerian history is a basic obligation of every militant/activist. "The falsification of the history of our country and its simplification by historians and publicists linked politically and ideologically with colonialism have often constituted a brake on the influence of the national movement." Of course, the reifying of history then began anew, and despite the more secular orientation of many of Ben Bella's top advisors, it was the *islahi* narrative that was adopted.

For example, on the critical question of Algerian identity, Charte d'Alger asserts: "Beginning in the eighth century, Islamization and Arabization gave our country the aspect which it has preserved to the present." The claim of a twentieth-century essence dating from the eight century would be problematic under any circumstances. Here it is particularly so because the concept—Arabo-Muslim—was itself introduced by the French. In addition, the term presumes, but fails to specify, the pre-eighth-century identity of the indigenous inhabitants, whom I shall refer to using the (imprecise or inaccurate) term "Berbers." The refusal to include a recognition of Berber identity likely owed to the place it had occupied in the colonial narrative; but may have been reinforced by recent actions by Hocine Aït Ahmed, a Kabyle, who had founded a rival party to the FLN, the Front des forces socialistes (FFS: Socialist Forces Front), in 1963, and led the insurrection referred to above. In such circumstances, the leadership would have had little inclination to explicitly include those who rejected their authority. Suffice it to say that the authors of these and subsequent documents employing the same terms were not only accepting categories created by colonizers they had only recently expelled; but they then proceeded to insist upon the Arabo-Islamic designation as one of the most intrinsic elements of the highly valued Algerian "authenticity." On the question of identity, therefore, the ecumenism of the 1 November 1954 proclamation had disappeared.

Of course, many of those among the revolutionary elite were not "Arabs," and hence the Charte d'Alger could not simply ignore them. The document appears to attempt to finesse the Berber question in the section on "Characteristics of Algerian society" by claiming that "Arabo-Muslim" is not an *ethnic* reference (i.e., presumably, it does not exclude Berbers or set up an ethnically based opposition between Arab and Berber) and "is in opposition to underestimating contributions prior to the Arabs' arrival," by an unspecified population, clearly not "Arabo-Muslims." It does assert an important civilizational role for what it calls the Central Maghreb going back three millennia to the Numidian kingdom. It also charts successive struggles against foreign domination—Roman, Vandal, and Byzantine—from the second century BCE to the eighth century CE, thereby constructing the basis for a narrative of long historical resistance to and expulsion of outsiders.[55]

The arrival of the Arabs and Islam, on the other hand, could not be put in the same category as these other invasions, for that would have suggested that they and the religion they brought should have been resisted in the same way, an extremely problematic contention in a society overwhelmingly composed of practicing Muslims fiercely proud of their religion. To solve this problem, the Charte d'Alger adopted the story created by the *islahis* to reconcile the narrative of a millennia-old history of "national" resistance with the fact of a devout Muslim population: "in the seventh century, the speed and depth of the process of Islamization and Arabization which began cannot be explained except by the liberating role of this religion and this new civilization. A people who were so ready to fight would not have accepted it had it not brought them liberation, social advancement, cultural enrichment, prosperity, and tolerance." In this way, the potential conflict between the narratives of historic resistance to external invasion and the embrace of Islam by the indigenous population of "free men" was resolved.

Islamic culture and the common language (Arabic), therefore, are the unifying factors that history forged across the region. Having established this unity, the narrative asserts, "we will go forward, and with respect for our Arabo-Islamic traditions, we will build socialism," with the reference to socialism constituting a warning to those who might try to use religion in a way that the political elite defined as hostile to progress. The discourse thenceforth sought to reconcile Islam and socialism as a means of legitimizing the regime's policies and of mobilizing the people—both secularists and the pious—behind it, by eliminating the basis of opposition of those who argued that socialism was inauthentic: Western in origin, atheist in content, and in contradiction with Algeria's Islamic heritage.

Also in keeping with the *islahi* narrative, the Charte d'Alger asserted both the existence of an Algerian state and a unity or coherence of Algerian society prior to the French invasion: "Algeria already constituted a differentiated state. Islamic culture, an unchanged social hierarchy, a common/shared legal organization, all constituted a link among the members of the Algerian community, a link reinforced by the social hostility manifested by a military caste of foreign origin"—a reference to the Turkish governing class.[56]

As for the beginnings of constructing or elaborating a narrative of the foundational story, this text signals that 'Abd al-Qadir's leadership and resistance will be the historical reference point, with armed resistance a central organizing theme. The text claims that the Turkish bureaucracy disappeared quickly in the face of the French invasion,[57] thus opening "the way across the *national* territory for *authentic Algerian* forces, who took the reins of the armed resistance to the invader" (my emphasis). Note also in the following passage, the twentieth-century concepts that are used to characterize events of the 1800s: "By ending the difference between tribes, *makhzen* and *tribus raia* [protected tribes], 'Abd al-Qadir destroyed the ancient ties of exploitation established to the detriment of the masses of peasants and aspired to unify [them] through action against the enemy and around a single central authority of the country. By putting in place the bases of a modern economy he clashed with anti-national tendencies of the feudalists." The language of nationalism and of class struggle so important to the socialist vision of *part of* the postindependence elite was thereby woven into the story of the earliest resistance to the French.

The text insisted that the defeat of the Algerian resistance by the French in the nineteenth century was the result, "not of the efficiency of the French military, but of the absence of a real central leadership, the weaknesses and internal contradictions of the resistance at the time, regional particularisms and the treason of the feudalists"; in short, the absence of unity. "To confront any external aggression, the revolution had to create all the conditions necessary for the unity of the people to unmask those whose dirty interests led them to betray their country."

The importance of the people's unity and the futility of political (as opposed to militarized) approaches to colonization run throughout the text, although it will be recalled that the 1 November proclamation had left the door open for negotiation. The Charte d'Alger argued that all of the parties active prior to 1954 had shown their limits in that they were nonrevolutionary, which also meant in this text and others that they were out of touch with the masses. Worse, it claimed, the political parties "constituted the principal obstacle to the involvement of the people" in the revolutionary struggle. After the launching of the revolution, "the Messalist current [i.e., the followers of the nationalist leader Messali Hadj] for its part rapidly slipped into counterrevolutionary positions," but "the strike of July 1956 demonstrated the unity of the Algerian people around the FLN."[58]

The Charte d'Alger admitted that the national liberation movement had not been fully prepared for the struggle; it had not envisioned all of the implications of a liberation war. Still, it argued that the Algerian people "unanimously" felt the struggle was being waged correctly. As for the leadership, on the other hand, until the Congress of Soummam, "There was more unity of intention than unity of action. . . . Soummam constituted the first attempt at a coherent conception of the revolution." Finally, in a clear interruption of the unity narrative, the text did admit that independence "coincided" with a violent internal crisis: "The sabotage of the administration and the economy by the [French] OAS [Organisation de l'armée secrète],[59] the lack of an institution prepared to manage the country, the transformation of the units of the ALN under the weight of last-minute volunteers, the political maneuvers of the provisional executive, and the role of murky forces are some of the factors that played a role in the internal crisis of the FLN." Perhaps the internal fighting as well as its results were still too recent to ignore even in a narrative focused so heavily on unity.

John Ruedy argues that there was significant dissatisfaction with the Charte d'Alger, especially on the part of Boumedienne and the large ANP delegation to the FLN Congress. As for the reasons for that opposition, some blame the Marxist tone of the Charte's analysis, a discourse that was alien to Algeria's cultural heritage and that suggested that the path Algeria was taking was being laid out by foreigners. Another school focuses on the military, which it claims was hostile to socialism because of the petit bourgeois background of many of its officers. Others hold that it derived from a concern that a strong party threatened the hegemony of the army.[60]

What is certain is that from the time he took the reins of the ALN, Boumedienne stressed what he called "revolutionary legitimacy," meaning the right of those who had fought in the liberation struggle—of which he was a prominent example—to hold power. This formulation was intended to contrast with the "historic legitimacy" of those who had been present at the creation: the original founders of the FLN. Although Ben Bella enjoyed historic legitimacy according to this classification, most of those who came to power with him post-revolution did not. In response, the Charte d'Alger recast the term "historic legitimacy": "there are no historic leaders except those who spilled their blood for the liberation, those who today work and sweat anonymously to rebuild the country." Indicative both of unity and of the way the revolutionary story would be narrated, the Charte also used what became a famous slogan: "Un seul héros, le peuple." There would be no individual personalities in the telling of the revolutionary narrative, only one hero, the Algerian people as a whole.

Establishing the Postindependence Institutional Framework

Ideological and personal power struggles could be waged through charters and declarations, but leadership legitimation required inculcating the emerging official narrative into the broader population. In Algeria, the colonial legacy severely complicated such a prospect. At the time of the French invasion in 1830, Algeria's literacy level was comparable to that of France;[61] however, as time passed, the colonizers destroyed more than 80 percent of the mosques and other religious institutions in the large cities that had provided education.[62] As a result, one of the key demands of the first nationalist political party, the Étoile nord-africaine (ENA),[63] was access for Algerian students to education at all levels, and the creation of Arabic schools. After the establishment of the AUMA in 1931, there was a concerted effort to open such schools, and within sixteen years a national network of 147 madrasas had been established. Arabic language and religious studies were, however, the primary subjects taught. Science and technical subjects received little if any treatment.[64]

At independence illiteracy still stood at 88 percent, while the small elite was bifurcated, the product of two different types of institutions: the French school and university or the Islamic madrasa and university. "The nature of their education and their respective general culture imposed a division of labor between them. The *arabisants* monopolized symbolic power, the school and the media, and the *francisants* moved into the administration, the security services, and the modern technical, scientific, and economic institutions."[65] The way these two educational traditions were managed by successive post-independence leaderships created or exacerbated tensions that later came to constitute clear challenges to the notion of a unified Algerian people.

Following independence, a high commission for the reform of education was established. At its first meeting on 15 December 1962, the basic objectives of the future Algerian school system were defined as: gradual Algerianization of the teaching corps; gradual Arabization of curriculum and instruction; the unification of the educational system, meaning putting an end to the fragmentation that had existed under the French; a scientific and technical orientation of education; and the democratization of public instruction, which meant not only opening schools where there had been none before (particularly in the rural areas), but also creating the social conditions and supporting infrastructure required to provide equal educational opportunities to all Algerian children. Unfortunately, the pressures on the schools caused by the massive post-independence increase in demand allowed for only partial measures to reduce the gaps between the announced goals and the existing system. In fact, until 1975, the educational system was characterized by the absence of a global educational and instructional policy. Aside from some hasty and sectoral measures, the colonial system was largely preserved or renewed.[66]

With very few trained Algerian teachers, the regime faced a massive task in developing instructional materials and training cadres. To fill the huge, initial void, foreigners from around the world were imported to teach anything and everything. These *coopérants*, as they were called, may have been well intentioned, but the language barrier often limited their contributions.[67] There were insufficient numbers of arabophone instructors, and although a number of Arab states, most notably Egypt, supplied teachers, the Algerians' memories of them suggest that they were hardly the best and the brightest available. Moreover, given the dearth of qualified teachers, Arabic-language teachers generally doubled as religion instructors. Educators from a different national religious culture (even if overwhelmingly Arab and Muslim) were thus responsible for teaching Islam to young Algerians.[68]

Algerianization of the curriculum was also a fraught process, and was carried out unevenly. Certain disciplines like history and geography were not only Algerianized but also Arabized progressively. At the primary level, this proceeded quickly, but not so at the middle and secondary levels, given the dearth of qualified instructors.[69] Instructional materials also posed a huge challenge. Certain texts from the colonial period were adapted to the post-independence curriculum.[70] Decree 62–166 of 31 December 1962 established the Institut national pédagogique (IPN: National Pedagogic Institute), charged with the production and distribution of teaching materials, including textbooks,[71] but until 1970, many textbooks continued to be imported.[72]

If the stakes involved had been limited to the logistics and mechanics of instruction, there would be no need to devote space to education in this study of the national narrative. In fact, however, education is never value-neutral or an apolitical process, and in the case of schooling in post-independence Algeria, one cannot but be struck by the tremendous politicization of its evolution. One explanation for this is that two, potentially contradictory, goals underlay the efforts aimed at educational development; reasserting "authenticity" to help restore cultural attributes quashed or disfigured by the French colonizers; and embracing "modernity"—understood primarily in socioeconomic terms as throwing off the ties of dependency and developing a strong and sovereign state through socialism. As we have seen, both of these potentially contradictory terms—authenticity (coded in terms of Arabo-Muslim identity) and modernity (i.e., primarily the promotion of socialism)—were accorded an important place in the discourse.[73]

During the colonial period, not only had French been the language of instruction in colonial schools, but Arabic had been classified and treated as a foreign language. It should not be surprising then, that all of the foundational texts of the nationalist movement, from the Étoile nord-africaine's 1927 program of demands to the proclamation of 1 November 1954, were thought out, elaborated upon, and edited in French. The same was true of the Soummam platform, the constitutions of provisional institutions of the revolution voted by the members of the CNRA, the Evian accords that brought independence, and even the Tripoli program.[74] Language therefore had evolved as a marker of ethnic and educational differences, as well as social hierarchy associated with politico-cultural domination.[75] In addition, because of its inextricable link with Islam, the practice of which was the one characteristic all of those classified as *indigène* by the French shared, the Arabic language had taken on additional importance as a religious marker, indicative of the aspect of national patrimony that most deeply and firmly distinguished the colonized from the colonizer. It is therefore understandable why, after independence, there was a strong insistence upon giving, or, as some constructed it, returning, Arabic to its proper place.

In 1963, the study of Arabic was made obligatory in all programs and at all levels, and the first level of primary school was completely Arabized, although French continued to be privileged for the five elementary years.[76] However, in post-independence Algeria, Arabization meant not just teaching Arabic in schools, to which few had any objection, but also, according to its most determined proponents, converting it into the language of instruction in *all* subject areas. The leadership could have chosen a path of bilingualism, as Tunisia and Morocco had, but activists in Algeria deliberately sought to significantly reduce the role of French in education, government, and society more broadly. That goal required the development of textbooks in Arabic for teaching subjects that had previously been taught in French. In the absence of sufficient numbers of trained teachers, discussed above, subjects like history, geography, and philosophy were Arabized, but without training *arabisant* teachers in the subjects of instruction. In addition, the *islahis*, led by Tawfiq al-Madani, minister of religious affairs under Ben Bella, pushed for the creation of Islamic institutes to train those who would then propagate their religious ideology through future Arabized instruction. The pressure was so great that at one point Ben Bella himself insisted that "Arabization is not Islamization."[77]

State schooling came to play a major role in what gradually emerged as major sociocultural and political battles around the sensitive and fraught relationship between religion and language/ethnicity. Which Islam was to be taught in schools—that of the AUMA reformers, that of the traditional religious men, whose practices resonated among a large segment of the population, or the more cultural affiliation of the secularists? Similarly, which Arabic was being promoted? Classical Arabic, which virtually no one spoke? Algerian colloquial, which was widely spoken, but not written? Where would the languages generically referred to as Berber fit? What place would there be for French, in which virtually all of the political leadership as well as the technical and scientific cadres had been educated?[78] The major differences on these questions among the ranks and leadership of the FLN had been sublimated during the 1954–62 struggle. The emerging narrative tried to impose unity by denying diversity, but below the surface, the differences remained.

STATE FORMATION AND REGIME CONSOLIDATION UNDER BOUMEDIENNE

While some argue that the left-leaning francophone elite who had been so prominent since independence had alienated a large part of the Algerian population, it is not at all clear that Boumedienne's coup of June 1965 against Ben Bella had ideological bases. Rather, it appears to have been a part of the ongoing struggle within the ruling group over the power relationships among army, party, and state, which at that time remained fluid as key players often belonged to all three institutions. Ben Bella's drive to consolidate personal power also seems to have alienated many of his early supporters. Suffice it here to say that it was Boumedienne and the army who ultimately won out over Ben Bella and the party.

The "Proclamation of the Council of the Revolution, 19 June 1965" announced the coup. Its importance for the narrative going forward lies in its criticisms of the years since independence, which were intended to justify the overthrow of Ben Bella and legitimize the new leadership. The themes of unity and those who betrayed it, as well as the heroic role of armed resistance were notable. It claimed that at the time of independence, Algeria had been on the edge of the abyss; only the loyalty of true patriots had enabled it to avoid civil war. Yet after three years of national sovereignty:

> the country found itself turned over to . . . clashes between tendencies and claims revived by the needs of an old scheme of government, divide and rule. Dirty calculations, political narcissism, and the morbid love of power found their best illustration in the systematic liquidation of the country's cadres and the criminal attempt to discredit the *mujahidin* and the resistance. The ANP, worthy heir of the glorious ALN, will never . . . let itself be cut off from the people from which it emerged and from which it draws it force and reason for being.[79]

In this way, the coup was constructed as legitimate because it put an end to increasingly dangerous sedition (*fitna*, with its echoes of the narrative of the independence period), and reconsolidated the unity of the people and their relationship with the armed forces. In parallel, having overthrown one of the few remaining representatives of the *historic* legitimacy that he could not claim, Boumedienne thenceforth increasingly emphasized the importance of *revolutionary* legitimacy, which he could.

Education under Boumedienne

Economic policy, involving centralized planning and the nationalization of foreign capital, was in the forefront of the regime's drive to consolidate power, but educational policy, Arabization in particular, also played a critical role. Indeed, it was one of the key issues on which constructing or maintaining national unity, and by extension, regime legitimacy, turned. Had it been merely a matter of linguistic revival, the policy might not have been so contentious; however, because of the fractured composition of the post-independence elite and its power bases in the broader population, the role and use of language became a part of the larger socioeconomic and political struggles that emerged. Many of the young *francisants* were among the early revolutionaries who had used their education and language ability to contest the colonial presence. Not surprisingly, then, it was overwhelmingly those trained in French who were in a position to assume state administrative and technical positions at the time of independence.[80] The *arabisants*, on the other hand, tended to have had a traditional education in Arabic language and literature (and Islam), but they now sought to use their competency as one means of competing for state jobs.

Following the 1965 coup, Arabization was elevated to one of the principal objectives of the revolution. Foreign languages were to be allowed a complementary role, but "restoring" Arabic to what its proponents considered its rightful place as the national language came to be inextricably associated with national sovereignty, authenticity, and the country's Arabo-Islamic identity. Boumedienne then proceeded to appoint a key proponent of this conception of Arabization, Ahmed Taleb Ibrahimi, as minister of education, a post he held until 1970, when he was named to head the similarly influential Ministry of Culture and Information. The son of Sheikh Mohamed Bachir Ibrahimi, a former leader of the AUMA, Ahmed Talib was a leading voice among those whose vision of Algeria focused on its Arabo-Islamic identity and who were traditionalist in their curricular and pedagogical orientations. In 1970, as president of the national commission charged with the overhaul of the educational system, he defined the values he felt should structure the educational system as follows: "Islam is the value of values in Algerian life; the other values owe their importance, their existence and the consideration that they enjoy only to their being in harmony or having links parallel with Islam, or because they have their origins in Islam or are subject to it."[81] In addition to Ahmed Taleb Ibrahimi, other ulama held the key positions of minister of justice (Boualem Benhamouda) and minister of original education and religious affairs (Mouloud Kassim Naït Belkacem, 1970–79). Ben Bella's former advisor Mohammed Harbi characterized these men as "apostles of linguistic Jacobinism" who advocated policies that hid or suppressed "the diversity of the roots and cultures at the base of Algerian society."[82]

In the same camp, if not a member of the ulama, Abdelhamid al-Mehri, was appointed secretary-general of the Ministry of Primary and Secondary Education in 1970. Associated with the more religious wing of the FLN, he emerged as the most vocal advocate of Arabization.[83] As the policy continued to evolve, on 6 November 1973, a National Commission on Arabization was established under the aegis of the FLN. It was headed by the party's chief of information and guidance, Mohamed Cherif Messadia, as fierce a proponent of Arabization as he was an opponent of socialist-oriented policies.

Nevertheless, the composition of the governments/cabinets under Boumedienne continued to reflect both major sociopolitical trends. Most notably, in the mid-1970s, as the flaws of the Arabization program became increasingly obvious, Redha Malek, a secular leftist who had helped author the Tripoli program, was made minister of culture, and Mostefa Lacheraf, another leftist reformer, was, to the great consternation of the Islamists, named minister of education in 1976 specifically to oversee a review of the fraught Arabization efforts to date.

In the meantime, those who had done their studies in Arabic benefitted from the opening of Arabized sections in the departments of history, philosophy, geography, sociology, and pedagogy at the university. However, as these students graduated and looked for jobs, they were often rejected by large companies or government ministries: the quality of their Arabized education had often been poor and with the predominance of *francisants* in the administration, a selection bias was often at work. Successive government decrees (24 April 1968 and 12 February 1970) did demand improved levels of Arabic proficiency among state employees, but continuing inferior employment opportunities created growing discontent among the *arabisants*, which ultimately triggered demonstrations.[84]

Far more can be said on the question of Arabization; however, for the purposes of this analysis, the final dimension of concern is the relationship between Arabization and religion. Many contend that Arabization constituted a kind of Trojan horse for the Islamization of education, as part of a broader societal project of one sector of the *arabisants*. While one should be careful about drawing hard-and-fast lines between societal categories, there were at least two trends among the *arabisants*. The more secular, but still largely socially and politically conservative pan-Arabists, generally referred to as Ba'thists in Algerian writings critical of them, were one of these. The other was the neo-salafist or Islamist trend, which was also socially and politically conservative, and rejected the secularism or socialism of much of the post-independence elite. Major figures from both groups had studied in the Arab world: among the Islamists, either at religious institutions, such as Cairo's al-Azhar or Tunis's al-Zaytouna; or among the secularists at Cairo or Damascus University. While the two may have differed on many issues, the importance of Arabic as a key basis of "authentic" Algerian identity was not one of them.

Among the *francisants* were those who had studied in Algeria or in France. Their tendency was generally toward either secularism or at least a non-*islahi* practice of Islam. In addition, many of the *francisants* were Kabyles, for whom Arabic was not a language spoken at home. While the introduction of standard Arabic into the curriculum did not have to pose an insurmountable problem, the concomitant campaign by some of the most vocal proponents of Arabization to eliminate French and to refuse official recognition of Berber languages and identity added another dangerous layer of politicization (and repression) to the Arabization process. It should be noted, however, that there was some fluidity among these groups.[85]

In sum, Arabization emerged as a significant sociopolitical issue and was instrumentalized in political power struggles. Although Arabization by definition involved the suppression of aspects of Berber identity,[86] it was reportedly particularly dear to Boumedienne, for whom, although he was a Chaoui (Berber) himself,[87] it represented a form of anti-colonial struggle. Yet, unlike some of the *islahi* proponents of Arabization, Boumedienne's vision was not that of returning to the language of the past, but on promoting the language of the future: a task that required progressives devoted to the goals of the revolution. His initial appointment of Ibrahimi to lead the effort may therefore appear paradoxical. It suggests either that his definition of progressives was quite flexible or that, in the context of the two broad, competing sociopolitical currents in the country, he expected the legitimacy he would derive from making such an appointment to more than offset the negatives.

In fact the evidence makes clear that in addition to Boumedienne's goal of breaking with the colonial past, the purpose of Arabization was to enhance the standing of a regime that suffered from a low level of legitimacy.[88] The monopolization by a largely francophone elite of positions in the bureaucracy continued to alienate the much broader nonfrancophone masses, while the president's socialist economic policies met with resistance from the more socially and religiously conservative countryside. As the parameters of the identity of the postindependence state continued to be forged, the Arabization policy was used by those who wanted to solidify Algeria's membership in a larger Arab world, and/or Islamic community (*umma*), against those who preferred an Algerian Algeria that, without denying its Arab or Islamic heritage, sought to preserve other elements of the country's identity, whether ethnic, non-Islamist, secularist or French-language-related. In the end, for Boumedienne, the most important dividing line was between those who supported and those who opposed "the revolution," and especially his leadership of it. In this context, Arabization intersected with identity issues and reached out in important practical and symbolic ways to build support, or reduce animosity, among a set of constituencies otherwise alienated or marginalized by the politico-economic path of the regime.

History and Historiography under Boumedienne

The political elite's view of the political stakes involved in scripting the Algerian historical narrative were discussed above in the analysis of the Charte d'Alger. Those who had come to power after 1962 and drew their legitimacy from participation in the war felt they had to circumscribe the legitimacy of the historic leadership if they were to succeed in presenting themselves as unchallenged leaders of a homogeneous people.[89] Controlling history, therefore, became an explicit state policy carried out in both discursive and institutional ways. In his speech of 31 October 1966, Boumedienne underlined the role that revolutionary legitimacy would play in writing national history by assigning three functions to 1 November 1954: serving as a dividing point between two historical periods; opening an era of progress; and founding the most glorious generation. Thus, 1 November became "a demarcation line that distinguished the partisans of an armed solution from the reformists, the partisans of collective leadership from those who defended le Vieux [Messali], and the unity of the movement against divisions and the cacophony of the political parties."[90]

One example of the triumph of Boumedienne's revolutionary legitimacy was the experience of the Ministry of Mujahidin (war veterans).[91] Established as part of the first post-independence government, it had been subsumed in 1964 under the Ministry of Social Affairs. Following the coup, it was reopened as a separate entity, thus signaling the importance of separate recognition of these fighters and their part in the revolution. In addition, to unite veterans, whose ranks had been plagued by factionalism under Ben Bella, the Organisation nationale des moujahidines (ONM: National Organization of Mujahidin) was reorganized. Its highest goal was "to work to perpetuate the spirit of November 1954, to give prominence to the revolution's lofty example, to eternalize its influence, and to instill its principles and values in the coming generations as a service to the country and in loyalty to the martyrs."[92] Part of its work, conferring the title of *mujahid*—that is, determining that someone had fought in the revolution—was highly sensitive and political, inasmuch as the designation commanded respect. The ONM was further charged with preserving the dignity and rights of the *mujahidin*, their families, and those of the martyrs. To that end, it was to encourage the writing of the history of the revolution, gathering documentation related to it, working to prevent the distortion of its history, and exposing the crimes of colonialism.[93] In 1972, it was appropriated resources to begin publishing its own journal, entitled *Awwal Nufimbir* (1 November).

In the same period, the state launched a full-fledged program of "Writing and Rewriting History." Its name and goals implied that the history of the revolution needed to be written, while all that had come before and had been "falsified" by colonial historians had to be *re*written.[94] The state also explicitly called for giving weight or value to an Algerian identity whose roots were the bases of a past generally reduced to its Arabo-Islamic character; this character, the approved narrative went, had survived into the colonial period through insurrections and the actions of the leaders of religious reform.[95] In this official version, the role of the various nationalist or anti-colonial political parties of the pre-1954 period was minimized or ignored. Instead, the role of the *islahi* ulama was rescripted to make them, and not Messali, the political ancestors of the revolution. In so doing, the regime not only attempted to strengthen its own exclusive claim to the right to rule, but also managed to court the Arabo-Islamist tendency among the elite and in society more broadly.

Holidays also played a part in writing or rewriting the revolutionary narrative. In 1966, a National Youth Day was established in the first week of July, although no specific date was set. By 1970, however, although the 1963 law establishing 5 July as Independence Day was never changed, Boumedienne celebrated that day as Youth Day instead, so that the 1 November holiday marking the launching of the armed struggle became the central national holiday. Soufi offers several possible explanations for this change, all related to suppressing the memory of personalities and events the president preferred not to highlight.[96] On the other hand, the anniversary of his coup against Ben Bella, 19 June, was proclaimed a national holiday (law 66–153).

Boumedienne expected that Algerian historians would follow his directives for writing national history. For example, in a speech of 8 May 1973, he insisted, "Historians need to call it [the revolution] appropriately the most glorious generation in the history of Algeria. . . . My goal is that my words will be recorded as historical reality."[97] In a speech of 1 November 1972, he placed the 19 June events in an historical chain beginning with the 1954 revolution and continuing to the agrarian revolution, the centerpiece of regime policy at the time.[98] In this way, the concepts of revolution and revolutionary legitimacy were both reinforced and reinterpreted. The revolution had begun with armed struggle, but post-independence, it continued on other fronts—economic, social, and political—in order to deliver the full promise of 1 November. It is also worth noting that article 110 of the new Constitution published in 1976 stipulated for the first time that guaranteeing the intrinsic rights of the *mujahidin* and their dependents and preserving their dignity were now obligations of the state and of society. In addition, it modified the presidential oath of office to emphasize the role of those with revolutionary legitimacy. It henceforth ran: "Faithful to the *supreme sacrifice and the memory* of the martyrs of our *sacred* revolution, I swear . . ."[99]

Another part of the initiative to take control of national history was the creation in 1971 of a fund for the national archives, as well as the Centre national d'études historiques (CNEH: National Center for Historical Studies), initially attached directly to the presidency. The CNEH was charged with overseeing historical studies and research, participating in the elaboration of teaching methods and in the writing of history texts. From 1976 on, any participation in an international conference on history required that the CNEH first be informed in order to ensure coordination and discipline by researchers.[100] To create a narrative that was more accessible to a larger audience, in 1972 a law was passed to create the National Museum of the Mujahid, which was to recover and preserve objects and documents related to the national liberation struggle, defined as the 1954–62 period.[101]

In this way, an official history administration was put in place. The Ministry of Culture dealt largely with ancient history, the Ministry of Religious Affairs had a privileged position when it came to the medieval period, while the Ministry of Mujahidin had exclusive control of the 1954–62 period and special rights to the 1830–54 period. Finally, there was the critical Ministry of National Education, which, according to Soufi, was the greatest provider of historical information through, its teachers, its inspectors, and the texts it edited.[102]

Research for this project located only one history textbook from the Boumedienne period, the 1970 third-year secondary school text *Al-Ta'rikh al-hadith, 1453–1815* (Modern History, 1453–1815). Painfully, in a paragraph that is reprinted in later editions as well, the introduction noted that given the stage of Arabization in the country, not all students would be able to benefit from the general presentation in the chapters. Hence, at the end of each chapter, there was a brief summary of the main points. The introduction further stated that the authors saw this book as merely a first attempt to fill the gap in educational materials. The text contained only a couple of chapters directly relevant to Algeria. The main message from the presentations, which cover "The Arab Maghreb before the Ottoman Expansion" and "The Spanish Interference in North Africa," is that there had been unity in North Africa under the Almohad dynasty (1160–1350), but it then collapsed into mini-states. The Spanish transferred their Crusader wars to North Africa after the fall of Granada, thus setting the stage for the establishment of Ottoman rule in Algeria. Thus the theme of the importance of unity, particularly against an aggressive outside Christian power, with all of its echoes of the French colonial past, was reinforced even in the presentation of an earlier period.

The 1976 Charte nationale

Following the coup in 1965, several uprisings had tested the regime's staying power. This instability, along with the need to address pressing issues of national economic development, had led the leadership to choose not to reengage popular participation at the national level. By late 1971, factionalism once again began to emerge in the alliances that underpinned the regime, this time based on economic philosophy, One group advocated continuing the socialist course, while the other sought a gradual political liberalization and a retreat from the heavy statist economic development path.[103] The Arabo-Muslim component was generally in line with this latter group, as it viewed the expropriation of property as anti-Islamic, and opposed anything that smacked of socialism, which it considered a dangerous, Western ideology. Rather than placating this group, however, the leadership decided to implement an initiative that in fact threatened their economic or political interests. Launched in 1972, the agrarian revolution, intended to extend socialism into the agricultural sector, was advocated by the other major faction in the regime as a means of mobilizing rural support and stemming the tide of rural-urban migration, which had been creating increasing social problems in the cities.[104]

After a decade in power, and given the emerging factionalism in the regime, Boumedienne apparently concluded that the people's role in the political process needed to be reevaluated. Local governing councils at the provincial and communal level had been established and elections had been held, but the National Assembly had not been convened.[105] The passage of ten years since Ben Bella's ouster offered a symbolic opportunity to reassess the course of the revolution and to set the course for the future. It was in this context that the promulgation of a new national charter was conceived. As a careful reading reveals, it was a document whose underlying narrative was intended to address the growing factionalism.

Boumedienne announced the initiative to draft a new national charter on 19 June 1975, and a wide-ranging debate followed. Indeed, the public discussion of the draft, which took place over several months, represented the greatest degree of popular participation in any government project up to that time (or since).

The eighty-thousand-word final product was overwhelmingly approved by a popular referendum held on 27 June 1976,[106] and then served as the basis for a new constitution, which was approved shortly thereafter.[107]

The 1976 Charte nationale began with an historical section underlining elements that had become central to the regime's national identity narrative.[108] First, it reasserted the existence of Algeria and the Algerian people as far back as Roman times. However, it was only after the arrival of the Arabs that the constitutive elements of Algerian identity were progressively added: its cultural, linguistic, and spiritual unity, in the form of Arabo-Islamic civilization. Again, this insistence on an unchanging Arabo-Muslim identity was no doubt intended to appeal to the more religiously conservative elements in the regime and the country uncomfortable with the socialist direction of policy.

As for the narrative of the revolution, like its 1964 predecessor, the 1976 Charte nationale mentioned the colonial invasion, the massive involvement of people from the deepest reaches of the countryside, and the theme of the historical continuity of resistance: "this is how the content of Algerian nationalism was forged, a nationalism that would only be radicalized as colonialism extended its system of oppression." It then reiterated the critique of the political parties active in the final decades of colonial rule, with their "bourgeois liberal utopias, sectarian demagoguery, taste for compromise, illusions and vague attempts regarding paths and means to ensure the building of the country and national independence." There are repeated references to the conservative or bourgeois forces that threatened the revolution, but there is no other reference to divisions in the ranks, either during the revolution or in its immediate wake.[109]

While not new, the Charte nationale's discrediting of the predecessors of the FLN as bourgeois counterrevolutionaries at this juncture served a different purpose than in the immediate wake of independence: it helped establish the ideological justification for Boumedienne's socialism, which was constructed as a continuation of Algeria's revolutionary path. Algeria's economic development strategy and the discourse associated with it are worthy of a separate study. Here, I consider only those elements that were critical to national identity and to constructing and enforcing unity.

The problem faced by Ben Bella, and by Boumedienne after him, in pursuing what was called a socialist revolution was threefold. First, as noted above, the concept itself was alien and, worse, Western. Perhaps more important, its principles—such as class struggle and collectivization—appeared to run counter to Islamic notions of a just society and a peaceful community. Third, the impact of these policies threatened many well-entrenched conservative interests. Socialism had therefore to be presented as a continuation of the revolution to legitimize it as the regime's approach to development.

To that end, similar values had to be shown to inform both systems; or rather, socialism had to be demonstrated to be culturally authentic, proceeding naturally from Islamic values. The Charte nationale therefore began by situating Algerian state and society within an Islamic framework. It reaffirmed that the Algerian people were Muslim, and that Islam was both the religion of state and one of the basic components of the country's historical identity. Furthermore, it was "the impenetrable fortress that enabled Algeria to remain steadfast in the face of attempts to harm its personality. The Algerian people were protected by Islam, the religion of struggle, rigor, justice, and equality; they took refuge in it in the darkest periods of imperialist domination, they took from it the moral energies and the spiritual force that preserved them from giving in to despair, and it endowed them with bases for victory."

The Charte then proceeded to argue that Islam was the natural basis for socialism as a development strategy. "The decline of the Muslim world cannot be explained purely by moral causes; other material factors—social and economic—foreign invasions, internal struggles, the rise of despotism, etc., played a role." Therefore, "to regenerate itself the Muslim world has only one option: to go beyond reformism and take the path of social revolution. Any project that has as an objective today the reconstruction of Muslim thought must, in order to be credible, engage in a much larger project: the total remaking of the society. The Muslim peoples will realize more and more that it is by strengthening their struggle against imperialism and resolutely taking the path of socialism that they will best respond to the imperatives of their faith and that they will reconcile action with principles."

To reinforce the natural affinity between Islam, indigenous culture and socialism, the next section argued that capitalism was fundamentally linked to the exploitation of man—something abhorrent to Islam, which seeks justice. Further, it insisted that "socialism in Algeria does not proceed from a materialist metaphysic, nor is it attached to any dogmatic conception that is foreign to our national genius. Its construction is identified with a blossoming of Islamic values, which are a fundamental constitutive element of the identity of the Algerian people." The Charte thus attempted to dispel any notion that socialism derived from a Western dialectic materialism, namely, communism or atheism, but instead proceeded from a vision and values that were an integral part of the Algerian essence.

For good measure, Arabic, so dear to the religiously conservative sectors, was also included as a part of this socialist march, being defined as an essential element in the cultural identity of the Algerian people. "It is impossible to separate our personality from the national language that expresses it . . . the generalized usage of the Arabic language and mastering it as a functional creative instrument is one of the primordial tasks of Algerian society on all levels of culture and on the level of socialist ideology." No mention was made of any other Algerian languages.

In this way, the regime made its strongest case for a socialist path that was still consistent with and supportive of "authentic" national identity and culture. Not only was there no contradiction between Islam and socialism, but in fact, socialism was a natural response by an Arabo-Islamic culture struggling for full independence, development, and social justice. In the constitution approved several months later, the preamble restated this in the following terms: "At independence the people committed themselves to the construction of the State and the building of a new society founded on the elimination of the exploitation of man by man with its goal, in the framework of its having opted for socialism, the development of man and the promotion of the popular masses."[110]

Educational Reform

For Boumedienne, national development required three simultaneous revolutions—industrial, agricultural and cultural. The 1976 Charte nationale conceived of education as the primary motor behind the cultural revolution; without it, no infrastructural or superstructural modernization was possible. Moreover, a cultural revolution was an essential component of the broader process of transforming and purifying the Algerian nation. As a basic element of Algerians' cultural identity, Arabic was critical to this revolution. Arabization would unify the Algerians in the use of one language for work, teaching, and culture. In the eyes of the drafters, it was an objective in keeping with the recovery of all the historical characteristics of the Algerian nation.[111]

Yet, the educational sector so central to this revolution was in crisis, deeply marked by the sociocultural and linguistic battles that divided various components of the ruling coalition. Whatever successes the Algerian state could point to on other fronts, by the mid-1970s, it was clear that the process of educational development, with Arabization at its core, was in disarray. While in theory Arabization did not imply a political program, in practice it had helped to politicize the classroom and curriculum. For example, civics had been eliminated and replaced by religious instruction,[112] while in Arabic language instruction, both the classical period, from the ninth to the fourteenth centuries, and the nineteenth and twentieth centuries, tended to be excluded in order to highlight a particular version of "national" content. In history, on the other hand, the emphasis was on the recent past, downplaying the importance of critical moments in world history and excluding from the history of the Maghreb certain crucial periods, such as those prior to the arrival of Islam.[113]

The legal basis for a major educational reform to respond to Boumedienne's concerns was promulgated just before the issuance of the Charte, through Edict 76–35 of 16 April 1976. According to this, every Algerian had the right to an education; schooling was obligatory for all children from six to sixteen years of age, and free at all levels; and the state guaranteed equality of access to post-elementary education, without limitation, except individual aptitude, on the one hand, and the means and needs of society, on the other.

Beyond these general elements, the law was to serve as the justification for a major change in presecondary education through the institution of the basic school (*madrasa asasiyya*, or *école fondamentale polytechnique*). At the time, schooling comprised six years of primary education, followed by four years of middle school and three years of secondary school. The new structure involved nine years (three cycles of three years) of fundamental skills and general knowledge instruction, as well as broad science and technical education, followed by secondary school. The rationale was that a nine-year single track for all would better train Algerian youth to meet the pressing demand for skilled manual labor, managers, and administrators.

For purposes of analyzing the evolving narrative, the philosophy or vision guiding this reform is of greatest importance. Article 2 of the law described the mission of the educational system. Carefully placed in the framework of "Arabo-Islamic values and socialist conscience," it was a restatement of both the axes of authenticity and modernity underpinning regime legitimacy. This mission was to include, among other things, responding to popular aspirations for justice and progress and awakening love for the homeland. The system was also to inculcate into the young the principles of justice and equality among citizens and people, and lead them to combat all forms of discrimination; provide an education that favored understanding and cooperation among people for universal peace and accord among nations; and develop an education in accord with human rights and fundamental liberties.

In 1977, Boumedienne called upon his longtime supporter Mustefa Lacheraf to take the helm as minister of education to reform the educational system in a way that would produce cadres capable of fulfilling their role in all three revolutions—industrial, agricultural, and cultural—in the context of the commitment to Arabization. Lacheraf was a well-known intellectual who had been one of the drafters of both the 1962 Tripoli declaration and the 1976 Charte nationale. Portrayed by some as opposed to Arabization, a charge to which he took great exception, Lacheraf instead sought to rationalize what had to date been a thoroughly unplanned and inchoate implementation of the language policy. His assumption of the education portfolio marked a pause of sorts in the process in order to reassess and reorganize efforts. Suffice it here to say that his criticisms of the existing system, which he submitted in two reports for the Ministry of Education, and his efforts to reform, not only the modes of Arabization, but the existing methods, instructors, and curricular materials, triggered waves of criticism and resistance, primarily from the Arabophone and Islamist segments of the elite.

The president accepted Lacheraf's proposals, but he did not publicly support him in the broader societal debate they triggered. As a result, although the government finally approved his plan, Lacheraf refused to implement it. After Boumedienne's death in 1978, Lacheraf left the ministry, and his reform program was shelved. As a result, instead of being introduced by 1982, the *école fondamentale* structure was not fully established until 1989.[114] Its content and implications for the national narrative in the 1980s are discussed in chapter 5.

CONCLUSIONS

Algeria's long experience with brutal colonial rule included violence to its history in the form of a French narrative that sought to portray the population as not only backward, but lacking peoplehood: divided into a fanatical Arab sector, on the one hand, and an oppressed original Berber population, on the other. France's mission, constructed with echoes of earlier Roman conquerors, was to bring civilization—economic and social progress—to this underdeveloped region. This colonial portrayal triggered the production of a counternarrative, which was first articulated by *islahi* ulama prior to the revolution. The counternarrative largely preserved the structure of the colonial story line, but reversed the heroes and villains of the French version, attributed to the people a clear and long-standing Arabo-Muslim identity, and insisted upon the tradition of an indigenous state and valiant resistance to would-be conquerors. Elements of the deep history of this narrative were absent in the earliest documents of the revolution. They were later adopted as part of the national narrative, but it was the revolution itself that came to be constructed as the founding story.

The first critical challenge in which the narrative participated came in the immediate aftermath of independence, when fighting between factions within the FLN-ALN underlined the broader contest for power that pitted the GPRA against Ben Bella and his supporters. This violent factionalism played out against the backdrop of a country devastated by the scorched earth policy of the OAS and by the vengeance exacted from those Algerians who had fought for France. The dramatic challenges this situation posed to regime consolidation were addressed in the narrative by an insistence on unity. For example, the 1962 Tripoli declaration, published just before independence, placed the theme of national resistance to colonialism front and center, and emphasized the national unity of the Algerians. It was through the "unity of combat" that "the nation rediscovered itself as an organic entity." Thus, as part of its battle against serious divisions on the horizon, the leadership chose to proclaim the existence of national unity, as if verbally conjuring it could succeed in making it so.

The constitution of 1963 continued both to make the revolution the central story of the nation and to insist upon the unity of the people. Islam was declared the religion of state and Arabic the official language. At this point, however, the Arabo-Islamic essence of the people insisted upon by the *islahi* narrative was not alluded to in the constitution, perhaps because of the strong influence of secularism among Ben Bella's closest advisors.

It was instead the issuance of the 1964 Charte d'Alger that formalized this characterization of national identity, asserting that "Islamization and Arabization gave our country the aspect which it has preserved to the present." Perhaps as an attempt to avoid alienating those elements for whom an Arabo-Muslim identity was not a comfortable fit—and their numbers (*francisants*, Marxists, secularists, many Berbers) were significant under Ben Bella—the text did attempt to reinterpret the meaning of the term, claiming that "Arabo-Muslim is not an ethnic reference," and insisting upon the important civilizational contributions of the Central Maghreb prior to the coming of Islam. The persistence of these divisions rendered critical the official narrative's insistence upon unity. The Charte d'Alger therefore emphasized the unity of the people during both the liberation struggle and the earlier period of armed resistance against the French. Moreover, to provide a basis of common action among a disparate set of factions and interests, it insisted that Algeria would move forward "and with respect for our Arabo-Islamic tradition, we will build socialism." The goal was to reach out simultaneously to the constituencies of these divergent sociocultural and political inclinations by offering (granted, potentially contradictory) formulations to each as a way of trying to ensure the center would hold.

Ultimately, however, the contradictions in the Ben Bella regime, combined with the tremendous challenges it faced in the wake of independence, led to Boumedienne's coup, which also required discursive legitimation. The 19 June 1965 proclamation of the Council of the Revolution portrayed the previous three years as an era of unpatriotic maneuvers that threatened the relationship between the state (or at least the military) and the people. Such a construction was particularly important for Boumedienne, who drew his legitimacy from his role in the ALN during the liberation war. Now in control, he oversaw a shift in the narrative from the "historic legitimacy" of Ben Bella, which he could not claim, to "revolutionary legitimacy," which he and the *mujahidin* embodied.

The 1964 Charte d'Alger had been the first document to insist on the importance for all activists of having a knowledge of history. Yet it was Boumedienne, who, in beginning, after seizing power, to put in place a range of institutions that glorified the revolution and the *mujahidin*, concretely demonstrated the keenest sense of the political importance of controlling the narrative. At the same time, he reintroduced into positions of power influential personalities from the Arabo-Islamic trend who had chafed under Ben Bella's more secular orientation. Both of these moves were aimed at consolidating his legitimacy among key constituencies.

Boumedienne's empowerment of the Arabo-Islamist tendency, in tandem with his continued advocacy of socialist development, only allowed the contradictions between these two broad camps to grow. By the early 1970s, the fracture lines had developed to that point that he was in need of reinforcing the governing coalition. One key task of the 1976 Charte nationale was precisely to reconcile, discursively, the apparent contradictions between critical constituencies. The "truth" of the narrative's claim of the unity of the people depended upon this, but so did regime stability. Hence, Charte nationale not only devoted significant space to its argument about the compatibility of Islam and socialism, but also spent a great deal of time wooing the two camps. It juxtaposed its insistence upon a unified Algerian people of Arabo-Islamic character unchanged since the eighth century with a progressive program of agricultural, cultural, and industrial revolution, including central roles for the peasantry, workers, students and women. It also extended the definition or sweep of the revolution and revolutionary legitimacy from just the 1954–62 period to a new set of goals associated with the longer-term implementation of socialism. Furthermore, it built on the official narrative's previous discrediting of the pre-1954 political parties by setting up an implicit parallel between those conservative or bourgeois forces that had opposed the FLN and those who opposed Boumedienne's initiatives to continue the revolution in the form of socialist economic development.

In sum, the factionalism—regional, ideological, cultural, or personal—that had manifested itself during the revolution posed continuing challenges to the leadership of both Ben Bella and Boumedienne. The official narrative, as one tool in the struggles over regime legitimacy and consolidation, underwent several subtle shifts in response, related to the content of national identity, the bases of unity, and the construction of the content and message of the national liberation war. Unity itself increasingly came to be defined in homogeneous cultural-religious rather than more inclusive terms, and it often seemed that the greater the dissension from the official portrayal of unity, the more loudly it was insisted upon or the more homogeneous its bases were proclaimed to be.

The rescripting of key themes in the official narrative during this period certainly seemed aimed at cultivating legitimacy and reinforcing regime stability. Nevertheless, more critical certainly were the economic rents the state could distribute to the citizenry courtesy of high oil and natural gas prices on the international market. Boumedienne died before the decline in oil revenues began to undermine the cohesion of the regime and the narrative that legitimized it. It is to that juncture of leadership transition that the discussion now turns.

5 ALGERIA FROM BENDJEDID TO THE DARK DECADE

The Narrative Fractures

AS BOUMEDIENNE LAY DYING, two diametrically opposed tendencies in the regime emerged to contest the succession. The first sought to impose tighter political control over the bureaucracy and to assert the primacy of the FLN over the administrative apparatus of the state. It drew its support from elements of the officer corps, the UGTA, the student left, a section of the *arabisants*, the clandestine Parti de l'avant-garde socialiste (PAGS: Socialist Vanguard Party),[1] and sections of the press. The second tendency favored terminating the socialist policies pursued since the early 1970s and moving to liberalize state economic policy. It was supported by a large portion of the administrative and technocratic elite, the private sector (bourgeoisie) and liberal professions, but had little support in the party, mass organizations, or the army. With neither tendency sufficiently powerful to impose its will, the army emerged as the arbiter.[2] Its candidate for successor was Chadli Bendjedid, a former officer in the external ALN in Tunisia and a loyal supporter of Boumedienne, who had appointed him commander of the Oran military district in 1964.

Despite this apparent sign of continuity, an extraordinary congress of the FLN held in the summer of 1980 adopted the slogan "Toward a Better Life," thus signaling a retreat from Boumedienne's austere revolutionary socialism. The state then gradually relaxed its grip over much of the economy, including dismantling the agrarian revolution by 1983. Within five years, Bendjedid, who had always supported the private sector, "quietly but thoroughly 'de-Boumedianized'" the power structure, by reactivating the FLN and creating a real national structure for the first time. Indeed, Bendjedid's ascent to the presidency set in motion an elite realignment of a magnitude not experienced since 1965.[3]

The discussion that follows begins with a detailed examination of this transition and its effect on the official narrative. The second juncture to be explored is a more explosive challenge, the riots of 1988, which led to the end of one-party rule. The final episode covered is the insurgency of the 1990s, known as the dark decade (*la décennie noire*, or *al-ʿashriyya al-sawdaʾ*). Narrative developments since spring 2011 are taken up in the Epilogue.

BENDJEDID CHANGES COURSE

It is not uncommon for successor regimes to stake out new identities, legitimating symbols, or points of reference. Boumedienne himself had done so in his development of the narrative of revolutionary versus historic legitimacy. Moreover, any wise economic manager might have decided in 1980 that Algeria's growing socioeconomic woes required a change in course, and Bendjedid's gradual opening to private enterprise was hardly the most dramatic economic policy change being implemented across the world at the time. However, in this case, the transition also took place against the backdrop of a rising regional tide of movements organized around a politicization of Islam. As the economic crisis triggered by the drop in oil and natural gas prices assumed cultural and religious dimensions, the regime reprised the strategy of instrumentalizing language and cultural policy.

The relatively more liberal tone of the new regime quickly opened the way for social protest. As early as winter 1979–80, *arabisant* high school and university students went on strike to protest the poor implementation of Arabization. These students tended to come from humbler backgrounds, while the *francisants* were disproportionately represented among the intellectual class.[4] Bendjedid's policy at the time was to "get out ahead" of the Islamists, who had become increasingly visible proponents of Arabization and whom he was concerned would capture the movement.[5] To do so, he took several initiatives. In his first cabinet, he replaced Redha Malek and Mustapha Lacheraf, both of whom, as the previous chapter discussed, were known as secular leftists, with two high-profile *arabisants*: Abdelhamid Mehri, referred to in the previous chapter, as minister of information and culture; and Mohamed Cherif Kharroubi, the *wali* (governor) of Greater Kabylia, as minister of national education.[6] Ahmed Taleb Ibrahimi remained as a presidential advisor. Bendjedid also Arabized the justice system, thus creating thousands of jobs for unemployed *arabisants*.

Spring 1980 brought even more serious demonstrations, this time from the other side of the cultural divide, in Kabylia. Many Kabyles, *francisants* and heavily represented in the capital and in the bureaucratic apparatus, sought the recognition of Tamazight, the most widely spoken Berber language, along with Arabic as a national language. They were also uncomfortable with or opposed to the Arabization policy and the politicization of Islam that increasingly accompanied it. The appointment of Kharroubi, a Kabyle, as minister of education, was of little comfort to them, since he was himself a zealous supporter of Arabization. The depth of Kabyle dissatisfaction was dramatically demonstrated by the 1980 anti-regime protests, centered in the city of Tizi Ouzou,[7] that came to be known as the *Printemps berbère*, or Berber Spring, which were more brutally suppressed than the student demonstrations of the previous fall.

In the ongoing power jockeying among regime factions, Bendjedid was actually able to use the spring 1980 events to his advantage, because they divided the political Left. The more secular wing of leftists sympathized with the Kabyles' grievances, while the more Arabist and nationalist wing was deeply opposed. As a result of the FLN's poor performance in response to the crisis, Bendjedid was voted full authority to restructure the leading organs of the party, thus significantly increasing his power. An extraordinary meeting of the FLN was then held, 15–19 June, during which Arabo-Muslim values were emphasized, while the Marxists and members of the PAGS came under strong attack.[8]

John Ruedy argues that the regime's course was dictated by the need to overcome leftists, Marxists, and "Boumediennists" concentrated in the labor movement, on university campuses, and among the youth movement who opposed the revised economic priorities of Bendjedid's consolidation strategy. In this contest, the president sought support among the *arabisants*, a group that was generally politically conservative but economically liberal, and whose main focus was cultural issues. The ethnic ramifications of this were clear, since the largely *francisant* Kabyles tended to be more heavily concentrated in secular or leftist circles. However, even had the Kabyles not been linked to the Left, Ruedy writes, "the regime still would have supported the Arabizers to the detriment of Kabyle cultural interests because it needed their help in dismantling the house of Boumedienne."[9]

The rise of political Islam in the 1980s was another factor in Bendjedid's choice of strategies. No longer were the culture clashes merely about access to jobs or economic philosophy A new kind of militancy led to conflicts between Islamists and Berberists or Marxists. Religious extremists began flexing their muscle in a variety of ways: organizing informal prayer halls; evicting state-appointed imams from their mosques; distributing tracts demanding an

Islamic government; and engaging in increasingly violent clashes on university campuses. A manifestation of the growing power of these groups came in early November 1982, when, following the police arrest of four hundred religious militants after the killing of a leftist student, "some 100,000 shouting, banner-waving Muslim demonstrators converged for Friday prayers on the downtown University mosque."[10]

The need to outflank the Islamists, as manifested in the government's further push on Arabization, was apparent in dramatic increases in support for funding for religious education at all levels. Islamic cultural centers were established by the state in each of the country's forty-eight provinces, and in fall 1984, the massive Emir Abdelkader University of Islamic Sciences, one of the largest mosque-universities in the world, was opened in Constantine. Another indicator both of Bendjedid's desire to coopt the fundamentalists and of the degree to which the culturally conservative factions had already defeated their competitors came with the promulgation of the Family Code of 1984. Repeatedly since independence—in 1963, 1966, 1970, 1973, and 1981—proposals for a unified national family code had been the subject of such intense polemics and contestation that the result had been paralysis. In 1984, however, a new law was passed by the National Assembly with almost no discussion. Much to the dismay of women activists, the new law "catered to social and political forces with a vested interest in the preservation of the extended patrilineal kinship structure sanctioned by Islamic family law."[11] With its passage, Algeria, whose female participants in the liberation struggle (*mujahidat*)[12] had been famous for their sacrifices and daring, came under the most regressive family law in North Africa.[13]

Bendjedid also drew on the symbols and emotive power of the revolution to help consolidate support. One initiative involved gathering the remains of tens of thousands of martyrs and reburying them in proper graves, erecting monuments across the country to mark important battles of the liberation war to memorialize them and their heroes, and collecting written documentation and oral testimonies regarding the 1954–62 period.[14] In addition, museums were built throughout the country devoted either to the revolution or to a prominent martyr. For example, dating to this period, the city of Oran has both the obligatory Mujahid Museum—a large exposition hall with a poorly organized collection of photos and revolutionary memorabilia—and the Musée national Ahmed Zabanah, which takes its name from an early martyr of the revolution from Oran.[15] It has partial floors devoted to everything from modern painting to flora and fauna of the region, but the central room, which is visible as one enters, is devoted primarily to mementos of Zabanah's life and martyrdom, although there are also pieces related to the revolution more generally.

Dwarfing all of the museums outside the capital, however, is the Riadh al-Fath complex, which towers above Algiers, with its monument to the martyrs, Maqam al-Shahid,[16] and the museum beneath it, the National Museum of the Mujahid, which was inaugurated in 1982 and then transferred to a new (and current) location in 1983. Here, several key points will be made that underline the political and symbolic importance the museum had in promoting the narrative in line with the leadership's concerns at the time.

First is the name itself: a museum that is devoted to those who fought to secure national independence, thus emphasizing the centrality of the revolution and respect owed those who participated in it. Upon entering one first encounters a wall with paintings or pictures of "the 22"—the group of nationalists who planned and launched the revolution. Next, to the right, is another entrance with paintings or photographs of other martyrs, with the dates of their births and deaths. As one continues there is a display of officially sponsored books on the war and then bound early copies of *El Moujahid*, the newspaper of the FLN, as well as a collection of publications by the AUMA.

The museum itself is laid out in a circle, and the historical part begins with the period just prior to the French invasion. It then moves to 'Abd al-Qadir and his resistance; subsequent revolts with paintings of their leaders; the AUMA, but virtually nothing on the rest of the early nationalist or anti-colonial movement, thus emphasizing the official narrative's construction of its role as the link between the revolution and earlier resistance. It then turns to the Sétif massacres of May 1945,[17] and, finally, to the revolution itself. Examples of French brutality are highlighted, including instruments of torture, lists of the names and details of all those guillotined, and a life-size diorama of the Challe and Morice lines.[18] The display also includes a partial wall devoted to the provisional government; pictures of the October 1961 anti-Algerian violence in Paris; photographs relating to the negotiations at Evian and of the destruction carried out by OAS.[19] It is worth noting that while there are some materials in French, most of the materials, descriptive or otherwise, are in Arabic. It seems clear, therefore, that this is meant both to be directed primarily to an Algerian audience, and to send a message that Algeria's identity is Arab.

Finally, there is the lower level. Here, photographs are forbidden, the stone is black granite, and the lighting low. Continuous *tajwid* (Quranic recitation) plays in the background, adding to the sacred character of the hall and recreating the atmosphere of a place where condolences are offered. In the center is a large stone from the Aurès Mountains, where, according to tradition, the first operation of the revolution was launched. Along the wall around the hall that surrounds the center stone are verses from the Quran in brass letters. Overhead, in a circle near the top of the dome, is the verse:

"Do not consider those who have been slain in the path of God as dead; rather they are alive and find their sustenance in the presence of their Lord" (Quran 3:169).

Clearly, the lower level is intended, not only to underline the nature of the sacrifice of so many Algerians over decades of resistance, but also to link this resistance prominently with the Arabo-Islamic identity elements that increasingly infused the narrative during Bendjedid 's presidency.

Implementing the *École fondamentale* Model

As noted above, pressures to resume the interrupted Arabization process were renewed after Lacheraf was replaced at the Ministry of Education, and work transforming the educational system to the *école fondamentale* (EF: basic school) model was begun. Before examining the content of the textbooks in use during the early to mid-1980s in order to ascertain what if any changes may have been made in the official state narrative for student consumption, several remarks are in order. First, an examination of the publication dates of books as well as the grade level for which they were intended (which identifies them as EF or not) reveals that some books published and used during the EF years, or as the system was being phased in, appear to have been carried over from the pre-EF period. Since the goal here is to examine what students were being taught in the context of particular critical junctures, the texts are discussed based on year of publication, rather than according to whether they are designated as EF texts or not. Husayn Hammad notes that one history text for the final year of secondary school in use in 1976 was unchanged as of 1991, thus surviving intact two historical reframings—the 1976 and 1986 chartes (the latter to be addressed below)—one major regime transition, and the 1989 end of the single party state.[20]

Seven history textbooks from this period were located: two from 1979, two from the early 1980s, and three from the late 1980s. The introduction to the first-year secondary text *Ta'rikh al-'alam al-hadith* (History of the Modern World; 1979–80) contended that it combined "simplicity of presentation with comprehensiveness of perspective and complete neutrality in presenting historical facts." It included little on either Algeria or North Africa, but in its coverage of European imperialism, it insisted that in the battles for influence in the Mediterranean, Algeria carried the banner of holy jihad, repelling attempts at control by the Spanish, French, and British (157).

The second-year secondary text *Ta'rikh al-'Arab al-hadith w-al-'alam* (Modern History of the Arabs and the World, 1979–80) started by saying that the authors offered the book as part of their "service to the holy national cause, that of giving Algerian identity its face of authentic Arab genius." Not surprisingly, the first chapter addressed the importance of the Arab world, stressing its unity, which was strengthened under Islam. Any divisions of the Arab homeland or the Arab *umma* were only a temporary phase.

The second chapter, "The Arab Identity from pre-Islamic Times to the Present," was a combination of the *islahi* and Arab nationalist narratives. It argued that Arabs had been moving from the Arabian Peninsula to North Africa even before the arrival of Islam, so there was already a mixture with the "original inhabitants." The most definitive event, however, was the arrival of Islam: "By accepting Islam, feelings of unity among all of them were born, rising above tribal and clan feuding. The result was the birth of the Arab people [*umma*], so that after a time the Arabs were united in a single state" (11). It then claimed that Islam and the Qur'an had "put an end to multiple local dialects and preserved the unity of thought and expression among members of the Arab *umma* from the Atlantic to the Gulf." The book then repeated the material on imperial competition found in the 1970 third-year secondary text *Al-Ta'rikh al-hadith, 1453–1815* (Modern History, 1453–1815), discussed in the previous chapter.

Just as important is its discussion of the nationalist movement. From the publication date, it is impossible to know whether this was originally drafted before Boumedienne died or not. What is clear is that by the time it was written, the regime had overcome its hypersensitivity regarding pre-1954 nationalist history, for it discussed the evolution of the political parties by name, even mentioning Messali Hadj in the context of dissension in the Mouvement pour le triomphe des libertés démocratiques (MTLD: Movement for the Triumph of Democratic Liberties) (186). It then turned to the announcement of the revolution (188), explaining that those who felt it was not necessary to have complete unity in the ranks of the revolutionaries before engaging in more positive action came together to form the Revolutionary Council for Unity and Action. They launched the revolution and announced the birth of the FLN. Messali and his followers are mentioned as the only ones who deviated from this decision. Unity is still important as a purported accomplishment of the FLN, and hence the story remains highly stylized, but the aversion to discussing this critical episode of pre-1954 nationalist history appears to have waned.[21]

On the question of national identity, the second-year middle school text *Ta'rikh al-Qurun al-Wusta* (History of the Middle Ages, 1983–84) is significant for the attention it devotes in a chapter on North Africa to the Amazigh (the Tamazight name for those who speak it).[22] It claims that the Amazigh are a people (*qawm*) "whose ancestry is said to be Arab," who have lived in North Africa "since ancient times." It then adopts the *islahi* narrative that they loved freedom and hence resisted invaders, from the Vandals to the Romans. They even put up more resistance to the Arabs than the Arabs had encountered anywhere else "until they understood Islam and realized the goal of the Arabs. When they understood, they embraced Islam, and brotherhood between them and the Arabs was solidified" (119). Thus while acknowledging the existence of the indigenous people and giving them a corporate identity, the text claims their ancestry as Arab and insists that they embraced Islam and Arabism once they realized the Arabs' goals.

The first-year middle school text *Ta'rikh al-hadarat al-qadima* (History of Ancient Civilizations; likely early 1980s), had three chapters of interest entitled: "The Countries of the Arab Maghreb and Amazighi Society"; "The Great Amazigh Kingdoms"; and "The Civilization of the Amazigh Kingdoms." The text called the Amazigh descendants of Noah, but said they settled in the *Arab* Maghreb (*sic.*; my emphasis).[23] It went on to insist on their being Semites, stress their love of freedom, and detail the exploits and resistance of Masinissa and Jugurtha in the fight against Roman imperialism. It referred to the Amazigh as "our grandfathers" who achieved a most sophisticated civilization. They even had "a democratic form of government based on free elections and authority derived from the people" (100). Thus, perhaps in response to the events of the Berber spring, the texts acknowledged the Berbers in a way earlier government texts had not, but only after asserting clear links to the Arabs.

As for other texts addressing aspects of identity, at this stage, Islamic and national education were combined in a single textbook.[24]As in the third-year middle school text *Al-Mukhtar f-il-tarbiya al-Islamiyya w-al-wataniyya* (Readings in Islamic and Civic Education, 1984–85),[25] their introductions stress the important role of Islam "in lighting the fire of jihad," meaning the revolution, and in preserving the Algerian people "in the face of successive attempts to destroy its resistance. In its [Islam's] name and following its call, millions of its people/sons hurried to give their blood and souls for the sake of liberating the homeland." Similarly, in the introduction to the 1985–86 fourth-year middle school civics text in same series, *Al-Mukhtar f-il-tarbiya al-Islamiyya w-al-wataniyya*, we find: "If we search for the real force that lit the sparks of the revolution in the Islamic homeland against occupation and exploitation from ancient to modern times we find no power save that of Islam."

In the 1985–86 seventh-year *école fondamentale* text book for the series, the twenty-third chapter was entitled "Remembering 1 November" (112). It began with the same verse from the Quran referred to above in the discussion of the National Museum of the Mujahid, regarding those who are killed for the sake of God, but are not considered dead. Like the third-year middle school text examined above, it also situated the launching of the revolution in an Islamic framework, calling those who launched it faithful believers (*mu'minun sadiqun*). It labeled that struggle an example of jihad, and asserted that 1 November "is among God's eternal days registered by His believing servants in every part of the Islamic world." Although the word "jihad" had certainly been used in the past to refer to the liberation struggle, the broader religious framing of the revolution—which was not a characteristic of the narrative under Ben Bella or Boumedienne—continued: "we celebrate the anniversary of this great day which has influenced our continuous jihad against the enemies of the religion and the homeland." God was called upon or referenced throughout the rest of the chapter.[26]

As for the question of unity, the texts stressed the related concepts of brotherhood and affection, as well as cooperation and mutual support among members of society. In chapter 4 of the 1984–85 third-year middle school civics textbook, a section entitled "obstacles to unity and solidarity," seemed to posit a religious, rather than an ethnic, basis for unity, criticizing *qawmiyya*, the word used at the time to refer to (secular) Arab nationalism, in a way which would have been unthinkable under Boumedienne: "we have learned that human societies today do not depend on a particular race or *qawmiyya*, rather, they are based on the idea of beliefs, creeds, which include many people of different races. Thus we realize the corruption of the call of *qawmiyya* and its backwardness today. *Qawmiyya* is not sound as a basis for concord and unity, because it nourishes a chauvinist solidarity [*'asabiyya*], and this is one of the most dangerous factors that drive people to dissension and difference" (29). Finally, "To achieve an Islamic society it is necessary to work to remove the obstacles that stand between Muslims and their unity: nationalist struggles, imperialist barriers, and cultural and *madhhabi* invasions.[27] The establishment of Islamic civilization restores equilibrium to human life because it binds people to their creator and is founded on the basis of faith in God." This entire formulation is quite striking: it abandoned the Arab nationalism and third world solidarity that had been the hallmarks of the Boumedienne period, and established Islam, not the ethnic or secular nation, as the primary basis of solidarity.

Formalizing a New Course

Clearly, by the mid-1980s, many of the political, economic, and identity principles laid out in the 1976 Charte nationale were no longer operative or were under siege. As part of the discursive and institutional transition from Boumediennism, in April 1985, Bendjedid established a commission to review the document. The text it produced, the 1986 Charte nationale,[28] played a significant role in reshaping or confirming the ongoing rescripting of the national narrative.

The Founding Story in the 1986 Charte nationale As in the textbooks cited above, the presentation of the national foundational story in the preamble to the 1986 Charte nationale reflected the enhanced role of Islam in Bendjedid's Algeria. The revolution of 1 November was "supported by the spirit of Islam" and evolved "in the context of the Islamic concepts of justice, liberation and progress." When the FLN's leadership was mentioned, it was characterized as working toward the people's "unify[ing] itself morally through its struggle and profound conviction that Islam is its religion, Arabic its language, and Algeria its fatherland," a famous phrase used by the *islahi* ulama in the colonial era. Moreover, 1 November 1954 was more than an armed uprising. "It was an historic revolution, the new emergence of an identity, the rebirth of a culture and the *reassertion of the values of Islam*" (emphasis added). Thus the text reinforces the Islamization of the revolution that we have seen above in the school texts.

Considerable space was also devoted to the revolution in the long historical section of 1986 Charte nationale, and here the evolution of national unity was a key theme. It mentioned the role and importance of the Étoile nord-africaine (ENA), Parti du peuple algérien (PPA), and Mouvement pour le triomphe des libertés démocratiques (MTLD) in paving the way for spreading the idea of independence throughout the country. It also noted the contribution of the Sétif demonstration on 8 May 1945 and the subsequent massacres to the perception of armed struggle as the sole path to national independence.[29] As for the revolution itself, it was described as "the extension and the crowning of all the forms of resistance against French occupation. It signaled the birth of a new era and "it opened the way to the unification of the ranks of the people in a battle which became one of the most important epics in the history of the twentieth century." The ideals of sacrifice and heroism demonstrated by the ALN and *musabbalin* and *fida'iyyin*[30] produced results "expressed in the unity of the people, the cohesion of its ranks and the coherence of the discourse addressed to them." "The greatest achievement produced by the liberation war was the consecration of national unity inside the established frontiers."

Unity in an Ancient State The 1964 Charte d'Alger had argued that an objective knowledge of Algerian history was a basic obligation of every militant, and the preamble of the 1986 Charte nationale called it "one of the fundamental components of national identity and a reflection of the *unity* of the nation." However, history was now important, not just beginning with the revolution or 'Abd al-Qadir, but "from the oldest of times to the present." Such an approach would "permit the nation [*umma*] to clarify the stages of the formation of national identity, which has been known from ancient times to be jealous of liberty [the traditional vague reference to Berber society without naming it that we have seen before], and for its rejection of any attempt at foreign invasion or imperialist expansion."

Immediately thereafter, and significantly, it stated more explicitly: "It is not merely by chance that the inhabitants of this area called [note the use of the past tense] themselves *al-amazigh*, meaning free men." This fleeting reference was likely included as a response to the 1980 *Printemps berbère,* mentioned above. Moreover, here, for the first time, an official text labeled the Algerian people "Arab and Muslim," as opposed to the arguably broader "Arabo-Muslim" characterization that had been used in previous documents. Islam was registered as the religion of state, and one of the fundamental components of the national identity, a fundamental element in the mobilization of the capacity of the resistance, and an impenetrable fortress. The Charte nationale insisted that the Algerian people took refuge in it in their most difficult times, and obtained from it the moral and spiritual force that ultimately brought them victory. Islam molded Algerian society and made it a coherent force, attached to the same land, the same belief, and to the Arabic language, which permitted Algeria to resume its contributions to civilization.

The body of the charter then restated the importance of the study of history: "At this stage of its development, and with a view toward conceiving rational solutions to current and future problems, the orientation of the Algerian revolution intends to accord increased interest to national [*watani*] history, both ancient and modern.[31] An in-depth study of all of this history will enable the generations of today and tomorrow to appreciate the moments of grandeur and power, to determine points of strength and causes of decline." What followed was a long presentation of the regime's version of Algerian history—and implicitly, identity—beginning with prehistoric times.

This was the first such document to give extensive coverage to the country's ancient or pre-Islamic history. The Numidian heroes Masinissa and Jugurtha received detailed attention.[32] This is the period that the school textbooks reviewed above—but never this text—referred to as Berber kingdoms; thus, the extended discussion seemed aimed at recognizing the achievements of the region prior to the arrival of the Arabs, perhaps as a way of attempting to placate Berber activists, while at the same time reaffirming the degree of "state" formation in "Algeria" stretching back more than two thousand years. The text highlighted what one would call today the developmental aspect of the state under Masinissa, who built a powerful entity that commanded respect throughout the Mediterranean basin: he exploited political, military, and diplomatic means to achieve national unity; built an army and a fleet to deter attempts at occupation and to secure foreign trade routes; sedentarized the nomadic populations by introducing them to agricultural practices and techniques, including developing irrigation. Nor did he ignore the cultural dimension of state-building: "He expressed his profound love for independence as well as his determination to mobilize people against the greed of foreigners through the slogan he used: Africa for the Africans." Again, the text's insistence on an attachment this long ago to liberty, defense of the land, and resistance to foreign domination clearly, if indirectly, referred to Berbers and reinforced the notion that we have seen in earlier documents that resistance had always been a characteristic of the "Algerian people."

The next major historical period addressed was the arrival of Islam. The importance of the *islahi* formulation of the history of this period has already been noted. Increasingly, however, this episode was used by the more extreme Islamists as an alternative founding narrative. In other words, the *umma* was transformed from an Algerian one, which (re)gained national sovereignty in 1962, into an Islamic one, whose origins dated to the arrival of Islam in North

Africa.[33] Certainly, the leadership was not proposing such a radical replacement of the founding story, but the fact that it received extensive treatment in Charte nationale is just one more example of the degree to which the regime was reaching out to religiously conservative elements as a base of support.

The Charte nationale stated that the inhabitants found in Islam "a message with content that was at one and the same time religious, spiritual, political, and social—different from those known up to that point. They adopted it with an unprecedented passion, as was proved by the rapid and total disappearance of all the other beliefs. The combination of the appeal of Islam and the similarity of social organization between the Arabs and the people of Numidia led to a "civilizational symbiosis that gave birth to a harmonious human component, coherent in terms of religion, culture, society, and politics." "The introduction of Islam and its organic link with the Arabic language marked the beginning of a new era, which brought decisive transformations into the region and fused the social, economic, and cultural structures in the crucible of Arabo-Islamic civilization." In this way "Algeria," again constructed as existing at this time as a political entity, was able to resume the civilizational march that had been halted by Roman domination. In other words, Islam and Arabic helped restore Algeria to its former glory.

Finally, a separate section devoted to "The Islamic Dimension in the Algerian Revolution" was included, which began with an assertion that the most difficult task of the post-independence period had been tracing "a path leading to harmony between authenticity and modernity." Although the regime had already begun to move away from its socialist past, the text warned: "No regime hostile to emancipation or combating socialism, nor feudalism or capitalism should use its adherence to Islam to serve its interests or achieve its goals." This meant that Islam could not be used to justify exploitation. Then, as if to counter any concern about ethnic superiority or exclusion, the text argued that the Arab dimension of the Algerian revolution accepted no kind of discrimination and implied the domination of no race.

To sum up, the 1986 Charte nationale made the most detailed case to date in an official document for Islam's role as the great unifier of Algerians and of Arabic and Islam as the most basic components of Algerian identity. In so doing, it was certainly intended to cultivate support for the government among the growing numbers of increasingly vocal Islamists. Perhaps in response to the Berber Spring, the Charte also included the first official recognition of Amazigh identity, but it was framed in such a way as to represent little deviation from the identity narrative's overwhelming focus on Islam and Arabic. The Algerian people's "attachment to socialism as an aspiration" was also specified as the third key component—after Islam and Arabic—of Algerian identity, but in practice socialism was in the process of being dismantled. Social justice had been a basic element in the official narrative since independence, and socialism had been central to the narrative under Boumedienne. Perhaps too politically sensitive to banish entirely, it continued to be invoked as part of the leadership's legitimation formula, but it was a concept increasingly emptied of significant content in practice.

École fondamentale Textbooks Redux

Several history texts published around this time are worth examining to see how they parallel or depart from the narrative in the 1986 Charte nationale and the texts used prior to its issuance. The 1986–87 seventh-year *école fondamentale* history textbook *Al-Ta'rikh* focused on the ancient period. While it referred to the Amazigh, it mentioned other names for them, Libyans (*Libiyyun*) and Berber. More important is the way the presentation constructed Islam as a unifying factor. For example, "in the ancient Maghreb the inhabitants formed a single people, and Islam increased these ties" (22); the persistence of "some dialects"[34]—presumably referring to Berber languages—does not mean that there is a difference between the "sons of one region and another." Islam rejects racialism and fights chauvinist solidarity (*'asabiyya*).[35] The textbook then quoted from the Quran:"O people, we have created you, male and female, and we have made of you peoples and tribes, that you may know each other; for the noblest of you in God's sight is [he who is] the most righteous" (Quran 49:13). Thus there seemed to be an openness to some elements of diversity as long as the unifying element was Islam and none of these other identities was stressed.

Thereafter, the text referred to the people as *Maghariba*, which simply translates as North Africans.[36] It repeated much of the history of Jugurtha and Masinissa in the texts from the early 1980s, but did not refer to their kingdoms as Berber or Amazighi. Only when it discussed the resistance of the *Maghariba* did it say that they spoke a language called Tamazight.[37] The final chapters of the book addressed the coming of Islam, the Prophet, and the Righteous Caliphs.[38] In the 1986–87 eighth-grade *Al-Ta'rikh textbook*, the chapter on the spread of Islam to the Maghreb repeated the story of how the Amazigh—who are referred to as such in this text—received it, and it called the Rustumid kingdom the first "*Islamic national* [*watani*] state" (my emphasis).[39] Although it continued to refer to the region as the *Arab* Maghreb, the region's Islamic character pervades the description.

The 1988–89 ninth-grade *Ta'rikh al-Maghrib al-'Arabi al-hadith* (History of the Modern Arab Maghrib) stated in the introduction that it was intended to deepen the sense of national belonging, and lead the students to realize "the role of the people in making history. Critical junctures are written by the hands of the people in a way that mixes sweat with blood." Like previous texts, it stressed the "stateness" of Algeria prior to the French invasion, but with an Islamic character: 'Abd al-Qadir's state, whose constitution derived from Islam, "is considered the first Arab state with nationalist [*qawmi*] and national [*watani*] aspects established in the period of modern European imperial supremacy in the Arab homeland."

Turning to twentieth-century resistance, the text made only an oblique reference to a victory of revolutionaries over personalized leadership (i.e., Messali), but accorded an important role to the *islahi* ulama in "fighting against attempts to erase the national identity. They spread Arab culture and defended Islam against attempts at distortion. They concerned themselves with preparing a generation of Algerians who believed in the characteristics of the *umma* [people or nation]" (111). Ultimately, however, "it became clear *to the Algerian people* [my emphasis] that a political strategy was not useful, and this paved the way for the great Algerian revolution" (116). This was a democratic people's revolution that banished individual conflicts, so that all were fused in the jihad under collective leadership; it added to the efforts of earlier struggles to preserve Algerian authenticity and historic attachment. Thus, the Algerian people continue to be constructed as united, Arabo-Muslim, and engaged in resistance in order to reassert their traditional values. Clearly, there is a strong emphasis on the Islamic component of identity, although the relative emphasis between Arabism and Islam varies. The text makes virtually no mention of Algerian identity components beyond the Arabo-Muslim trait.

RESCRIPTING THE REGIME

The economic reforms put in place under Bendjedid failed to solve the country's problems, and tensions continued to build as a result. The economy was shrinking, unemployment was growing, in part due to layoffs forced by the economic efficiency campaign, and wages were frozen, while prices soared. Simultaneously, a new group of private entrepreneurs who had profited from Bendjedid's liberalization policies conspicuously lived increasingly prosperous lives, while the mass of the population saw its standard of living continue to deteriorate. The cultural wars over the roles of religion, language, and identity both proceeded from and added to these other conflicts. Serious protests, which began among students in 1986, soon spread to other parts of the population and continued through 1987. In early October 1988, strikes led to rioting and massive destruction of government and other property. State repression in response was brutal. By the time order had been restored on 10 October, hundreds of Algerians had been killed, and thousands arrested, many of whom were tortured.

In response, Bendjedid ousted several top officials who had been particular targets of popular wrath and outlined a strategy for reform, which included making the government responsible to parliament for the first time. The FLN Party Congress held in late November and early December 1988 voiced serious opposition to the proposed reforms, which significantly reduced the FLN's power. Nonetheless, Bendjedid was nominated by the party for a third presidential term, and the voters elected him later that month.

In the meantime, a new constitution was drafted, which institutionalized a major break with the past. As regards the structure of the state and economy, perhaps the most notable changes were these: the virtual elimination of the language of socialism; the introduction of a new discourse referring to basic rights of the citizen, although unlike the 1976 Constitution, it removed any explicit guarantees of the rights of women; the complete disappearance of a political role for the FLN, thus ending the one-party state and opening the way for greater political pluralism; and the reduction of the army to a strictly military institution responsible for national defense. Algerians overwhelmingly approved the changes in a February 1989 referendum.

As for the narrative, one of the most notable changes in the new constitution concerned the role of Islam. In the preamble, the "epic of Islam" was mentioned as an historical period, and the Algerian people were referred to as strong in their spiritual values. Algeria was called a land of Islam, but also "an integral part of the Great Maghreb, an Arab, Mediterranean, and African country." These were not new terms, but their use together suggesting a more diverse basis of national identity, combined with the absence of the previous emphasis on Arabo-Islamic referents, was striking. It appears to be a reflection of the demise of the monopolistic discourse of an authoritarian state in which the partisans of a singular Arabo-Muslim identity had gained increasing power, both within and outside government. Islam was still the religion of state, and practices that were contrary to Islamic morals were forbidden, but so were feudal, parochial, or exploitative practices, the mention of which preceded the mention of Islamic morals in the text.[40]

The Constitution did reassert a number of the other basic elements of the narrative. For example, article 59 reaffirmed the state's respect for the symbols of the revolution, for the memory of the martyrs and the dignity of their dependents and those of the *mujahidin*. It also repeated that "The 1st of November is one of the high points of its [the Algerian people's] destiny, the end point of a long resistance against aggressions against its culture, values, and personality." Yet it also stated that 1 November "anchors the struggles of the present in the glorious past of the nation," thereby implying that there are lessons for the difficult present to be drawn from the revolution. Its history appears to be invoked as evidence that the Algerian people, united, were capable of overcoming the trials of the present.

As we have seen, an otherwise faceless "people" had long had a central role in the narrative, but the way in which "the people" were to be engaged in the state was scripted quite differently in the 1989 Constitution:

> Having campaigned for liberty and democracy, the people intend through this constitution to create institutions based in the participation of the citizens in the running of public affairs that will achieve social justice, equality, and liberty of each and all. In approving this constitution, a work of its [the people's] own genius, a reflection of its aspirations, the fruit of its determination, and a product of profound social changes, the people intend to consecrate more solemnly than ever the primacy of law.

It is not that the people were ever absent from the narrative, but the type of agency ascribed to them here, most notably, participation in "the running of public affairs" and the focus on more meaningful citizenship, was a significant departure from the past.

Before moving to the next critical juncture, it is worth noting two 1991 laws that reinforced the narrative of the revolution. One, largely symbolic, designated 18 February the National Day of the Martyr of the National Liberation War. The second had far deeper ramifications. Over the years, a series of laws had been passed providing for various forms of support for liberation war veterans and their families; however, the first law to fully define a proliferating set of categories of benefits and beneficiaries was finally passed in 1991 (Law 91-16). Among its general provisions, it articulated the goal of establishing principles to govern the *mujahidin*, *mujahidat*, and martyrs' dependents,[41] as well as the protection and preservation of historic and cultural patrimony of the national liberation war.

The law's significance lay in its use of the narrative of the liberation struggle to formalize the intersection of the requirements of regime legitimation with economic distributive capacity. This was not new, nor was it unique to Algeria. What was unusual was the role that participation in the revolution, the founding story, played in both. Initially, involvement with the FLN in the armed struggle against the French had been used to justify the right of those in power to rule. Subsequently, however, the experience of war participation (whether real or fabricated) assumed near mythic proportions and demanded comparable respect. More concretely, it came to be used by a significant sector of the population as grounds for insisting upon the far more bankable economic benefits of promised state financial support in return.

Finally, as for school books in use after this major shift in government structure and discourse, it is worth examining one text published in 1990–91, but which apparently had not been changed since 1976.[42] Entitled *Al-Ta'rikh al-Mu'asir* (Contemporary History), it was used in the final year of high school. In its treatment of Algeria, it presented the post–World War II story as inexorably leading to the FLN's emergence. The people were united, with a strong nationalist spirit, mobilized by the Sétif massacres of May 1945. Messali was not mentioned, but the role of the reformist ulama and the PPA/MTLD was. The suffering and the heroism of the people throughout the revolution was stressed, as was the role of the ALN, which was called the majesty of the Algerian people. The text devoted a number of pages to the Evian accords, criticizing them as putting Algeria in a neocolonialist situation, and then, as one would have expected in a text produced under Boumedienne, it noted several post-1965 developments that ended this neocolonialism. The goal of the revolution was portrayed as not just ejecting imperialism, but also ridding the country "of the effects of capitalism, such as class differences, the control of a minority over the majority, [and] ignoring the peasantry." Thus, the language and emphases of the Boumedienne regime were clear. This book was written before the sensitivity regarding Messali had completely disappeared,[43] but it also came before the Islamization of the revolution and before the excessive emphasis on Arabism as a singular identity for all Algerians. That this textbook continued to be used for the final year of high school, part of preparation for the all-important baccalaureate exam,[44] is quite amazing for a state/regime so apparently concerned with controlling the narrative.

THE DARK DECADE

The Constitution was the last major document issued before the descent into internal insurgency.[45] The explosion of October 1988 turned out to be only the opening act in what deteriorated into a bloody civil conflict that called into question all the values—religious, cultural, economic, and political—that the leadership had long officially promoted. The new Constitution's adoption of political pluralism simply allowed for the legal surfacing and expression of tensions and conflicts that had driven the increasing numbers of student, Berber, Islamist and other demonstrations as the 1980s unfolded. The trigger for the next stage was the results of the first round of parliamentary elections in December 1991, which put the Front islamique du salut (FIS: Islamic Salvation Front) in a position to win a majority of seats. In response, the military cancelled the second round of these elections, scheduled for January 1992, and put an end to Algeria's democratic experiment. Bendjedid was removed and replaced by a military-backed collective leadership, the Haut comité d'État (HCE: High Committee of State), which ruled from 14 January 1992 to 31 January 1994. Violence grew increasingly widespread. Even one of the historic chiefs of the Algerian liberation struggle, Mohamed Boudiaf, whom the Algerian military had called back from exile to serve as the first president of the HCE, was assassinated, while giving a speech, on 29 June 1992.[46] By the mid-1990s many analysts outside Algeria wondered how much longer the military regime could hold on against its armed Islamist opponents.

Algerian History and Education in the 1990s

The events of October 1988 were critical in breaking the hold of the single party and its monopolistic legitimation discourse. Soon, voices that had long been marginalized or suppressed began to be heard, many of them broaching traditionally taboo subjects, primarily those concerning the internal divisions that had existed among the leaders of the revolution. The results were dramatic, particularly for the scripting of the founding story: "the public revelations of the internal rifts in the FLN-ALN ranks between 1954 and 1962 opened the way for another social history of Algeria," Rabah Lounissi writes.[47] The swift descent shortly thereafter into domestic insurgency, which demonstrated the weakness of the state, was also in part responsible for the new, greater latitude in writing history. Algeria became a dangerous place for intellectuals to live, but a corollary of the state's inability to provide security was its impotence in policing the narrative as it once had. Thus, we find a fracturing of certain elements of the previous versions, as well as lack of coherence in presentation.

That said, even in the context of reduced state authority, the educational system continued to be heavily influenced by the legacy of the FLN's approach to education.[48] For example, although the language of the 1989 Constitution had presaged a shift in the monopoly of a certain view of "Arabo-Islamic heritage" as centrally defining the nation, textbooks that had been written in the context of this monopoly continued to be used. The *école fondamentale* textbooks had all been written under Bendjedid 's regime, with its increasing insistence upon an Islamized narrative; and the curricular restructuring implemented under the *école fondamentale* system had included the incorporation into the regular state educational system of previously separate Islamic schools.[49] As a result, Islamic education had been introduced as a separate subject, to be taught through all grades, separate from instruction in moral and civic values with which it had previously been integrated.[50]

Some history textbooks were revised during the 1990s to reflect narrative rescripting,[51] ending the relative anonymity of many of the key participants in the revolution. Hitherto, the official line had been that it was fought by "the people, the only hero," led by the FLN. However, the ninth-grade *école fondamentale* text mentioned Ferhat Abbas, rehabilitated Messali Hadj (although as we have seen, he had gradually returned to the narrative in the late 1970s), and included short biographies of a number of prominent FLN leaders, even some who were still alive, regardless of later political developments or affiliations.

As for questions of identity, the 1998–99 seventh-grade *Kitab al-ta'rikh* (History Book) was focused on antiquity and appeared to value the pre-Islamic (i.e., Berber) past. It gave separate treatment to a specifically Maghrebi (North African) dynamic, rather than presenting the region's history as if its source had always been the Mashriq (Levant, i.e., Arab countries east of Egypt),[52] a favorite frame of the Arabo-Islamic tendency. It devoted significant attention to the history of Numidia and its prominent personalities, and its cultural diversity, including the Roman era, as well as the various periods and acts of resistance. In terms of identity, it continued the practice seen in the last set of books of referring to the people and area as the Maghreb and *Magharibа*. It mentioned the Amazigh and Berbers in connection with the pre-Islamic period, although not in the rest of the text, where the people are all simply *Magharibа*. The theme of unity was engaged, inasmuch as various "plans" or initiatives to unify the Maghreb were mentioned, accompanied by such section titles as "Unity Is the Basis of the Stability and Flourishing of the Maghreb" (107) and "Unity Frightens Imperialism" (108).

The introduction to the 1992–93 sixth-grade history textbook *Al-Ta'rikh* summed up its most important lesson—unity and resistance—by saying that it focused on "the rejection by the Algerian people of French colonialism and resistance through the entire colonial period." It claimed that the country's people constituted " a single Algerian society, united in language, religion, customs, and tradition" (9). Islam was mentioned, but in the context of French attempts to undermine it by destroying mosques, and trying to obstruct the teaching of Arabic by destroying Quranic schools. Unlike in previous texts, there was no religious coloring given to 'Abd al-Qadir's resistance or state. The Algerian people rejected French colonialism, initiated many popular revolts, and were heroic and willing to die. Finally, they were convinced that the only way to secure their freedom was through armed resistance. The text was notable for how much space and detail it devoted to the anti-colonial struggle. The coverage in history textbooks of the revolution, and of Algerian history in general, was gradually expanding.[53]

During this period, *école fondamentale* grades 1–9 used separate textbooks for religion and civics,[54] although the two subjects remained together at the secondary level.[55] The fact that the 1988–89 first-year secondary school text *Al-Mukhtar f-il-tarbiya al-Islamiyya w-al-wataniyya* (Readings in Islamic and Civic Education) was still taught in the mid-1990s is just another example of how the narrative as scripted in textbooks may lag behind what is presented in government documents more immediately responsive to changing circumstances. Some of the paragraphs from the text's introduction were taken verbatim from the books of the mid-1980s, discussed above. Not surprisingly then, the introduction affirmed that "the bases of socialism, which flourished and advanced in all fields . . . derive from the principles of Islam . . . and are part of our authenticity, the components of our identity, which imperialism tried in vain to destroy." Here, socialism was still alive and well and proceeding from solid Islamic bases, even though at it had, for all practical purposes, been abandoned years earlier by the leadership.

State Language and Practices as the Violence Continued

In addition to its armed responses to combat the insurgency, during the early 1990s, the regime undertook a number of other steps to reassert its legitimacy as the inheritor of the revolution and guarantor of its ideals, and to reconsolidate support by expanding its commitments to key sectors of the population. One initiative in June 1993 under Ali Kafi, the second president of the Haut comité d'État,[56] involved establishing five new holidays linked to the revolution.[57] Another, also in 1993, was the creation of the Organisation nationale des enfants de moujahidines (ONEM; National Organization for the Children of *Mujahidin*), which further expanded the state's institutional infrastructure in support of liberation war veterans and their families. Then in August 1995, the National Center for Studies and Research on the National Movement and the Revolution of 1 November 1954 was inaugurated, charged with documentation, research, publication, and distribution related to the national movement and the revolution.

Given the centrality of the liberation war to the nation's past of violent struggle, it is not surprising that it would be invoked during the violence of the 1990s. Indeed, both sides drew on symbols and language from the past both to claim the patriotic *mujahid* designation for themselves and to paint the enemy as traitors.[58] For example, the Islamists referred to their opponents using the old term *hizb fransa* (the "party of France"), which appears to have been coined by Boumedienne to perpetuate suspicions about the loyalties of those who had been educated in French schools prior to 1962, some of whom were accused by the ulama during and after the war of betraying their people. This same term had been used by *arabisant* graduates to refer to the largely *francisant* government administration, in which they found only limited job prospects. For its part, the state referred to the Islamists as *anciens et nouveaux harkis* (former and new *harkis*): the *harkis* were those Algerians who had cooperated or fought with the French during the liberation war, and hence the term had become synonymous with "national traitors."[59] General Liamine Zeroual, the minister of defense who was appointed president in January 1994, used this terminology in his 1995 presidential campaign, saying that the members of the insurgent Islamist groups, in addition to being criminals, traitors, and mercenaries, were sons of *harkis*.[60] The 1995 law concerning potential clemency for the ongoing bloodshed also consigned all groups and individuals who had committed violent crimes—none of whom were presumed to be state actors—to the category of terrorist, subversive, or criminal.

The Platform of National Understanding and the 1996 Constitution

By 1996, President Zeroual was seeking to reach an internal peace accord through negotiations among the major parties—although not with the FIS, which had stood to win the 1992 elections, with which the regime was still unwilling to deal. The result of these efforts was the September 1996 Plateforme de l'entente nationale (Platform of National Understanding), in which, to shore up support for the state during this difficult period, significant changes were introduced into the official narrative regarding basic elements of the political system and of "the people's" identity.

In keeping with the tradition of invoking the revolution, the Plateforme first described "the people," whom it mentioned in nine of fourteen articles, as "faithful to the message of 1 November 1954 and to the oath to its martyrs." However, it then proceeded to applaud their adoption of the goal of building a pluralist democracy, thanks to their national values. The elections of 1995, which had confirmed Zeroual as president, were characterized as the first that had allowed Algerians to express their free democratic and sovereign choice, a choice that "gave the Algerian people its *first legitimate institution*" (my emphasis). Such a portrayal is remarkable, since it implies that institutions in place prior to these elections were illegitimate. Through these elections, the Algerian people "forcefully reaffirmed their resolute attachment to unity and to building a strong and democratic state strengthened by its national values of tolerance, dialogue, and understanding." Thus, the concept of the unity of the Algerian people, long scripted in ethno-religious terms, now included, or presumed, a set of civic values that underpinned a new pluralist system and its institutions.

It is significant, though hardly surprising, given the ideology of the armed opposition, that in addressing identity the text made no reference to an Arabo-Islamic essence. Instead, in the context of what it described as terrorist violence that had affected the entire population, the state appropriated the right to determine what did or did not violate Islam. Thus, articles 22 and 23 insisted that the Algerian state would continue to mobilize all means in order to permanently preserve and promote the "true" values of Islam based on tolerance, brotherhood, equality, solidarity, liberty, justice, and progress; it would also be watchful to prevent places of worship from being used for any activity other than their original purpose. The state's role regarding religion was not, therefore, simply to draw inspiration from and uphold Islamic values; rather, it would also now define these values, and in a way that placed those who had violently challenged it beyond the limits of acceptable creeds and, by implication, outside the identity boundaries of the national community as well.

In order to consolidate the new pluralist political system, respect for basic components of national identity were given priority, and, in a clear departure from the past, not only Islam and Arabism, but also Amazighism (*Amazighité*, or *al-amazighiyya*) were specified. Article 27 of the Plateforme stated that "the Algerian nation will proceed in the process of crystallizing its national personality and identity, which encompasses Amazighism, the heritage of all Algerians." Article 28 continued: "The state oversees the rehabilitation of Amazighism and the promotion of the Amazigh language in the different educational, cultural, and communication sectors." Finally article 29 stipulated that "[l]ike the other components of national identity, it is in the interest of the nation to keep Amazighism beyond partisan and politicized usage."

The stakes involved were tremendous, for official recognition of a Berber component of national identity had been fiercely resisted by the Arabo-Islamic current for years. The inclusion of Amazighism here and in the new Constitution that followed derived in part from the new discourse of pluralism in the face of vicious, armed intolerance. More important to the official recognition of Berber cultural demands and to the introduction of these changes into the official narrative were the general opposition of Kabyles to the Islamist insurgency and the political activism of the Berber Cultural Movement (MCB). For example, on April 22, 1995, an agreement had been reached between the government and the representatives of the Amazigh movements of Kabylia, the Aurès, and the Mzab,[61] whereby a High Commission for Amazighism was to be created. This agreement came in the context of a school boycott launched in September 1994 by both teachers and students in Kabylia aimed at securing official recognition of Tamazight. It also came in the immediate wake of massive demonstrations in Kabylia to mark the fifteenth anniversary of the Berber Spring.[62] The spread of the boycott and demands for recognition of Tamazight to the Aurès and Mzab came as Algeria was experiencing some of the worst of the violence of the *décennie noire*. Given the continuing identity-focused activism of the MCB during this period of internal conflict, as well as its fervent opposition to the Arabo-Islamic trend, the regime had a clear political interest in effectively responding to their demands.

The new Constitution, approved by referendum in November 1996, formalized the most important elements of the Plateforme. With regard to unity and national identity, the inclusion of Amazighism was a major change. Beyond that, article 42 is of greatest interest. While stressing the right to form political parties, it forbade using such parties as a platform to attack fundamental liberties or basic components of national identity (whether Islam, Arabism, or Amazighism). This article is also notable because it eliminated any misunderstanding as to whether the state controlled religion, or the reverse.[63] The Constitution also outlawed parties' instrumentalizing Islam, Arabism, or Amazighism in partisan propaganda, just as it forbade "subservience to foreign interests or parties." This latter injunction certainly targeted Islamists who had ties with outside Salafi or Muslim Brotherhood–related groups, but it also reflected long-standing suspicions about a continuing alliance or affinity with France among other quarters.

As for the narrative of the founding story, the section on respect for the revolution and martyrs was unchanged from that of its predecessor. What was new were several stipulations regarding candidacy for the presidency. In the past, the candidate had had to be Muslim and of a specified age. This text, however, required that those born before July 1942 demonstrate that they had participated in the liberation war, while those born after July 1942 were required to prove that neither they nor their relatives had taken part in acts hostile to the revolution. Both requirements should be read as an official reaffirmation of the centrality of loyalty to the revolution to political legitimacy.

CONSOLIDATING RECONCILIATION?

Zeroual ultimately decided not to run again for the presidency and called for early elections in 1999. Abd al-'Aziz Bouteflika, a member of the Oujda clan of the revolutionary period, and perhaps best known for having served as foreign minister under Boumedienne at the age of twenty-seven, was the army's candidate, in a field that was severely reduced by last-minute withdrawals over concerns of electoral fraud. Shortly before the vote a new Law of the Mujahid and Martyr (*shahid*) (5 April 99–07), superseding the 1991 law, was passed. The text began by restating the state's glorification of the martyrs and respect for the symbols and monuments of the revolution. It also guaranteed the dignity of the *mujahidin* and the dependents of martyrs, reaffirming that their rights were a debt that society owed them and that the state would guarantee. The law both laid out the state's responsibilities and detailed the various monuments, buildings, and other historic sites considered symbols of the revolution to be protected.

The timing of its promulgation suggests that this legislation sought to reinforce the state's claim to legitimacy with the concerned families in the context of the ugly internal conflict, although the violence had already begun to wane by 1999. In addition, however, the Organisation nationale des moudjahidines and the ONEM had continued to be important bases of regime electoral support.[64] The fact that this law was passed just before the 1999 presidential polls suggests a deliberate attempt to turn out and secure the vote of this critical sector.

Following his election, Bouteflika oversaw the issuance of two additional documents as part of the process of conflict resolution and reconciliation. The first was the Law on the Reestablishment of Civil Concorde (no. 99–08). Like Zeroual's Law of Clemency (no. 95–12), which it superseded, there was no mention of religion, or of any particular affiliation of those who committed crimes during the dark decade: they were again referred to as terrorists, subversives, or criminals, and the law outlined the various penalties (or amnesties) for different types of crimes. It was Bouteflika himself who apparently changed the broader discourse regarding these people, and instead of referring to them as bandits with a price on their heads, characterized them as "brave and worthy children of Algeria." While this was no doubt an attempt to facilitate the reincorporation of repentant members of the various armed Islamist groups into the national fold, it outraged many other Algerians who counted friends and family among the victims of the violence. Just as important in undermining the tough language of the law was the fact that some of those who "repented" were—again as a means of cooptation—given housing or jobs unavailable to many average young people who had no record of anti-regime or communal violence.[65]

More important for the evolution of the official narrative was the 2005 Charte pour la paix et la réconciliation nationale (Charter for Peace and National Reconciliation) and its portrayal of the Dark Decade. In keeping with previous texts, the preamble described Algeria's history as a series of struggles by its people to defend their liberty and dignity. Here, however, instead of the traditional construction of this heritage as a means of confronting economic, political, and cultural challenges, the narrative claimed that this history of struggle had made the country "a land of respect for the values of tolerance, peace, dialogue, and civilization." The intent would appear to be to demonstrate what a gross departure from this "norm" of tolerance the 1990s had been: "For more than a decade, Algeria's evolution has deviated from its natural course by an *unprecedented* [my emphasis] criminal aggression [apparently implying that it was even worse than colonialism], seeking to erase the gains of the Algerian people and even call into question the national state itself." It claimed that the majority of Algerians quickly understood the threat posed by this "aggression," which "attacked its nature, its history and its culture."

The text then appropriated religious language to discredit those who had attacked the state by first referring to what happened as a grand *fitna*, meaning strife or sedition. It further insisted that the struggle was about "security of life and property, and dignity:" "all that Islam makes sacred and that the law protects," thereby not only discrediting those who, in the name of Islam, had committed crimes, but also linking Islam to state (secular) law. "This turmoil instrumentalized religion as well as a number of Algerians for anti-national goals." Throughout its history, and contrary to the theses of those who were responsible for the violence, Islam had been "a source of light, peace, liberty, and tolerance, and a unifying cement." "This barbarous terrorism is in contradiction to the authentic values of Islam and Muslim traditions of peace, tolerance, and solidarity." Thus, subtly, the text rescripts the long legacy of resistance to outsiders and turns it inward. Recalling the long-standing theme of *le seul héros, le peuple*, it contended that "This terrorism has been vanquished by the Algerian people, who want to transcend this *fitna* . . . and reestablish peace and security." It then credited God for the outcome: "The terrorism has been, through the grace of God, the all-powerful and merciful, fought and brought under control." Thus, again, characteristic of this new period, in order to delegitimize its opponents, the state invoked an "authentic" Islam of which it was the proponent and protector; those who opposed it were engaged in terrorism.

In response to the experience of *fitna*, the text stressed unity as a basis of power: through unity as well as through "its spiritual values and secular morals," "the Algerian people have overcome the most sorrowful trials to write glorious new pages in their history." It then continued the tradition of making "the people" the primary actor, recognizing the families of martyrs, the victims of terrorism, recalling people's fierce resistance, abnegation, and sacrifices for the survival of the country. Perhaps more controversially, given the charges by some of state involvement in the violence, it praised "the patriotism and sacrifices of the National People's Army [Armée nationale populaire: ANP] and the security forces." Indeed, the first subsection after the preamble defended the actions and reputation of the security forces and put them above question.

> The Algerian people render homage to the ANP, the security services, as well as all the anonymous patriots and citizens who aided them for their patriotic involvement and their sacrifices which saved Algeria and preserved the gains of the institutions of the republic. By sovereignly adopting this Charter, the Algerian people affirm that no one or nothing whether in Algeria or abroad, is authorized to use or instrumentalize the wounds of the national tragedy to attack the institutions of the People's Democratic Republic of Algeria [République algérienne démocratique populaire: RADP] to weaken the state, damage the honor of all the agents who served it with dignity, or to hurt the image of Algeria internationally.

In this way, the people and the security forces were in the same camp, having struggled nobly against a vicious enemy. The violence to which they had been exposed was reminiscent of episodes from the colonial period, hence there were echoes in it of the founding story in this attempt to reinforce the legitimacy of a major instrument of state power.

Educational Reform, 2002

As the violence continued to abate, attention turned to reviewing educational programs. In 2000–2001, the National Commission for Reform of the Educational System worked on this for nearly a year, and from 2003–4, a national commission for programs attached to the Ministry of National Education was charged with overhauling programs in all disciplines.[66] The result was a comprehensive reform in curricula and textbooks at all levels between 2003 and 2006.[67] The two principal poles of this reform were efforts to respond to the demand to teach Tamazight, which an April 2002 constitutional amendment had finally designated a national language,[68] and a reworking of the content of Islamic education and civic and moral education in line with the new emphasis on tolerance and citizenship increasingly emphasized by the state as central to Algerian values.[69] Thus, the reform continued the process of expanding the national identity framework to be more inclusive of Amazigh identity.[70] Just as important, since many Algerians held the previous religion curriculum partially responsible for the terrible violence of the 1990s, the program overhaul sought to rescript the bases of religious identity to include dialogue, openness, and respect for the rights of minorities.[71] Apart from these two changes, the educational mission as expressed in the 2002 reform paralleled its predecessors. It invoked the founding story as providing its inspiration, and insisted that the school system should contribute to perpetuating the image of the Algerian nation through, among other things, "the awareness that it elicits and develops throughout all of Algerian society of its *essential unity*" (my emphasis).[72]

In the context of this reform, the 2004 and 2008–9 first-year middle school *Kitab al-ta'rikh* (History Book) focused on the ancient period, making several references to Berbers, but none to Amazighism. Parts 1 and 2 of the 2004 second-year middle school *Kitab al-ta'rikh*, on the other hand, concentrated on what it called the Islamic Maghreb. It mentioned both Berbers and Amazighiyya, but did not differ in the long-standing narrative about fierce indigenous resistance to the Arabs only until their goal of bringing Islam was understood.

The 2006 fourth-year middle school text in this same series was devoted entirely to Algerian history. The introduction established understanding French colonialism as the goal, and hence the focus was on what the French had sought to do in Algeria, including falsifying history, suppressing Arab identity and Arabic, which is referred to as Algeria's national (*qawmiyya*) language. In a remarkable departure from the narrative of unity during the revolutionary struggle, this text detailed the groups who had fought with the French, including Algerians, although it argued that many were conscripted. There was also brief mention of the differences with Messali, but in a significant first, it referred to him as a leader (*za'im*) of the nationalist movement, who was not fated *(lam yuktab)* to lead the revolution or support it. Despite the new openness regarding these topics, there was nothing about the coup against Ben Bella or any of the other instability surrounding independence. Indeed, the post-independence period received very little attention: a handful of dates and post-independence, but no historical context.

Toward the end, the issue of unity was addressed, but this time in the broader framework of the larger Arab homeland. Algeria is described as devoting all its efforts to a unity struggle, which is part of a shared destiny uniting the Algerian people with its brother Arabs. A few references were made to Algeria's Islamic identity, but there was more of a balance with Arabism, just as there were numerous references to Algeria's African and or North African identity.

The 2004 second-year middle school civics text *Al-Tarbiya al-wataniyya* reinforced the long-standing importance of unity, sacrifice, and respect for martyrs and national symbols. However, as was clear in the first unit, national unity was now portrayed in terms of solidarity and cooperation among individuals and societies, as well as customs and traditions symbolic of a common spirit (*ruh jama'iyya*). The second unit's discussion of the basic components of Algerian identity included the now common triad of Islam, Arabism, and Amazighism, along with elements evocative of the founding story: pictures of the Algiers Maqam al-Shahid monument, the flag, national currency, and the national anthem, which it described as symbols of sovereignty, independence, and the unity of the nation (*umma).*

Civics texts all stressed the importance of solidarity and collective work, both in the present as well as in the past. For example, the 2006 fourth-year middle school textbook *Al-Jadid f-il-tarbiya al-madaniyya* (What's New in Civic Education) argued that Algerians remained unified and steadfast, despite attempts by the French to assimilate them and sow dissension. On the question of identity, after asserting the new tripartite identity, it went on to mention a single homeland, a shared culture, and a long history. It also reprised the bases of Algeria's solidarity with those outside its borders, with the other countries of the Arab Maghreb, as an inseparable part of the Arab world, and as part of the Islamic world, "from Tangiers to Jakarta" (7–8).

As for religion textbooks, several observations are in order. First is the introduction of new sections on violence and extremism. The 2004 second-year middle school textbook *Al-Mufid f-il-tarbiya al-Islamiyya* (What's Beneficial in Islamic Education) contended that Islam had warned against both of these forces because they corrupt and destroy social relations. It then gave examples of violence and extremism in everyday life: a lack of acceptance of other opinions, an insistence that people do things God has not required, a ruthlessness in dealing with people, and anger in arguments or disagreements (22). This behavior was contrasted with Islam, a religion of moderation and kindness. The second unit in the book focused on social cohesion and solidarity, using examples taken from the life of the Prophet Muhammad and the Muslim community in Medina. In the same vein, the 2005 third-year middle school version of the same text included a section on brotherhood in Islam and another on "tolerance and generosity" in which students were told to emulate the example of the Prophet. The 2006–7 fourth-year middle school textbook in the same series also had a chapter on peace, which teaches that it is a principle base of Islam, and that war is a deviation. The 2007 third-year secondary school text *Al-Mufid f-il-'ulum al-Islamiyya* (What's Beneficial in Islamic Sciences) dealt with Muslim relations with non-Muslims, insisting that Islamic legislation had been exemplary in this regard, because the Muslim values of human dignity insist upon peaceful coexistence. Yet problems in consistency of message remained. For example, although the 2006 second-year secondary school text *Al-Wadih f-il-'ulum al-Islamiyya* (What's Clear in Islamic Sciences) decried excess and extremism in one section, arguing that they result from a limited understanding of Islam, in another it repeated the Prophet's injunction not to imitate Christians and Jews, warning about the cultural invasion that they might bring (44–45).

In sum, the texts of this period manifested several significant departures from their predecessors. First, the presentations of the revolution were more detailed, including a somewhat different approach to Messali as well as a preliminary broaching of the topic of those Algerians who had fought with the French, suggesting the widening breach in the wall of prior official historical orthodoxy. Second, the inclusion of Amazighism and Tamazight indicate a major shift in the official identity narrative, even if Algeria's place in the Arab world continued to be stressed. Finally, and equally important, there was the emphasis on tolerance, moderation, and human rights, a product of the imperative of reinforcing a broader set of national identity values intended to protect the country from a recurrence of the violence of the dark decade.

CONCLUSIONS

Boumedienne's unexpected death came at a time when the Algerian state was on the verge of a marked decline in the value of its primary source of budgetary support: revenues from natural gas. That crisis alone would have been challenging for any leadership. In Algeria, however, it was accompanied by deepening social conflict over cultural, linguistic, and ethnic identity, which intersected with the growth of an increasingly militant Islamism.

In response, Bendjedid sought to change course on both the economic and cultural/religious fronts. Both discursively and in practice, he gradually moved away from the revolutionary socialism that had been the hallmark of Algeria's sociopolitical identity since Ben Bella, giving freer rein to a long-repressed private sector. At the same time, to insulate himself from opposition to this shift and to consolidate his power, he ended Boumedienne's strategy of attempting to balance (or alternate carrots and sticks with) the more secular, often *francisant,* sector, on the one hand, and the partisans of a more conservative Arabo-Islamic identity, on the other. The discursive legitimation of these shifts is clear in the documents examined here. In the 1986 Charte nationale, the most dramatic change in the narrative during this period involved Bendjedid's attempt to ride the tide of surging Islamism. In the process, the official construction of Algerian identity focused overwhelmingly on an unchanging essence specified as Arab and Islamic, rather than the somewhat broader (if still problematic) Arabo-Islamic characterization used previously. As for the non-Arab segment of the population, textbooks of the period and the 1986 Charte made a few symbolic bows to Berber sensibilities, perhaps in an attempt to placate that sector of the population following the 1980 *Printemps berbère,* but they did not significantly alter the fundamentals of national unity promoted by the regime.

Under Bendjedid, the narrative of the revolution was expanded to incorporate a fuller presentation of the various political parties prior to 1954, including mention of Messali, suggesting that the saliency for regime stability of the battles over at least the early history of the national movement had been superseded by events. More important for the legitimacy struggle was the official Islamization of the revolution. Religious language and imagery were added to the narrative to give the national faith a more central role in the account than had ever been the case before. Finally, there were the continuing, concrete efforts to cultivate the *mujahidin* constituency. To that end Bendjedid initiated a series of symbolic (museums, reburials) and material measures related to the liberation war, its fighters and martyrs, to reinforce support among this critical sector.

Ultimately, however, regardless of its attempts to consolidate power, economic crisis unleashed the riots of October 1988, which in turn brought an end to one-party rule. The regime was shaken to its core, and hence the narrative that accompanied the subsequent political changes shifted significantly. First, there was a clear retreat in the emphasis on religion and on Arab identity. They did not disappear entirely, but national identity was attributed additional markers, including a new language of participatory citizenship. The revolution continued to be the point of historical reference, but it was used as an anchor for confronting the challenges of the present. Its ideals were invoked as a guide. The liberation struggle was pointed to as evidence that Algerians, united, were capable of overcoming the severe economic and political crisis of 1989.

These narrative reframings were reflections both of what had been overthrown by the events of October 1988 and of what was projected for the future. Unfortunately, the pluralist system promised in their wake by the 1989 Constitution was to have a short life. The descent into a violent insurgency called into question, not just key elements of the narrative, but the very existence of the state itself. Ironically, it was at this point that the *école fondamentale* educational system was finally fully implemented, with the new textbooks largely reflective of the pre-1989 narrative. Following the outbreak of serious violence in the early 1990s, some history books were revised, reducing the heavy emphasis on religion instituted under Bendjedid, and placing a greater emphasis on specifically Algerian history. Moreover, as a result of the weakness of the state and the greater openness to new voices, more stories of the early nationalists, the revolution, and individual revolutionaries began to make their way into textbooks.

As for the narrative of the revolution, during the worst period of violence, the regime seemingly tried to reconsolidate support by creating holidays and institutions that exemplified its devotion to the *mujahidin*. At the same time, a battle began over control of the language of the revolution, which was reinterpreted to apply to the ongoing violence. There was also an official move to control the meaning of Islam itself. Government documents insisted on defining it as a religion of peace and tolerance, and on labeling those who engaged in violence in its name as criminals and terrorists (implying "apostates").

Official publications continued to stress the unity of the Algerian people. To participate in combatting the insurgency, this unity continued to be constructed as based in pluralism and presuming the values of tolerance and dialogue. In order to consolidate the new pluralist political system, the language of the 1996 Plateforme de l'entente nationale specified Amazighism, along with Islam and Arabism, as deserving of respect. Such a recognition of the non-Arab sector of the population was an obvious result of the opening provided for by the 1989 Constitution, but it also served regime survival interests by attempting to bridge the political and cultural divide with the Berberist movement, with which it shared an opposition to the armed Islamist insurgency. These elements were all then formalized in the 1996 Constitution.

The final stage of emerging from the dark decade came with Bouteflika's election in 1999. Ensuring this involved reaching out again to the vital constituency of the families of martyrs and *mujahidin*, with the new law further outlining their benefits and rights. At this stage, however, the echoes of the revolution were different. As before, Bouteflika's 2005 Charte pour la paix et la réconciliation nationale portrayed the Algerian people as heroic fighters—but now against enemies the state defined as violators of Islam, not foreign invaders. Just as important, in this rescripting of elements of the founding story, instead of armed resistance (violence) being basic to an heroic national identity, the liberation war was portrayed as making Algeria "a land of respect for the values of tolerance, peace, dialogue, and civilization." If history is also destiny, then this reconstruction of the past was intended to open the way to a peaceful future.

As the country continued to move out of the dark decade, the textbooks published in the 2000's reinforced most of these points. Algeria's own history received more coverage, including increasing references to its Amazigh heritage. Civics books focused on pluralism, participation, and solidarity; and religion texts stressed the centrality of peace, moderation, and tolerance to "true" Islam. That said, as noted earlier, there were important holdovers from previous periods that conveyed messages contradictory to those being promoted by the newer texts.

Finally, as for the larger struggle to control history, the constitutional revision of 2008, the primary aim of which was to ensure that Bouteflika could be elected to the presidency for a third term, also amended Article 62. Following the sentence unchanged from the 1996 Constitution regarding the State's responsibilities "toward the symbols of the revolution, the memory of the martyrs and the dignity of their dependents and the *mujahidin*" the amendment stipulated that the state "also works to promote the writing of history and its teaching to the young generations." Left open was the question of how the state's commitment to this long-standing preoccupation, and now constitutionally binding obligation, might be addressed going forward. More important for a country in which battles over key components of history and identity had recently turned deadly, it also failed to stipulate just what the parameters of the successful fulfillment of this requirement might be.

6 NARRATIVE RESCRIPTINGS AND LEGITIMACY CRISES

THROUGH SPEECHES, SCHOOL TEXTBOOKS, and a range of other official documents, those who have ruled Egypt and Algeria since their revolutions in the middle of the twentieth century have rescripted the founding story, revalued its constituent elements, and reconfigured the definition of national unity. To be sure, coercion in various forms has been fundamental to addressing challenges to the political order, as has regime socioeconomic performance. Nevertheless, the myriad examples of reshapings of the founding myths or reframing of notions of identity and national mission explored in the previous chapters strongly suggest that the leaderships in both countries have believed in the importance of the narrative and used it in their attempts to consolidate or maintain power.

We therefore return to the central questions posed at the outset. Which types of junctures, challenges, or crises have been most likely to trigger significant narrative rescripting, and what forms have the changes taken? When, instead, is there more of a change in emphasis or a reinterpretation of existing narrative elements, drawing on the multivocality of official symbols and tropes? What insights into state capacity can be gleaned from a review of the way such changes are introduced, and, in particular, into the role of curricular reforms?

WHAT KINDS OF CRISES AND WHAT KINDS OF RESPONSES?

As we saw in chapter 1, Ann Anagnost contends that it is particularly during periods of crisis that gaps in the national narrative may appear, while James Wertsch offers evidence of narrative rescripting as the result of intra-elite struggles. Sam Kaplan's work suggests that the nature of the crisis, whether it is sudden or more gradual, is significant. To attempt to draw some generalizations regarding the origins and nature of narrative revision revealed in this study, I shall first group the examples from the cases into three major categories of crises or challenges: leadership changes/transitions, wars, and internal instability.

Leadership Changes

The examples of leadership changes examined here may be subdivided into uncontested successions, contested successions, and coups.

First, let us consider examples of uncontested successions: the transition from Sadat to Mubarak and Bouteflika's election after Zeroual fall into this category.[1] The most striking element in reviewing the narratives in the immediate wake of these transitions is that there were no dramatic departures. Sadat's assassination was a violent shock, but there was no question over the line or legitimacy of the succession, at least among the political/military elite who would have been in a position to contest it. Instead, Mubarak continued the narrative of the revolution's flexibility. He only gradually revised the account of the 1973 war to make himself, not Sadat, the symbol of a battle that had been constructed as an heroic victory. The other example, the transition from Zeroual to Bouteflika in Algeria, also produced no significant changes. The country was still in the throes of the Dark Decade (although the worst was past and processes of reconciliation had already been initiated), Bouteflika was the choice of the military—the kingmakers in Algeria—and his succession was confirmed by an election, albeit flawed.

The record when we come to contested successions, however, is quite different. Here we have the establishment of the first post-revolutionary governments in Egypt and Algeria; Sadat's assumption of the presidency after Nasser; and Benjdedid's replacement of Boumedienne.

The process of establishing a new leadership in post–July 1952 Egypt was doubly contested, and a new founding story, one that rejected the characterization of the change of regime as a coup, instead insisting that it was a revolution, was quickly established through a series of documents and new policies. For example, the agrarian reform law published in its wake targeted two levels: first, it sought to undermine the power base of the members of the ancien régime and began to cultivate new bases of support for the Free Officers; and second, it established a different political and economic orientation from that of the monarchy. At the same time, however, another battle was under way, a power struggle within the ranks of the Free Officers themselves. In response, Nasser used his manifesto *Falsafat al-thawra* (Philosophy of the Revolution) both to set out clearly the principles of the revolution—all of which marked a dramatic political departure from the past—and to position himself as its leader. In contrast, the newly evolving founding narrative did not reformulate or call into question the parameters of who was Egyptian. To the extent that there was a shift in the identity narrative, it was limited to the upper levels of power: with the monarchy (of non-Egyptian origin) gone, it contended, the country was now finally ruled by its own, and was therefore on a course to achieve social and economic justice.

The immediate post-independence power struggle in Algeria was of a different order, since the new state was born out of a bloody and divisive national liberation struggle, which was not only a war against the French and those Algerians allied with them, but also at times between factions of Algerian nationalists themselves. The political contestation continued with the summer 1962 battles that followed formal independence. Once the physical confrontations had ended, the considerable task of consolidating political power seemed to demand a taming of the contending factions through controlling the history of the war, which was soon established as the new Algeria's founding narrative. As for the question of identity, the persistence of factionalism, and the leadership's awareness of the continuing dangers it posed would seem to explain, at least initially, an attempt at balancing the demands of the *francisant* and *arabisant*, and traditionalist and revolutionary sectors of the population.

The two remaining examples of contested successions are those in which the leader died unexpectedly. In Egypt, Sadat assumed the reins of power immediately upon Nasser's death, and was confirmed as president shortly thereafter. However, it soon became clear that a faction comprising some of the most powerful members of the political elite sought to control, if not oust, him. Sadat certainly outmaneuvered them politically, but he also justified his move with a creative framing. He used Nasser's post-1967 admission that the revolution had made mistakes to introduce the notion of the revolution's flexibility and ability to correct itself. He ultimately redefined this corrective "movement" by which he sidelined his opponents as a "corrective revolution." Sadat also sought to delegitimize his foes by branding them "centers of power" (*marakiz quwa*), a pejorative originally coined by Nasser. In contrast to his predecessor's discourse of "citizenship," he imposed more traditional family and religious identities on the narrative of the revolution almost immediately upon assuming power. In this way, he sought to reinforce his position against those lined up against him by appealing to a constituency that had been marginalized or suppressed by the Nasserist regime, in effect redefining the terms of national belonging.

In Algeria, Boumedienne's death also triggered a contested succession, which pitted members of different regime factions against each other. One faction was clearly interested in moving away from the austere socialism of the Boumedienne period, while the other sought to impose tighter political control over the bureaucracy and assert the primacy of the FLN over the administrative apparatus of the state. The military ultimately stepped in as arbiter, and selected Bendjedid. There was no attempt to rewrite the revolutionary narrative as part of the transition, nor was there an immediate change in the identity construction of the population. However, the slogan "Toward a Better Life," adopted by the FLN for an extraordinary congress held in the summer of 1980, was the first sign that the liberalizers would have the upper hand, at least in terms of economic policy. In the period that followed, of course, Bendjedid succeeded, not only in reorienting economic policy in a more liberal direction, but also in instrumentalizing a new emphasis on religio-cultural identity policy to reinforce his power in the face of the increasing societal power of political Islam.

As for coups, we have Boumedienne's overthrow of Ben Bella and Syria's secession from the United Arab Republic.[2] The 1965 Algerian coup could well be viewed as the next stage in the FLN leadership's working through the factionalism and power jockeying that had remained below the surface after the summer of 1962. Perhaps more than any other leader examined here, Boumedienne seems to have believed in the power of controlling the historical narrative, and so it was under him that a revolutionary story that brooked no counter-narrative was more fully fleshed out and institutionally reinforced. he clearly felt the need to restructure the narrative basis of regime legitimacy in order to consolidate his position; so he explicitly shifted it from historic to revolutionary legitimacy. With that revision, Boumedienne moved to the center of the revolutionary story those who had fought in the revolution and marginalized or downplayed those who had actually brought the national movement to the point where armed struggle was launched. However, this was only part of his strategy. To balance the various sociopolitical orientations vying for power in the FLN, he sought to enforce a construction of national identity and unity that made room for both traditionalists and secularists (absent better shorthand terms). To that end, the narrative of economic modernization continued to be Marxist, while that of cultural affiliation was Arabo-Muslim. It was an uncomfortable juxtaposition at best, and the very real threat of its disintegration probably explains why there continued to be no room for deviation from it, why the regime continued to insist upon homogeneity. Indeed, by this time, the identity narrative, insofar as it addressed ethnicity, rigidly insisted upon an ethnic Arab homogeneity, and an exclusion of Berber components, rather than a more flexible or inclusive notion of unity.

Turning to Egypt, the Syrian secession (*infisal*) was an unusual coup, for it both succeeded and left the leader of the UAR in power, if only in the Egyptian part of the joint state. That said, it was a terrible political blow. Whatever hesitations Nasser had initially had about agreeing to the union, it had greatly enhanced his and Egypt's regional power and prestige. As a result, not surprisingly, the coup makers had to be discredited. They could not be delegitimized on ethnic grounds, because they were Arabs, and the hegemonic narrative about identity proclaimed unity among all Arabs. As a result, another formula had to be found to mark them as outside the fold. To that end, they were labeled counterrevolutionaries, linked with economic classes and forces opposed to the Arab revolution. While the promulgation of the so-called socialist decrees had preceded the secession—indeed, they were part of the backdrop to it—Nasser responded to the *infisal* by moving ahead even more aggressively in promoting Arab socialism, primarily by issuing the influential *Al-Mithaq al-watani* (The National Charter). This distinction among Arabs, between those who were with the revolution and those who represented reaction and were allied with imperialism, permeated Egyptian political discourse thereafter, continuing until the 1967 disaster.

Wars

For the purposes of this analysis, there are two major types of wars: those ending in defeat and those whose ending is defined as victory. As for defeats, in the case of Egypt, we have the 1948 Palestine war and the 1967 war. I did not discuss the 1948 Arab-Israeli war here, but the Free Officers' narrative clearly cited defeat in Palestine as one factor justifying the 1952 overthrow of King Farouk.

In the case of the 1967 war, Nasser's immediate response to defeat was to offer to step down. That his offer was rejected was probably as much a result of fear of losing a leader whom many loved as of lack of alternatives in the context of such a national disaster. Perhaps the shock of the defeat itself explains the fact there was no significant change either to the founding story or to notions of national identity, even in the context of compromised sovereignty through Israel's occupation of the Sinai. Or perhaps the narrative symbols and story lines, which included Egypt's long history of struggle, were viewed as sufficient to accommodate the mobilizational demands at the time. Either way, the only narrative innovation at this point involved admitting that mistakes had been made, and that corrupt or criminal "centers of power" (*marakiz quwa*) had emerged that had to be eliminated, although this short-term solution was rejected by students and other activists as insufficient. At the same time, the unity of the home front continued to be proclaimed and insisted upon as critical to the rebuilding of the economy and the military required if the country was to liberate its occupied territory. In the short time that followed before his death, Nasser began to shift his policies on the economy, initiating a gradual turn away from socialism, and on the Arab-Israeli conflict, inasmuch as he accepted the Rogers Plan. We shall never know where this path would have led him had he lived, but he appeared to be embarked on courses that would at some point have required significant reformulations of elements of the narrative in order to maintain the erstwhile revolutionary regime's legitimacy.

The cases of the outcomes of the 1956 and 1973 wars are not as clear cut as 1967. Strictly speaking, from a militarily standpoint, both of these wars ended in Egyptian defeats. Nevertheless, as we have seen, in 1956, the United States and USSR forced a ceasefire and the ultimate evacuation of British, French, and Israeli forces, such that Egypt retained its sovereignty and Nasser succeeded in asserting control over the Suez Canal Company. Viewed in this light, 1956 was a political victory, and it was certainly constructed as such in the narrative. The war's outcome was rescripted as a triumphal conclusion to the Egyptian people's long history of struggle, fulfilling the revolution's promise of full sovereignty and independence. Most important for the narrative, in the wake of 1956, Egypt's Arab identity and regional role certainly received greater emphasis, and its revolution was increasingly constructed as a model for the Arab world and beyond.

The 1973 war manifests similar elements of victory and defeat, but no significant restructuring of the founding story followed. It did, however, allow Sadat to integrate an extension, of sorts to the national narrative. Thanks to support from the United States, Israel had been able to push Egyptian forces back across the canal; however, it was the initial crossing and destruction of the Bar Lev Line that came to define the war for the Egyptians. Hence, by "destroying the myth of Israeli invincibility," the war was claimed as a glorious, heroic episode. Although he had already consolidated his power, Sadat had been as desperate to escape from Nasser's shadow as he was to make peace with Israel by altering the regional status quo. He could not have known it in advance, but the initial success of "the crossing" gave him a military success that he used to great symbolic effect to establish a reputation of strength and daring paralleling Nasser's. Following the 1973 "victory," he continued to stress Egypt's power and regional role, but he shifted the construction of the country's identity toward one that emphasized, not a program of ultimate Arab political unity, but instead Egypt's many sacrifices for Arab causes, as if its own interests perhaps lay elsewhere. At the same time, he continued to insist upon the country's religious and moral values as primary parameters of national identity. Arabism was never excluded, but the priority of identity components was clearly rearranged to appeal to different internal and external bases of support than those upon which Nasser had relied.

Internal Instability

The cases cited exemplify two types of internal instability: extended insurgency and one-time shocks. We have two extended insurgencies: the Dark Decade of the 1990s in Algeria and the Islamist challenge to Egypt in the late 1980s to early 1990s. One-time shocks are represented by the 1977 bread riots and 1986 conscript riots in Egypt and the 1988 riots in Algeria.

The 1990s in Algeria triggered important developments in the narrative. The regime and the insurgents sought to discredit one another, using language from the time of the revolution. Terms vilifying those who had thrown their lot in with France, such as "party of France" (*hizb fransa*) and "son of a *harki*" (*ibn harki*), were resurrected and became common again. In the meantime, the FLN's monopolistic hold on power had been broken. There was thus scope for the reemergence of figures who had played prominent roles in the revolution, but were rarely mentioned by name, having been deliberately excised from the founding story by means of the hegemonic trope "un seul héros, le peuple." However, this change owed in the first instance to the developments of 1988–89, not to the impact of the internal insurgency, except to the extent that it even further weakened the power of the state to control the narrative. The other notable change during this period was the willingness of the state officially to accept Amazighism as a characteristic of Algerian identity. The Berber Spring of 1980 had brought Amazighism forcibly to the leadership's attention, but Bendjedid had made no serious attempt (only a couple of passing references in the 1986 Charte) at offering fuller inclusion or recognition. However, as the regime was in need of allies against Islamist extremists, and Berber ethno-political activists had long been the nemesis of the Arabo-Muslim politico-cultural lobby, recognition of Berber identity was an effective means of securing allies. Another notable regime initiative to try to dampen support for religious extremism during this period involved regular proclamations in speeches and official documents of the fact that tolerance was inherent in Islam, thus identifying as criminals those who espoused violence in the name of religion.

The extent of the violence in Egypt in the 1980s and early 1990s did not reach the same levels as Algeria witnessed, and there was no appeal to the founding narrative in the leadership's official statements, but there was at least one similarity to the Algerian response: the Mubarak regime also sought to discredit those who used violence against it by labeling them as criminals who had departed from the practice of true Islam. Sadat had already initiated some of these themes during his presidency when, thanks in part to policies he himself had initiated, political Islam began to attract more and more adherents. In both the Algerian and Egyptian cases, the regime described what was happening as sedition (*fitna*), which automatically branded those engaged in it as opponents of the broader Muslim community. It was also during this period in Egypt that education's primary function was redefined in national security terms: teaching tolerance and other values that were defined as historically characterizing Egyptians was adopted as necessary to maintaining political stability.

As for examples of one time shocks to domestic security, in the case of both the 1977 bread riots and the 1986 conscripts riots, official discourse depoliticized the episodes by minimizing or denying any economic motives, and by dealing with those involved as criminals. The 1988 riots in Algeria, on the other hand, were quite another matter, for they shook the regime to its core, and forced a major opening of the political system. The FLN monopoly was ended and the new Constitution promulgated in February 1989 heralded a multiparty system. This crack in the monolith of state power ultimately opened up the possibilities for other forms of discourse as well, since the regime's control of the narrative of the revolution gave way. The effect was most obvious outside official outlets, where new civil society discourse began to appear. However, even in the official narrative, a greater toleration of long-suppressed elements was clear: school texts devoted more space to the revolution and to the early nationalist movement, even to the long-banished Messali Hadj. Just as important, although the FLN retained popular respect for making the revolution, the cadres of the party into which it had evolved clearly suffered a major blow to their prestige and influence.

NARRATIVE FLEXIBILITY VERSUS NARRATIVE CHANGE

The cases cited in this study bear out Nels Johnson's contention that "ideological changes are usually changes of emphasis and connotation in the system of dominant symbols."[3] Evidence from many of the challenges or crises discussed suggests that the multivocality or flexibility of the basic story lines and symbols facilitates not only incremental shifts but also significant redefinitions (albeit less frequently) of them or in their constituent elements.

As for more striking changes or new story lines, the answer that has gradually emerged through this exploration is that significant modifications are most likely to emerge in the context of a threat to a regime characterized by preexisting factionalism within its ranks, or when it faces significant opposition from below. The examples here strongly suggest that the composition and coherence of the leadership group or regime coalition at any given point is far more influential in determining whether rescripting is produced than is the specific nature of the crisis or challenge—war, economic crisis, internal insurgency—involved.

Establishing completely new narrative strategies of legitimation is quite rare. Indeed, the only examples we have encountered in this work are those of the initial emplotting of founding stories. In Algeria, the narrative was forged through the liberation struggle, which was subsequently established as the new official founding story, even if it did draw on elements from the *islahi* historiographic tradition. In the case of Egypt, the founding story was that of the initial overthrow of the monarchy; however, with a program and vision that differed significantly from what had preceded it, the narrative of the Free Officers' revolution quickly set itself apart as a new beginning. It did not deny Mehmet Ali's role in laying the foundations for a modern Egyptian state, but the corruption and collusion of his descendants with the British provided the opening for the establishment of a new founding narrative, that of the 23 July Revolution.

Beyond these examples, the most significant shifts in the narrative have come in the context either of contested leadership succession, when the regime itself is severely divided, or when domestic crises (usually a combination of economic and political factors) have produced or mobilized significant opposition to the regime. In the first instance, we have the transitions from Nasser to Sadat and from Boumedienne to Bendjedid. In both cases, a gradual reshaping of the narrative served to reframe what was an effective gutting of the economic justice content of the revolutionary narrative by introducing economic liberalization; at the same time, there was an introduction (in Egypt) or strengthening (in Algeria) of the role of religion and religious language in the narrative.

As for severe domestic political economy crises, in Algeria, the result was the introduction in 1989 of a greater flexibility or pluralism into representations of aspects of the revolution, along with a reframing of the role and identity of the FLN as alone entitled to lead the state, and of citizenship as the basis of belonging. Then, as the breakdown took more violent forms, in order to discredit the Islamists, the state not only shifted from (Arabo-Muslim) identity-based to citizenship belonging, but also formally accepted Amazighism as part of the country's identity heritage.

Finally, victory in war, or the ability to snatch political victory from the jaws of military defeat, served to reinforce the narrative. Nasser used 1956 both to bolster Arabism and to emphasize that Egypt could defeat imperialism, and the heroic crossing of the Suez Canal in 1973 enabled Sadat to shore up the existing story line. More surprising is that striking defeats, like the 1967 war for Egypt, did not result in any significant restructuring or rescripting. Perhaps this is explained by the lack of significant internal political fracture lines before the war. Or, given that the defeat was at the hands of a long-standing external enemy, perhaps the tendency/inclination to close ranks and reassert existing "truths" is actually a more logical and understandable reaction, at least in the short term.

Regime Capacity

This study is primarily concerned with understanding efforts at the regime or leadership level to rescript the official narrative. It does not attempt to explore the other side of the equation: how such attempts are received by the population at large. However, anecdotal evidence makes clear that state efforts are often at best insufficient or ineffective; indeed, official insistence on messages that depart significantly from perceived reality may actually further alienate the audience rather than generate or reinforce legitimacy.[4] In addressing the role of educational institutions in particular, the fine ethnographies of Gregory Starrett, Linda Herrera, and Fida Adely all demonstrate how teachers and students may, for reasons of political or religious orientation, resist elements of the official narrative and introduce interpretations of their own.[5] Beyond those studies, however, the exploration of the Algerian and Egyptian educational systems undertaken here reveals significant deficiencies in state scripting, suggesting the limits it may face.

One basic issue is the reach of the educational system at any given time. Post-revolutionary Algeria and Egypt counted universal education as a national goal, but both faced significant hurdles in implementing it. Lack of resources was one major constraint. The numbers of children to be served were huge, requiring a tremendous expansion in physical infrastructure. In addition, there was the question of providing instructors. In Algeria, the dearth of teachers was so great that the country was forced to import educators who spoke none of its languages. It would be hard to overestimate the disastrous implications of such inappropriate staffing.

Then there was the question of teaching materials. In Egypt, which had long been a regional center of publishing, the transition to a universal system of education with nationalist content did not require the importation of textbooks. In Algeria, on the other hand, the absence of instructional materials forced a continued reliance on texts left over from the French colonial period, many of which were completely lacking in indigenous content. Given the multiple crises the first post-independence Algerian government had to deal with simultaneously, it is unsurprising that it was not until the 1970s that the country began to produce its own schoolbooks.

Yet the initiation of indigenous textbook production was no panacea. The lack of experienced educators and pedagogues was reflected in the content of the texts. Many were poorly written or produced, inappropriate for the grade level and/or boring. In Algeria, the insistence upon Arabization and its dreadful implementation meant that many children were not prepared for a classroom conducted in standard Arabic. Indeed, many Algerians today regard the disastrous way Arabization unfolded as partly responsible for the subsequent disruption and alienation that contributed to the Dark Decade.

Even in Egypt, however, where there was no challenge of Arabization, the process of expanding the number of schools and teachers was far from easy. At the time of this writing, more than sixty years since the Free Officers came to power, Egypt has still not been able to push beyond the 50–60 percent level of literacy, a terrible commentary on state educational reach. The problem owes in part to continuing levels of poverty and the demands of rural life, all of which tend to keep children out of school or lead them to quit early. The high levels of population growth that have characterized much of the post-1952 period have also played a role, placing an ever-increasing burden on existing educational infrastructure and staff.[6] However, the fact is that Egypt's successive leaderships have been responsible for creating and then tolerating the country's disastrous public school system, significantly weakening the most important institutional channel for influencing children's sense of identity and belonging.

These problems, while illustrative of weaknesses in state capacity, are not the only types of inadequacies that may have affected the respective regimes' abilities to inculcate an official narrative through the schools. In both cases, new elements are introduced into the narrative with varying degrees of speed. In some instances, such as Egypt immediately after the revolution, new textbooks rewriting Egyptian history were already being introduced by 1954. Likewise, in the wake of the Syrian secession, textbooks were quickly revised to introduce the official version of the end of the UAR. In the case of Algeria, on the other hand, some eight years passed after independence before educational materials with an indigenously generated message were produced. Then, just as problematic, the lag time in the implementation of the *école fondamentale* (basic school) system meant that by the time the newly created materials were being introduced, not only had the economic narrative of socialism that had been promoted under Boumedienne been superseded, but the FLN monopoly on political power itself was on the verge of imploding. Yet the socialist narrative continued to be conveyed by educational materials into the mid-1990s. Similarly, Egyptian students in the late 1970s would have found the textbook language left over from the Nasser period promoting socialism dissonant with Sadat's post-1974 open door economic policy (*infitah*). Finally, as we have seen, insistence on Islam's creed of tolerance and moderation was often contradicted in Algeria by exhortations against being influenced by Christians, and in Egypt by charges of sedition (*fitna*).

Educational reform can be extremely contentious, especially when basic societal values are in dispute. One indicator of state capacity, at least in authoritarian regimes, is the ability to produce a coherent or unified official narrative. This ability may be influenced by the degree of consensus among the elite on central political, economy, cultural, and/or religious issues. There may be agreement on some, but significant divergence on others. The balancing act or the compromise that results can involve the production of a story some of whose elements are inconsistent. Contestation can also lead to significant delays in producing new materials. In the Egyptian case, particularly following the peace treaty with Israel, there have been repeated claims of outside interference in shaping the roles of Islam, Arabism, and Palestine in school texts.

All of these examples of constraints on state capacity concern only the state's power to influence the narrative through changes to the curriculum, which is, of course, only one means by which the official narrative is conveyed. It is for that reason that this study has examined a range of official texts that have contributed to shaping the narrative over time. It is possible that speeches, which are carried by state media, and are the most obvious vehicle for swift introduction of changes into the narrative, have been more important in reaching large numbers of people than national charters or constitutions. What is clear, however, is that even given the importance of a monopoly on "legitimate education" in shaping the identity and sense of patriotism of a population, states are never all-powerful. Leaderships have clear interests in shaping popular understandings of the economy, religion, culture, justice, and governance as part of their strategies to secure and maintain power, and the national narrative is one potentially powerful tool to be used to those ends. Yet political elites face constraints on their capacity and limits to their vision. They may make poor decisions, or the public may resist even their best attempts. In sum, a leadership's intent is one thing, but the results of its efforts, no matter how well planned or crafted, may well bear little resemblance to its initial goals.

EPILOGUE
THE OFFICIAL NARRATIVE AND THE "ARAB SPRING"
The Limits of Revolution

THE UPRISINGS IN THE MIDDLE EAST AND NORTH AFRICA that began in Tunisia in late 2010 have been the most dramatic internally generated—as opposed to externally triggered (by invasion)—crises in the recent history of the region. In both Egypt and Tunisia, the broad-based nature and intensity of the calls for an end to the regimes provoked the relatively swift departures of Presidents Husni Mubarak and Zine El Abidine Ben 'Ali, rather than any sustained campaign to mobilize symbols or themes from the official narrative to support attempts at political survival. Emblematic of the bankruptcy of vision of these corrupt regimes, perhaps the most memorable line from the period was Ben 'Ali's hollow, tardy response to the massive anti-regime demonstrations in Tunisia: "*Ana fihimtkum*" (literally, "I have understood you".

Before concluding, it is worthwhile exploring what changes in the official narratives have been introduced in Egypt and Algeria during this turbulent period, as their respective experiences put them on opposite ends of the spectrum of "Arab Spring" outcomes. Egypt has been at the center of developments since its 25 January 2011 revolution, when it entered a period of what the previous chapter termed a contested succession. Mubarak's ouster led first to eighteen months of military rule, followed by elections won by Muhammad Mursi, the country's first civilian president. However, Mursi's presidency was cut short by a massive oppositional campaign that triggered his removal by the army on 3 July 2013 and replacement by an interim government with a thin civilian veneer, which then countenanced vicious repression against the Muslim Brotherhood. At the other end of the spectrum, Algeria witnessed numerous demonstrations at the same time as the initial unrest began in Tunisia. Yet it avoided the regional wave of uprisings, in no small measure due to Algerians' fear of a new episode of violence, and to swift state efforts to address popular economic distress and obstruct large-scale political demonstrations.

ALGERIA

The possibilities of the December 2010 protests and self-immolations in Algeria developing into a more sustained opposition movement like that in neighboring Tunisia soon dissipated. Flush with natural gas revenues, the government moved quickly to undercut the bases of protest by reinstating key food subsidies. Perhaps even more important, the lingering trauma from the violence of the 1990s prevented the mounting of sustained protests even in the context of broad, deep popular dissatisfaction. In addition, the efforts of the one party that did attempt to organize weekly protests, the Rassemblement pour la culture et la démocratie, a secular and largely Kabyle party, quickly triggered ethnic antagonisms, which also worked against the emergence of a larger oppositional movement. Nevertheless, clearly prompted by the regional ferment, President Abd al-'Aziz Bouteflika gave a speech on 11 April 2011 in which he promised deep political reforms and a revision of the Constitution after the spring 2012 parliamentary elections. Although there have been rumors about the possible content of the revisions, no official draft had been released at the time of this writing (February 2014).

Thus, although there are concerns about possible smuggling of weapons from Libya, across what is in many places a porous border, the Algerian regime was not forced to confront broad domestic agitation for change. Indeed, its major challenge has not been so much the "Arab Spring" as the "Algerian leadership winter": the problem of an ageing political and military elite. Bouteflika's health problems seemed to rule out yet another presidential term, but who was likely to (be allowed to) succeed him raised questions over future stability.

In his 2012 speech marking the sixty-seventh anniversary of the massacre at Sétif (8 May 1945), Bouteflika reinforced numerous lines of the traditional official narrative, while introducing no innovations. He repeatedly used the language of martyrs and of the trials and suffering to which Algerians had been subjected, weaving together the challenges of the revolution with those of the Dark Decade of the 1990s. He claimed that Algeria had reacted positively to the march of history in carrying out its great liberation movement, in achieving broad sustainable development, adopting an authentic democracy reinforced recently by an ambitious program of socioeconomic achievements and political reforms aimed at consolidating a state of law. Further, he warned that Algerians, especially the younger generation, needed to understand that the freedom, liberty, stability, progress, and democracy that the country enjoyed were the fruits of enormous sacrifices which needed to be appreciated in order to be preserved.[1]

The most notable development during this period with potential implications for the historical narrative was the fiftieth anniversary of independence. In keeping with its long-standing intent to control the narrative of the revolution, and certainly with its eye on the approach of this momentous celebration in 2012, the government passed a law on 17 February 2011 outlawing the production and use of any film that sought to discredit religion or the national liberation war, its symbols and its history, or that glorified colonialism, hurt the public order or national unity, or incited hatred, violence, or racism. Article 6 of the same law stipulated that the production of films related to the national liberation war and its symbols was subject to the prior approval of the government, with violators subject to a fine of between five hundred thousand and one million Algerian dinars (roughly U.S.$6,300–12,600). This law was widely criticized by filmmakers and other members of civil society, and a number of projects were blocked, including a screenplay about Larbi Ben M'hidi, one of the founders of the FLN, which had been sent to the Ministry of Mujahidin in November 2010. After the passage of several months, the filmmaker made repeated inquiries and was finally told that the screenplay had disappeared and there was no file about the project to be found.[2]

As the anniversary approached, there were numerous critiques in the opposition press of the apparent lack of appropriate preparations. Nevertheless, in the days prior to it, the streets of the capital were filled with the national flag and with the official logo of the fiftieth anniversary. The area around the Grande Poste in central Algiers was prepared to host a series of concerts. On the anniversary itself, there were numerous celebrations in Algiers, among them: one at the Riadh al-Fath complex, where the Maqam al-Shahid monument is located, and another at the National Library, which hosted a conference on "Algeria at 50."

The major celebration in Algiers was staged at the Casif of Sidi Freij to the west of Algiers (where, ironically, the French had invaded in 1830). Three huge screens showed a parade of images of French colonization and its crimes, 'Abd al-Qadir's resistance, and the War of National Liberation. The projections then moved on to highlight the agrarian revolution, free health care, and the abyss of the 1990s. One segment also featured a huge national flag unfurled by hundreds of young Algerians marching in the shape of the country. The president's speech was accompanied by pictures from the archives of his life, after which he was "caped" with a mantle made in Lebanon, a tribute that, one photographer commented, seemed more appropriate for a king from the past. Indeed, a critical account asked whether it was Algeria or Bouteflika that was being feted.[3]

The festivities of the day, whether appropriate or not, could not change the reality of the country as the anniversary passed. The situation was aptly described in *El Watan* in the following terms: "one of the most beautiful national liberation struggles watches, impotent in the face of the wreck of its ideals: rather than celebrating its achievements, the country lives the rhythm of riots, the young throw themselves into the sea [hoping to reach Europe], administrative cadres flee by the tens of thousands while others, desperate and worn out by the disarray regularly set themselves on fire. Fifty percent of the economy is in the informal sector; the administration is ruined, and the justice system has become the symbol of national shame."[4]

Despite concerns about poor health, in early spring 2013, a new initiative appeared pushing for yet another term for Bouteflika. Then, in mid-April he suffered a stroke, and in a supreme irony for an FLN veteran (although not for an Arab head of state), he was evacuated to France for the kind of medical care of which Algerians back home could only dream. He finally returned after an absence of eighty-three days, but his poor health seemed to put an end to speculation about a renewed presidential mandate. Nevertheless, Bouteflika and his supporters demonstrated continued determination to control or postpone the looming succession struggle. In the end, popular apathy, fear of the unknown, and, no doubt, official manipulation secured the still ailing leader a fourth term in the April 2014 elections. Left unanswered, however, were myriad pressing questions about what lay ahead.

How long can the revolution in its current narration survive as Algeria's defining story? The hegemonic reified version of the national liberation war has certainly begun to give way to more nuanced and often painful explorations, some of which have already influenced the crafting of the official story, as we saw in chapter 5. However, the question remains of how a foundational myth transitions, not just from one leadership to the next, but from the generation of its authorship to that of the postrevolutionary generation, and the attendant implications for the future evolution of regime power. Malika Rahal beautifully captured the challenge in the following terms: "[T]he event itself loses its intensity as it enters into the past. This distancing means a loss of sorts, and it is painful, indeed unacceptable, for some. But it is unavoidable and necessary today so that the younger generation will be able to construct its own past and imagine [and make] its own future."[5] It remains to be seen who will lead that transition and how they may rescript the official narrative of the revolution to assert their own legitimacy as they do.

EGYPT

As shown in chapter 3, the economic, political and social resonance of the 1952 revolution had already waned significantly well before Husni Mubarak was forced to relinquish (*yatanahha 'an*) the presidency in February 2011. As a result, the emergence of a movement with a new mission of transformation, which made a point of emphasizing the unity of Egyptian Muslims and Christians, could claim the designation of "Revolution" as a point of departure for a new era of "bread, freedom, and social justice," the most common slogan of the demonstrators. What has followed has been a battle over political succession conducted by several principal actors struggling for power and legitimacy: the military, the Muslim Brotherhood and other Islamist parties, the security forces and remnants of the previous regime (including the National Democratic Party), a handful of other small political parties led by the previous generation, and last, and, unfortunately, often least, the original young revolutionaries. A reading of official statements and the press from this period makes clear the competing narratives and goals stemming from the anger of the revolutionaries, the anxiety of many of the non-Islamist sectors of society, remnants of the previous regime, and the rising power of the Islamists. In short, events in Egypt since 25 January 2011 clearly meet the definition of a contested succession, and we should therefore expect to see significant attempts at rescripting the founding story, and perhaps even some aspects of national identity. In considering these developments, the discussion is divided into three periods: the rule of the Supreme Council of the Armed Forces (SCAF), which assumed responsibility for governing Egypt on a transitional basis until the June 2012 election of a new president; the twelve months of the presidency of Muhammad Mursi; and the post-Mursi transition.

The movement that sought to oust Mubarak quickly became known as the 25 January revolution. The military was hailed during the initial three-week uprising for refusing to fire on the Egyptian people. The demonstrators repeatedly called on the army to intervene to respond to their desire to remove Mubarak.[6] The army ultimately obliged, and despite some episodes of hideous behavior—most notably, but not limited to, forced virginity tests of female protestors—

the slogan that seemed to summarize the protestors' view of the military was summed up in the regularly repeated slogan "*Al-sha'b w-al-gaysh id wahda*" (the army and the people are one hand). Of course, according to traditional political science criteria, regardless of the mass mobilization that had prompted it, what 25 January initially accomplished was little more than a coup: a partial removal of the power structure under Mubarak—the arrest and then trial of only the president, his sons, and a few top corrupt ministers/businessmen, along with the closing of the NDP. Nevertheless, a new story of revolution had entered the narrative. What remained was to see how its parameters and content would develop. Would it, like the 1952 revolution, ultimately evolve into something much deeper, or would it ultimately leave the rest of the power networks—military, bureaucratic and economic—in place?

The SCAF made no attempt to repress the narrative of revolution; indeed, it served their interests to have people believe that they had made a revolution and that it had succeeded. Indeed, the military chiefs had no interest in promoting a narrative of the revolution as an ongoing process. Beginning in the early days of the mass mobilization, several civil society initiatives were launched to document the revolution.[7] At the same time, however, the SCAF issued numerous statements in an attempt to take control of the narrative, in no small part in order to shift blame for violent acts during its initial days from the *baltagiyya* (thugs associated with the previous regime, of which the military had been a central part) to mysterious "third parties" and "foreign forces." Part of the rationale was to join its narrative with a critique targeting its biggest critics: the Egyptian human rights and activist organizations documenting military and government abuses, whom it accused of carrying out foreign agendas as the price for receiving foreign funding.[8]

As for the larger narrative, the temporary constitution that was approved by popular referendum in March 2011 introduced no changes to the basic identity elements that we have seen over time. However, there were some initial moves aimed at modifying how history was to be taught, as the committee charged by the Ministry of Education to edit the textbooks for the sixth elementary and third preparatory levels announced several proposed changes in April 2011. For example, it was reported that Lieutenant General Sa'ad Shazly, the chief of staff of the armed forces during the 1973 war (who had quarreled with Sadat over Camp David and had been exiled) was to be readmitted into state texts, as was General Muhammad Naguib, the first president of the republic, beginning with the fall 2012 semester. On the other hand, pictures of Suzanne Mubarak, the former Egyptian first lady, and paragraphs devoted to the recently dissolved NDP were to be removed. It was also reported that a chapter on the 25 January revolution would be introduced into the third-year preparatory textbook, along with lessons on the revolution into the sixth-year elementary textbook. The report of these decisions, which originally appeared in al-*Yawm al-Sabi'* of 20 April 2012, also stated that the Curriculum Development Center had prepared some four thousand pictures from the revolution for possible addition to the books. However, interviews with people involved with textbooks in summer 2011 indicated that such announcements had been premature,[9] and the textbooks made available online for the 2012–13 academic year remained unchanged from those for the previous year. That said, the *thanawiyyah 'ammah* (end of high school) exams in June 2011 did require that students answer the following question in the Arabic exam: "Egyptians all together, Muslims and Copts proved that they have taught the world how revolutions are. Write a letter to the youth asking them to preserve this spirit of national unity in order to build a new Egypt."[10]

There were also numerous instances of attempts to rename places and institutions to remove traces of the Mubarak regime. For example, ten days after Mubarak was deposed, Prime Minister Ahmed Shafiq ordered streets to be renamed after "martyrs," although this, like many other proposals seems to have gone largely unimplemented. On 21 April 2011, an Egyptian court issued a verdict requiring the removal of Husni and Suzanne Mubarak's names from all public places, but this was soon challenged and suspended by another court on 5 June. Around the same time the Ministry of Education promised to rename some 549 schools around the country that bore the name of some Mubarak family member.[11] However, a backlash by Mubarak supporters, followed by the continuing uncertainty over the political future were probably responsible for the delays or continuing contestation over such moves.

Meanwhile other attempts at influencing the course of narrative development could be observed in formal events. On the anniversary of the 1952 revolution, Field Marshall Husayn Tantawi, the de facto ruler of Egypt at the time, gave a speech in which he praised the youth who had led the uprising and promised to help move the country toward democracy through parliamentary and presidential elections. On the other hand, during the 2011 celebrations marking the 1973 October war, Tantawi used his remarks to rescript certain aspects of the war, the most significant of which was to downplay Mubarak's role, which had been expanded during his presidency, and return primary credit for the "victory" to Sadat's leadership.[12] Indeed, Sadat's widow, Jihan, commented positively on the way her husband had been treated by the SCAF in this first post-Mubarak celebration, in contrast to how he had been portrayed by the previous regime.[13] Nevertheless, sentiment elsewhere in society continued to chafe under the continuing military rule: false starts, missteps, and heavy-handed security brutality, most notably in the massacre of Christians in the Maspero district in October 2011, undermined the narrative of the people and the army being "one hand."

Parliamentary elections were finally held from November 2011 to January 2012. Although unsurprising, it was nonetheless disturbing to some sectors that the Muslim Brotherhood, a party outlawed and suppressed under Nasser, given freer rein under Sadat, and then alternatively coopted and repressed under Mubarak, swept some 50 percent of the seats, while even more religiously conservative (salafist) parties took another 25 percent. Then, in late spring 2012, the long-awaited presidential elections were held in two stages, and the Brotherhood's candidate, Dr. Muhammad Mursi, eked out a victory of 51.73 percent to 48.27 percent over Ahmed Shafiq, who was viewed as a candidate of the previous regime.

It is no small irony that it was a candidate of the Muslim Brotherhood, whose leadership had initially rejected participation in the 25 January Revolution, who became the first postrevolutionary president. Mursi's early speeches made some references to the revolution, but also indicated a strengthening of religious content in the official identity narrative. For example, in his 24 June inaugural speech, from his repeated use of quotations from the Quran and Abu Bakr, the first successor to the Prophet Muhammad as leader of the Muslim community, to his many additional references to God, the Islamic coloring of the language was clear. At the same time, the language of citizenship was absent; the president instead used blood relational references (my people, my tribe, my sons, my brothers), or simply "people of Egypt" in addressing the audience. He did mention the concept of national unity several times, but without offering specific parameters.

During his speech in Tahrir square on 29 June, where he took the oath of office before the people (as opposed to before the Constitutional Court), Mursi did make numerous references to the 25 January revolution. He saluted its martyrs and recognized Midan al-Tahrir and other squares in which the revolution had taken place. He continued by stating that since the beginning of the twentieth century, the blood of men had watered the roots of (what would become) the trees of freedom.[14] However, he then mentioned sacrifices made in the 1950s and 1960s in what appeared to be a clear reference to the repression of Nasser's regime, thereby angering Nasserists as well as many in the military. This speech was also replete with religious language, but was not punctuated by the relational references of the first speech. Instead, Mursi most often addressed the audience as "people of Egypt," although at the very beginning he addressed "the free world, Arabs, Muslims, beloved ones, people of Egypt, brothers and sisters, sons and daughters, Muslims in Egypt, Christians in Egypt, respected citizens, wherever you are, in Egypt or abroad." Later in the speech he exclaimed, as he had at the very opening, "O revolutionaries, we shall continue the work" in "a modern constitutional patriotic civil state." The second phrase was particularly significant, because since the beginning of the regional uprisings, Islamists associated with the Muslim Brotherhood (as opposed to most salafists) in Egypt and Tunisia had been careful to talk about seeking a *civil* state (*dawlah madaniyya*), in which all would be equal as citizens, as opposed to an Islamic state (*dawliyyah Islamiyya*), in which one's religion would in part determine one's status.

All eyes were then on the first celebration of the anniversary of the 23 July revolution following the election. Here, the signals regarding the narrative appeared to be mixed. In a speech on 22 July 2012, Mursi termed the 1952 revolution "a turning point in the history of modern Egypt." He recognized its goals and lauded some of its achievements and contributions, which he said represented the "beginning of Egyptian self-determination" and provided "a model for other liberation movements throughout the Arab and Muslim world." However, he went on to state that "the revolution's first steps toward democracy retreated over the past thirty years due to corruption and oppression, which sapped many of Egypt's national resources." It had not delivered the sound democracy it had promised.[15] Note here that he attributed the failures to only the previous thirty years, that is, the period of Mubarak's rule. He did not directly attack Nasser or Sadat. He also stated that because of the failures of the past thirty years, the Egyptian people had had to correct the country's path, and so they undertook the revolution of 25 January to set matters right.[16] This line seems to echo Sadat's rescripting of the 1952 revolution and the need for a "correction."

Despite the sparring that had taken place between the SCAF and the Muslim Brotherhood over the previous year and despite the growing anger in civil society over the role of the SCAF, in this speech Mursi constructed the role of the Egyptian military in a positive light: the army had taken the side of the people in the 25 January revolution and stood beside them to establish the "Second

Republic" on the basis of democracy, freedom, justice, and the rule of law. He also referred to the 25 January revolution as an extension of the Egyptian struggle for a free life and complete democracy. The SCAF, however, responded by posting a statement on its Facebook page criticizing as deception all attempts to attack or deliberately distort the 23 July revolution. The Egyptian armed forces had been the guarantor of safety and security for Egypt for thousands of years, it claimed, and only someone who was ignorant or a traitor would deny their role. These forces had taken the side of the Egyptian people in the 25 January revolution, so it was a revolution of the people and the army. The SCAF statement then paid tribute to the traditional list of achievements of the July 1952 revolution such as the agricultural reform and the High Dam, and took exception to Mursi's statements, attacking those who "try to distort the revolution and its memory."[17] That said, in keeping with the rewriting of Mubarak's role initiated during the SCAF period, in the first celebration of the anniversary of the 1973 war following Muhammad Mursi's election (which Jihan al-Sadat reportedly helped organize), Egypt's first civilian president, accompanied by top military officials, laid a wreath at Sadat's tomb in a televised ceremony.[18]

A dramatic and dangerous confrontation came in late November–early December 2012, when Mursi arrogated to himself powers he asserted were above judicial review. The president, whose Muslim Brotherhood had had significant reservations about the 2011 uprising against Mubarak, nonetheless sought legitimacy (or cover) for his moves by asserting that he had acted in order to save the revolution. As part of his declaration, he announced a "Revolution Protection Law," which he claimed would guarantee the rights of the 25 January martyrs and injured revolutionaries and ensure the retrial of regime officials accused of killing protesters.[19] Those opposed to him, of whatever political or religious stripe, likened him to a tyrannical pharaoh, and claimed that it was their rejection of his move that was in keeping with the needs of the revolution.

As for official documents, it is worth mentioning two telling modifications made in high school civics textbooks for 2013–14 under the Mursi government. In the books for grades 11 and 12, the picture of Doriya Shafiq, an early twentieth-century Egyptian women's rights pioneer, was deleted, apparently in response to objections from religious satellite channels because she was not wearing a *hijab*.[20] Pictures of those killed during the 25 January revolution were also removed.[21]

Far more important, however, was the new Constitution that had been hammered out in the months following the parliamentary elections. The debate over the committee drafting the new Constitution, and the document's content had made the process a particularly contentious one. Ultimately, most of the non-Islamist members of the Constituent Assembly resigned in protest over what they viewed as an excessively Islamist composition of the drafting committee. The result, therefore, was hardly surprising.

The draft constitution was approved by a hastily organized referendum that was widely resisted by the liberal or more secular opposition.[22] While there were serious reservations about other aspects of the document related to the role of the president and the military, the focus here is only on the elements with direct import for the narrative of the revolution and of identity. The text began: "We, the people of Egypt, in the name of God and with the assistance of God." It went on to salute the 25 January Revolution,[23] through which Egyptians sought to reject injustice and assert "all rights granted by God before being prescribed in constitutions and universal declarations of human rights." "Having restored a fresh spirit of unity between Egyptians, men and women, the people's revolution continues toward building a modern democratic state, while preserving Egypt's spiritual and social values, its rich and unique constituents." Its list of the principles upon which the new state was to be built included a number of traditional elements from the narrative: "Arab unity is a call of history and of the future, and a demand of destiny. Such unity is to be reinforced through the integration and fraternity with countries of the Nile Valley and of the Muslim world, both a natural extension borne out of the distinctiveness of Egypt's position on the global map." It also repeated that men and women were equal, although the word "citizenship" did not appear until article 6. Article 9 decreed safety, security, and equal opportunities for all citizens, without discrimination; and article 33 reiterated that all citizens were equal before the law.

It was the place of religion in the new Constitution that most clearly introduced elements aimed at modifying the traditional identity narrative. The reassertion in article 2 that Islam was the religion of state and Islamic *shari'a* the principle source of legislation was to be expected, even if it was not welcomed by more liberal activists. However, several new provisions gave particular pause to those concerned with building a civil rather than a religious state. For example, article 4 stipulated a role for Al-Azhar, while article 219, one of the most controversial of those dealing with religion, specified Sunni doctrines as the basis for defining what constituted *shari'a.* Article 3, which stated that "The canon principles of Egyptian Christians and Jews are the main source of legislation for their personal status laws, religious affairs, and the selection of their religious leaders," was "widely touted by members of the Constituent Assembly and supporters of the draft constitution as a 'concession' to the sensibilities of the Coptic community,"[24] but for those seeking a civil state, it marked a clear retreat. Article 6 forbade establishing political parties that *discriminate* on the basis of sex, origin, or religion, but unlike its predecessor it did not outlaw parties *based on* religion, while article 44's prohibition of insulting or abusing religious prophets, without further specification, was regarded as opening the way to repression of freedom of expression.

The process by which the Constitution was completed and then hastily submitted for popular referendum outraged many who viewed President Mursi as increasingly violating his promise to be a president of all Egyptians in favor of policies and practices suggesting a Brotherhood-based government. In the meantime, the president increasingly sought to delegitimize the opposition, often referring to them as supporters of the Mubarak regime *(fulul)*, conspirators, enemies of the people, or thugs. In a speech on 6 December 2012, he repeatedly called his opponents a minority unable to accept the will of the majority that had been expressed through elections. He also appealed numerous times to legitimacy *(shar'iyya)*, now defined as the legitimacy of the ballot box. Indeed, while placing himself in the line of revolutionary achievements in a 23 November speech, in an interview on 29 November, he insisted that "revolutionary legitimacy" was over, and that now it was the "popular legitimacy" earned through elections that had precedence.[25]

As a result, as the anniversary of the 25 January Revolution approached, Mursi elected to give an address to the nation the day before, 24 January, the Prophet Muhammad's birthday. For its part, the opposition called for and mounted demonstrations on the revolution's anniversary to protest against the government and the new Constitution. In response, the Brotherhood used the occasion to launch a new social initiative called Together We Build Egypt, but its impact was eclipsed by the opposition protests, which turned into clashes leaving tens of dead and leading the president to announce a state of emergency in Port Said, Suez, and Ismailia.

As the spring unfolded, the rhetoric on both sides intensified, with the president continuing to refer to opponents of his government as enemies and increasingly labeling them in ways suggesting that they were outside the fold. Just as important, people around him from the Brotherhood or other religious currents accused opposition members of not being true Muslims, a dangerous charge with potentially violent repercussions in a country like Egypt. On the other side, dissatisfaction with the Mursi government, whether because of its Ikhwan coloring or its generally poor performance in critical areas of basic governance, finally led to the initiation in May of a signature campaign entitled Tamarod (*tamarrud*: rebel) aimed at collecting signatures in support of early presidential elections. It set 30 June, the one-year anniversary of Mursi's taking office, for a massive demonstration to push for an end to his rule. Claiming a total of twenty-two million signatures by June's end, Tamarod's efforts brought Egyptians into the streets on 30 June in numbers far surpassing those that had forced Mubarak's ouster. The standoff between Mursi, who refused any concessions, and the protestors, demanding the end of his presidency, did not last long, because the military intervened on 3 July, removing Egypt's first elected president not only from office, but also from view.

The Brotherhood and Mursi's other supporters were outraged and labeled his ouster a coup against the legitimacy of the ballot box. Those who cheered on the military intervention insisted on a different narrative. In their account, vast numbers of Egyptians—staggering exaggerations of which claimed as many as thirty million—had gone into the streets to demand change, and their clear withdrawal of legitimacy from the elected government trumped whatever had happened at the ballot boxes the previous summer. Indeed, for Mursi's opponents, to call 30 June a coup was heresy. Instead, this was a new revolution, one that was intended to save Egypt from the disastrous course he and the Ikhwan had set it on. In that sense there were echoes of Sadat's corrective revolution, although the massive popular involvement gave this revolutionary reset far greater resonance.

What followed would have been simply a fascinating example of battling narratives, had it not turned into the bloodiest period of internal repression in the modern history of the country. Mursi's supporters refused to back down and established two long-term sit-ins, whose participants proclaimed they were ready to die for the cause of ousted president's return. However, the army's key role in his removal meant that any attempt to overturn the results of the Tamarod campaign would have to be endorsed by the military. As the sit-ins and demonstrations of Mursi supporters continued, unmoved by the establishment of a new temporary government, which insisted that they had to disband, state media outlets moved into high gear in setting new parameters for national identity and unity. The message was a simple but devastating one: the Egyptian people had made their will clear in calling for Mursi's ouster. Those who supported Mursi's return, therefore, were not really part of the Egyptian people. As they continued their sit-ins, official portrayals of them quickly evolved from marginalization or exclusion to active criminalization—they were charged, as a group, with being terrorists. While there was evidence to suggest that a few of those in the major sit-ins did have weapons, the determination by the authorities—military and civilians—to treat the problem as a security issue rather than a political one left only one possible outcome: suppression by force. The first episode, on 27 July, left sixty-six dead, but the bloodiest events were the destruction of the two major sit-ins at Rabi'a al-'Adawiya and al-Nahda squares on 14 August, the death toll from which, according to government sources, surpassed six hundred. Simply serving to confirm the image already widely portrayed, some Brotherhood members and other Islamists continued their opposition by engaging in attacks on police stations, churches, schools, and government buildings throughout the country.

The atmosphere that had encouraged the internal repression, which was heartily embraced by many who had earlier called themselves liberals, leftists, or defenders of human rights, then turned outward. The official narrative of a battle against domestic terrorism was rejected by many foreign observers and powers, who began to raise the possibility of sanctions or other punitive measures. In response, the internal rhetoric increasingly drew upon themes from earlier episodes of external threats to the country: the insistence upon Egypt's sovereignty, its independence in decision-making, and its historic genius and greatness reached xenophobic levels.

In January and February 2011, pictures of Nasser had been raised by protestors as expressions of nostalgia for a founding revolutionary leader and the program of social and economic justice he had proclaimed. By July 2013, Nasser's picture was being raised next to that of the new military strongman 'Abd al-Fattah al-Sisi, perhaps as a way of suggesting the power and heroism of the army, but also, certainly, because Nasser had imprisoned (although never massacred) the Ikhwan in 1954. As the Egyptian media adopted a single narrative focused on the country's continuing struggle against terrorism, broadcasts repeated verbal and visual paeans to the patriotism and sacrifices of the police and the military. With the passage of time, perhaps the cruel irony will be more obvious to more of those who went into the streets in 2011 to call for Mubarak's ouster: the corruption and brutality of the police had been a major factor in triggering the 25 January revolution; and the missteps and repression of the army had led young revolutionaries, some of whom paid with their lives, to call for an end to its rule in 2011 and 2012. By July 2013, however, yesterday's villains had become the heroic martyrs and defenders of another, very different, "revolution," as the state announced its intention to rename streets after members of the police and security forces killed in the confrontations with "terrorists." Rarely have the powers of a hegemonic narrative and the utility of the multivocality of its constituent elements been more clearly, effectively, and disturbingly, on display.

NOTES

CHAPTER 1: RESTOR(Y)ING THE STATE

1. A reference to Samuel Huntington's *The Third Wave: Democratization in the Late Twentieth Century* (Norman: University of Oklahoma Press, 1991).

2. See, inter alia, Samuel Huntington, "Will More Countries Become Democratic?" *Political Science Quarterly* 99, no. 2 (1984): 193–218, and Elie Kedourie, *Democracy and Arab Political Culture* (Washington, D.C.: Washington Institute for Near East Policy, 1992).

3. See, e.g., *Authoritarianism in the Middle East: Regimes and Resistance*, ed. Marsha Pripstein Posusney and Michele Penner Angrist (Boulder, CO: Lynne Rienner, 2005), originally a special issue of *Comparative Politics* (January 2004). And see also the contributions in *Islam and Democracy in the Middle East*, ed. Larry Jay Diamond, Marc F. Plattner and Daniel Brumberg (Baltimore: Johns Hopkins University Press, 2003); *Democracy without Democrats? The Renewal of Politics in the Muslim World*, ed. Ghassan Salame (London: I. B. Taurus, 1994); and *Political Liberalization and Democratization in the Arab World*, ed. Rex Brynen, Bahgat Korany, and Paul Noble (Boulder, CO: Lynne Rienner, 1998).

4. Fayez Yousef Hammad, "The Resiliency of Arab Authoritarianism and the Arab-Israeli Conflict: The United States' Role in the Cases of Egypt and Jordan" (PhD diss., University of Southern California, 2008); Jason Brownlee, *Democracy Prevention: The Politics of the U.S.-Egyptian Alliance* (New York: Cambridge University Press, 2012).

5. See esp. Eva Bellin, "The Robustness of Authoritarianism in the Middle East: Exceptionalism in Comparative Perspective," *Comparative Politics* 36, no. 2 (2004): 139–57.

6. In Arabic, Muhammad 'Ali.

7. In June 2012, Egypt elected its first civilian president, Muhammad Mursi; however, he was removed from office through a combination of popular uprising and military intervention on 3 July 2013 and replaced by a temporary civilian president, 'Adli Mansur, although the military, led by Vice President and Minister of Defense General 'Abd al-Fattah Al-Sisi, wielded broad powers. We take up the changes in Egypt since the 25 January 2011 revolution in the Epilogue.

8. See Khaled Fahmy, *All the Pasha's Men: Mehmed Ali, His Army and the Making of Modern Egypt* (Cairo: American University in Cairo Press, 2002).

9. James P. Farwell, *Persuasion and Power: The Art of Strategic Communication* (Washington, D.C.: Georgetown University Press, 2012), 107.

10. Anne Showstack Sassoon, *Gramsci's Politics* (Minneapolis: University of Minnesota Press, 1987), 109–25, 232. More generally, however, see *Selections from the Prison Notebooks of Antonio Gramsci*, ed. and trans. Quintin Hoare and Geoffrey Nowell Smith (New York: International Publishers, 1971).

11. Barry Smart, "The Politics of Truth and the Problem of Hegemony," in *Foucault: A Critical Reader*, ed. David Couzens Hoy (New York: Blackwell, 1987), 157–74. On Foucault's thinking on power, see esp. *Discipline and Punish: The Birth of the Prison* (New York: Vintage Books, 1979).

12. See Claire Sutherland, "Nation-Building through Discourse Theory," *Nations and Nationalism* 11, no. 2 (2005): 186, 191. For a fuller discussion, see Ernesto Laclau and Chantal Mouffe, *Hegemony and Socialist Strategy: Towards a Radical Democratic Politics* (New York: Verso, 2000).

13. Teun A. van Dijk, *Discourse and Power* (New York: Palgrave Macmillan, 2008), 29.

14. Anne-Marie Brady, "Introduction," in *China's Thought Management*, ed. Anne-Marie Brady (New York: Routledge, 2012), 2.

15. Ji Fengjuan, "Linguistic Engineering in Hu Jintao's China," in *China's Thought Management*, ed. Brady, 90.

16. Karel C. Berkhoff, *Motherland in Danger: Soviet Propaganda during World War II* (Cambridge, MA: Harvard University Press, 2012), 3. Berkhoff adapts his definition from Garth S. Jowett and Victoria O'Donnell, *Propaganda and Persuasion*, 3rd ed. (Thousand Oaks, CA: Sage, 1999), 6, 45, 290.

17. Peter Kenez, *The Birth of the Propaganda State: Soviet Methods of Mass Mobilization, 1917–1929* (New York: Cambridge University Press, 1985), 1, 5, 15.

18. Lillian Guerra, *Visions of Power in Cuba: Revolution, Redemption and Resistance, 1959–1971* (Chapel Hill: University of North Carolina Press, 2012), 3.

19. Matthew G. Stanard, *Selling the Congo: A History of European Pro-Empire Propaganda and the Making of Belgian Imperialism* (Lincoln: University of Nebraska Press, 2011), 24.

20. Ibid., 136.

21. David Monger, *Patriotism and Propaganda in First World War Britain: The National War Aims Committee and Civilian Morale* (Liverpool: Liverpool University Press, 2012), 86.

22. Anne-Marie Brady, "Talking up the Market: Economic Propaganda in Contemporary China," in *China's Thought Management*, ed. id., 60.

23. Berkhoff, *Motherland in Danger*, 8.

24. Ibid., 271, 278.

25. Maureen Perrie, *The Cult of Ivan the Terrible in Stalin's Russia* (New York: Palgrave, 2001), 3.

26. Yaacov Yadgar, "From the Particularistic to the Universalistic: National Narratives in Israel's Mainstream Press, 1967–97," *Nations and Nationalism* 8, no. 1 (2002): 58–59.

27. See James V. Wertsch, *Voices of Collective Remembering* (New York: Cambridge University Press, 2002). In chapter 3, Wertsch details the broad scope as well as the limited agreement and lack of overall coherence in this literature.

28. See, e.g., Jack Snyder, *From Voting to Violence: Democratization and National Conflict* (New York: Norton, 2000).

29. Ernst Cassirer, *The Myth of the State* (New Haven, CT: Yale University Press, 1946), 279.

30. Edmund Burke III, "Theorizing the Histories of Colonialism, and Nationalism in the Arab Maghreb," *Arab Studies Quarterly* 20, no. 2 (Spring 1998): 10.

31. Wertsch, *Voices of Collective Remembering*, 95, taking the term from L. P. Zamora, *The Usable Past: The Imagination of History in Recent Fiction of the Americas* (Cambridge: Cambridge University Press, 1998).

32. Benedict Anderson, *Imagined Communities: Reflections on the Origin and Spread of Nationalism* (London: Verso, 1983). Popular beliefs and polemics notwithstanding, this study has rendered the notion of "imagining the community" almost second nature for scholars.

33. Eric J. Hobsbawm, "Introduction: The Invention of Tradition," in *The Invention of Tradition*, ed. id. and Terence Ranger (New York: Cambridge University Press, 1983), 9.

34. Anthony D. Smith, "Nationalism and the Historians," in *Mapping the Nation*, ed. Gopal Balakrishnan (New York: Verso, 1996), 191.

35. Yael Zerubavel, *Recovered Roots: Collective Memory and the Making of Israeli National Tradition* (Chicago: University of Chicago Press, 1995), 7.

36. Ann Anagnost, *National Past-Times: Narrative, Representation and Power in Modern China* (Durham, NC: Duke University Press, 1997), 3.

37. See Israel Gershoni and James P. Jankowski, *Redefining the Egyptian Nation, 1930–1945* (New York: Cambridge University Press, 1995); Elliott Colla, *Conflicted Antiquities: Egyptology, Egyptomania, Egyptian Modernity* (Durham, NC: Duke University Press, 2007).

38. Lisa Wedeen, *Ambiguities of Domination: Politics, Rhetoric, and Symbols in Contemporary Syria* (Chicago: University of Chicago Press, 1999), 40 n21.

39. Wertsch, *Voices of Collective Remembering*, 68–69.

40. Ernest Gellner, "The Coming of Nationalism and its Interpretation: The Myths of Nation and Class," in *Mapping the Nation*, ed. Gopal Balakrishnan (London: Verso, 1996), 107–8.

41. Michael C. Hechter, *Containing Nationalism* (New York: Oxford University Press, 2001), 56, 63–64.

42. Burke, "Theorizing," 12.

43. Prasenjit Duara, *Rescuing History from the Nation: Questioning Narratives of Modern China* (Chicago: University of Chicago Press, 1995), 9.

44. Homi K. Bhabha, "Introduction: Narrating the Nation," in *Nation and Narration*, ed. id. (New York: Routledge, 1990), 1.

45. Of course, there are countries in which parts of the citizenry are not included in the narrative of unity. The case of the Muslim and Christian Palestinian citizens of the self-proclaimed Jewish state of Israel is one obvious example.

46. Max Weber, *The Theory of Social and Economic Organization* (New York: Free Press, 1964).

47. Ofra Bengio, *Saddam's Word: Political Discourse in Iraq* (New York: Oxford University Press, 1998).

48. Başak İnce, *Citizenship and Identity in Turkey: From Atatürk's Republic to the Present Day* (New York: I. B. Tauris, 2012).

49. Monger, *Patriotism and Propaganda*, 10.

50. Berkhoff, *Motherland in Danger*, 276.

51. Stanard, *Selling the Congo*, 44.

52. Anagnost, *National Past-Times*, 2

53. Wertsch, *Voices of Collective Remembering*, 81, 102–4.

54. Sam Kaplan, *The Pedagogical State: Education and the Politics of National Culture in Post-1980 Turkey* (Stanford: Stanford University Press, 2006).

55. Nels Johnson, *Islam and the Politics of Meaning in Palestinian Nationalism* (Boston: Keegan Paul International, 1982), 3.

56. Ibid., 4.

57. See, inter alia, Simha Flapan, *The Birth of Israel: Myths and Realities* (New York: Pantheon Books, 1988); Avi Shlaim, "The Debate about 1948," *International Journal of Middle East Studies* 27, no. 3 (1995): 287–304; and for an historical extension of the analysis, Sean McMahon, *The Discourse of Palestinian-Israeli Relations: Persistent Analytics and Practices* (New York: Routledge, 2010).

58. Kamal Salibi, *A House of Many Mansions: The History of Lebanon Reconsidered* (Berkeley: University of California Press, 1988). See also Ahmad Beydoun, *Identité confessionnelle et temps social chez les historiens libanais contemporains* (Beirut: Université libanaise, 1984).

59. See, e.g., Ayşe Gül Altinay, *The Myth of the Military-Nation: Militarism, Gender, and Education in Turkey* (New York: Palgrave Macmillan, 2004), and Tanil Bora "Nationalist Discourses in Turkey," *South Atlantic Quarterly* 102, no. 2–3 (Spring–Summer 2003): 433–51.

60. Bengio, *Saddam's Word*.

61. See, e.g., Joel Gordon, *Revolutionary Melodramas: Popular Film and Civic Identity in Nasser's Egypt* (Chicago: University of Chicago Press, 2002); Leila Abu-Lughod, *Dramas of Nationhood: The Politics of Television in Egypt* (Chicago: University of Chicago

Press, 2005); Walter Armbrust, "Audiovisual Media and History of the Arab Middle East," in *Middle East Historiographies: Narrating the Twentieth Century*, ed. Israel Gershoni, Amy Singer, and Y. Hakan Erdem (Seattle: University of Washington Press, 2006), 288–314; Douglas R. Boyd, *Broadcasting in the Arab World: A Survey of the Electronic Media in the Middle East* (Des Moines: Iowa State University Press, 1999); Hassan Remaoun and Mohamed Bensalah, eds., *Image, mémoire, histoire: Les représentations iconographiques en Algérie et au Maghreb* (Oran: Centre de recherche en anthropologie sociale et culturelle, 2007); Virginia Danielson, *The Voice of Egypt: Umm Kulthum, Arabic Song, and Egyptian Society in the Twentieth Century* (Chicago: University of Chicago Press, 2008).

62. Duara, *Rescuing History*, 32.

63. Adrian Oldfield, "Citizenship and Community: Civic Republicanism and the Modern World," in *The Citizenship Debates*, ed. Gershon Shafir (Minneapolis: University of Minnesota Press, 1998), 86.

64. Kaplan, *Pedagogical State*, 9.

65. As cited in Wertsch, *Voices of Collective Remembering*, 34.

66. Kenez, *Birth of the Propaganda State*, 16 and 83.

67. İnce, *Citizenship and Identity in Turkey*, 67, from Sefa Şimşek, *Bir İdeolojik Seferberlik Deneyemi: Halkevleri, 1932–1951* (Istanbul: Boğaziçi Üniversitesi Yayınevi, 2002), 145.

68. İnce, *Citizenship and Identity*, 70, from Şimşek, *Bir İdeolojik Seferberlik Deneyemi*, 157.

69. E.g., Eleanor Abdella Doumato and Gregory Starrett, eds., *Teaching Islam: Textbooks and Religion in the Middle East* (Boulder, CO: Lynne Rienner, 2007); Betty S. Anderson, "Writing the Nation: Textbooks of the Hashemite Kingdom of Jordan," *Comparative Studies of South Asia, Africa and the Middle East* 21, nos. 1–2 (2001): 5–14; Riad M. Nasser, *Palestinian Identity in Jordan and Israel: The Necessary "Other" in the Making of a Nation* (New York: Routledge, 2005); Elie Podeh, *The Arab-Israeli Conflict in Israeli History Textbooks, 1948–2000* (New York: Praeger, 2001); Nurit Peled-Elhanan, *Palestine in Israeli School Books: Ideology and Propaganda in Education* (New York: Tauris Academic Studies, 2012).

70. Gregory Starrett, *Putting Islam to Work: Education, Politics, and Religious Transformation in Egypt* (Berkeley: University of California Press, 1998); Linda Herrera, "Islamization and Education: Between Politics, Profit and Pluralism," in *Cultures of Arab Schooling: Critical Ethnographies from Egypt*, ed. Herrera and Carlos Alberto Torres (Albany: State University of New York Press, 2006), 25–52; Fida J. Adely, *Gendered Paradoxes: Educating Jordanian Women in Nation, Faith and Progress* (Chicago: University of Chicago Press, 2012).

CHAPTER 2: EGYPT UNDER NASSER

1. Mehmet Ali, who was born in Greek Macedonia to Albanian parents, ruled Egypt from 1805 to 1848.

2. *Ta'rikh Misr w-al-'Arab al-hadith* (The Modern History of Egypt and the Arabs), a textbook for the last year of high school.

3. Elliott Colla, *Conflicted Antiquities: Egyptology, Egyptomania, Egyptian Modernity* (Durham, NC: Duke University Press, 2007), 74 and 79.

4. Ibid., 177.

5. Ibid., 126.

6. Charles D. Smith, "Imagined Identities, Imagined Nationalism: Print Culture and Egyptian Nationalism in Light of Recent Scholarship," review of Israel Gershoni and James P. Jankowski, *Redefining the Egyptian Nation, 1930–1945* (New York: Cambridge University Press, 1995), *International Journal of Middle East Studies* 29, no. 4 (November 1997): 612.

7. Ibid., 612.

8. Gershoni and Jankowski, *Redefining the Egyptian Nation*, 82.

9. Ibid., 103.

10. Ibid., 124–26, 138.

11. Smith, 616 and 619.

12. Ibid., 616.

13. Anthony Gorman, *Historians, State and Politics in Twentieth Century Egypt: Contesting the Nation* (New York: Routledge Curzon, 2010), 159.

14. Isma'il, a grandson of Mehmet Ali born in 1830, ruled Egypt (and the Sudan) from 1863 to 1879, when he was forced by the British to step down.

15. 'Isam 'Ashur, *Al-Dasatir al-Misriyyah 'abr al-ta'rikh, 1837–2011 rihlat nidal* (Cairo: Dar Mirit, 2011), 211.

16. Ahmad 'Urabi, an Egyptian colonel in the army, led an ultimately unsuccessful revolt/revolution against foreign (European, as well as Turkish-Circassian) influence in Egypt in 1879–82, which subsequently came to be presented as the first example of an anti-colonial nationalist movement in Egypt.

17. 'Ashur, *Al-Dasatir al-Misriyyah*, 31 and 35.

18. *Al-Dasatir al-Misriyya, 1805–1971* (Cairo: Al-Ahram, Makaz al-Tanthim w-al-Mikrufilm, 1977), 155.

19. Muhsin Khudr notes that prior to the 1950s, *qawmiyya* was used to mean "national" in the sense of "Egyptian." See *Al-Ittijah al-qawmi al-'Arabi f-il-ta'lim al-Misri 1952–1981* (Cairo: Al-Hay'a al-Misriyya al-'Amma l-il-Kitab, 1992), 89.

20. In 1899, with the British in occupation of Egypt, what was called an Anglo-Egyptian condominium, but what was really British imperial rule, was imposed on the Sudan, which had been ruled from Cairo since the time of Mehmet Ali.

21. Gorman, *Historians, State and Politics*, 50.

22. Shlomit Shraybom Shrivtel, "Language and Political Change in Modern Egypt," *International Journal of the Sociology of Language* 137 (1999): 132. Egyptian territorial nationalists such as Salama Musa (1887–1958) also sought to make colloquial Egyptian Arabic the language of instruction (ibid., 134).

23. Sa'id Isma'il 'Ali, *Al-Hawiyya w-al-ta'lim* (Cairo: 'Alam al-Kitab, 2005), 227.

24. "As late as the 1940s, foreign languages were still the primary means of instruction in the education system" (Shrivtel, "Language and Political Change," 136).

25. Although generally translated simply as "civics," *tarbiya* has the sense of both upbringing and education, and *qawmiyya* (nationalism) was used to refer to Egypt alone at this time, as n. 19 above indicates. It only later acquired a pan-Arab connotation.

26. Khudr, *Al-Ittijah al-qawmi*, 174–75.

27. In 1953–54, there were 1,982,842 children in school, according to Amir Boktor, *The Development and Expansion of Education in the United Arab Republic* (Cairo: American University in Cairo Press, 1963), 1.

28. "Sons of my homeland" could also be translated as *abna' watani. Bani* is usually used to refer to members of a tribe.

29. 'Ashur, *Al-Dasatir al-Misriyyah*, 103–4.

30. Ibid., 105.

31. Ibid., 108.

32. Khedive Tawfiq ruled from 1879 to 1892.

33. *Kufr* literally means denying the existence of God. Here it is more likely a broader critique of King Farouk's lack of respect for religion and religious principles.

34. One of these postage stamps (234) shows a woman holding a sword and with chains on her arms broken. She appears to wear a pharaonic headpiece, but she resembles the French republican icon Marianne, not an Egyptian peasant woman.

35. P. J. Vatikiotis, *The Modern History of Egypt: From Muhammad Ali to Mubarak*, 4th ed. (Baltimore: Johns Hopkins University Press, 1991), 385–86.

36. The Muslim Brotherhood was founded in Egypt in 1928.

37. Gamal Abdel Nasser, *Falsafat al-thawra* (1953; Cairo: Maktabat Madbuli, 2005). The journalist Muhammad Hasanayn Haykal, a Nasser confidant, is generally credited with drafting *Falsafat al-thawra*. I am grateful to Kirk Beattie for helping me verify that this work actually first appeared in 1953, not in 1954 or 1955 as many extant versions of the book indicate. Page numbers for quotations from it are given parenthetically in the text.

38. Here Nasser refers to a 1952 attempt by King Farouk to prevent the Free Officers group from running a candidate in the elections for president of the Officers' Club.

39. Ihlam Rajab 'Abd al-Ghaffar, *Ta'rikh al-tarbiya wa nizam al-ta'lim fi Misr* (Dar al-Thaqafa l-il-Tiba'a w-al-Nashr, 1991), 194.

40. 'Ali, *Al-Hawiyya w-al-ta'lim*, 166.

41. Ibid., 166–67.

42. Cairo was the capital of the Fatimid caliphate from 969 to 1171. The Ottomans conquered Egypt in 1517.

43. The word *mamluk*, which literally means "owned," refers to a caste of soldier slaves, generally of Turkic or Circassian origin, who by 1250 had gained such power that

they claimed the sultanate in Egypt. They ruled until their ouster by Mehmet Ali following the Napoleonic invasion.

44. *Tawa'if* is usually translated as "sects," but here the text lists peasants, craftsmen, merchants, religious scholars ('ulama), Sufis, soldiers, and Mamluks as examples of *tawa'if.*

45. The reference here is to Turkish titles such as pasha and bey. That said, while they were no longer obligatory, many Egyptians continue(d) to use these titles to indicate various levels of respect in forms of address.

46. Mustafa Kamil (1874–1908) was leader of the Egyptian Nationalist Party. Muhammad Farid (1868–1919) succeeded Kamil as leader of the Nationalist Party. Sa'd Zaghlul (1859–1927) was a nationalist activist who led the Egyptian delegation to the Paris peace conference in 1919, which demanded independence; he served in several government positions, including that of prime minister in 1924.

47. Nazih Nasif Al-Ayyubi, *Siyasat al-ta'lim fi Misr: Dirasa siyasiyya wa-idariyya* (Cairo: Al-Ahram Center for Political and Strategic Studies, 1978), 41. In 1956, there were 1,986,000 children in primary schools, 318,000 in preparatory schools, and 109,000 in secondary schools.

48. The 99 percent + support these referenda purportedly received made it clear that the exercise was aimed at mobilization and the illusion of popular input, not a free and fair outcome.

49. Ahmad Isma'il Hijja, *Al-Ta'rikh al-thaqafi l-il-ta'lim fi Misr* (Cairo: Dar al-Fikr al-'Arabi, 2002), 292 and 294.

50. It is also worth noting, however, that large landholders ("feudalists") are never identified as Egyptian in the 1956 *Al-Tarbiya al-wataniyya* textbook, although the peasantry always are (see, e.g., 237).

51. Avaris, in the northwestern part of the Nile Delta, was the ancient Hyksos ("foreign rulers") capital of Egypt.

52. "President Gamal Abd El Nasser: Plastic and Applied Arts," *Bibliotheca Alexandrina,* http://nasser.bibalex.org/NasserCulture/Arts_Main.aspx?x=7&TP=0&CS=0&lang=en (accessed 18 August 2013). The stamps can be viewed on this archival site and are numbered, respectively, 222, 213. 214, 215, and 216.

53. Ibid., stamps numbered 190–93, 183–87, 163, 165, 141, and 173.

54. Nasser made a special point in this context of noting that unity included Arab Christians, who, he insisted, had joined the Muslims in resisting the Crusaders (2).

55. Khudr, *Al-Ittijah al-qawmi,* 93 and 101.

56. Ibid., 99 and 112.

57. Ibid., 158–59.

58. Ibid., 162–65.

59. Ibid., 166–67.

60. Ibid., 169–71.

61. http://nasser.bibalex.org/NasserCulture/Arts_Main.aspx?x=7&TP=0&CS=0&lang=en, postage stamps numbered 134–36, 138, and 140.

62. As we shall see in the next chapter, this is a theme that was used even more extensively by Sadat.

63. United Arab Republic, *Al-Mithaq al-watani* [The National Charter] (N.p.: Maslahat al-Isti'lamat, 1962). Page numbers for quotations from this are given parenthetically in the text.

64. Gorman, *Historians, State and Politics*, 61.

65. *Al-Mithaq al-watani* notes that although the Ottomans imposed this weakness and disintegration in the name of religion, religion (Islam) is innocent of this.

66. Gorman, *Historians, State and Politics*, 57.

67. Ibid., 92–93.

68. Al-Ayyubi, *Siyasat al-ta'lim fi Misr*, 41.

69. "Bayan al- Ra'is Gamal 'Abd al-Nasir ila al-sha'b w-al-umma bi-i'lan al-tanahhi 'an ri'asat al-jumhuriyya," 9 June 1967, in

"President Gamal Abd El Nasser: Speeches," Bibliotheca Alexandrina, http://nasser.bibalex.org/Speeches/SpeechesAll.aspx?CS=0&lang=ar (accessed 21 December 2013), 1. The page numbers refer to the text as it printed out from the online source.

70. "Khitab al-Ra'is Gamal 'Abd al-Nasir," 23 July 1967, ibid., 1. The page numbers refer to the text as it printed out from the online source.

71. Vatikiotis, *Modern History of Egypt*, 411.

72. R. Hrair Dekmejian, *Egypt under Nasir: A Study in Political Dynamics* (Albany: State University of New York Press, 1971), 165.

73. Gamal Abdel Nasser, "Mandate for Change," in 'Ashur, *Al-Dasatir al-Misriyyah.* The page numbers given in parentheses in the text refer to its reproduction there.

74. Amal Andrawus, *Al-Siyasat al-ta'limiyya fi Misr* (Cairo: Dar Farha l-il-Nashr w-al-Tawzi', 2004), 175.

75. Throughout Nasser's presidency, stamps and coins with pharaonic themes, including the Sphinx and the pyramids, were issued. One depicted Nasser's face next to the Sphinx. A coin with a pharaonic archer was issued to commemorate the founding of the UAR.

76. A notable exception was a 1,900-year commemorative stamp was issued in 1968 for St. Mark, the disciple who according to tradition brought Christianity to Egypt, where he was martyred in 68 CE.

CHAPTER 3: EGYPT UNDER SADAT AND MUBARAK

1. Raymond Baker, *Egypt's Uncertain Revolution under Nasser and Sadat* (Cambridge, MA: Harvard University Press, 1978), 124.

2. Decision of the prime minister, 578 of 1971. *Al-Jaridah al-Rasmiyyah*, 25 March 1971. Sadat's speech is quoted from "Address by the U.A.R. President Designate Anwar

El Sadat before the National Assembly," 7 October 1970, http://sadat.umd.edu/archives/written_works.htm (accessed 21 December 2013), 11.

3. Kirk Beattie, *Egypt during the Nasser Years: Ideology, Politics, and Civil Society* (Boulder, CO: Westview Press, 1994), 62–63.

4. Raymond A. Hinnebusch, *Egyptian Politics under Sadat: The Post-populist Development of an Authoritarian-modernizing State* (New York: Cambridge University Press, 1985), 41.

5. "Bayan al-Ra'is Muhammad Anwar al-Sadat ila al-umma," 14 May 1971, in "President Anwar Sadat: Speeches," Bibliotheca Alexandrina, http://sadat.bibalex.org/speeches/speechesall.aspx?CS=0 (accessed 21 December 2013), 14. Page numbers reflect the hard-copy printout. It is worth noting that Nasser also used such terms, but much less frequently—at least before 1967.

6. Amani Qandil, *Siyasat al-ta'lim fi-wadi al-Nil w-al-Sumal wa-Jibuti* (Cairo: Muntada al-Fikr al-'Arabi, 1989), 25.

7. "Khitab al-Ra'is Muhammad Anwar al-Sadat fi iftitah al-dawra al-jadida l-il-mu'tamar al-qawmi al-'amm l-il-Ittihad al-Ishtiraki al-'Arabi," 23 July 1972, in "President Anwar Sadat: Speeches," Bibliotheca Alexandrina, 1. Page numbers reflect the hard-copy printout.

8. "Bayan al-Ra'is Muhammad Anwar al-Sadat," 28 December 1972, in "President Anwar Sadat: Speeches," Bibliotheca Alexandrina, 1. Page numbers reflect the hard-copy printout.

9. "Khitab al-Ra'is Muhammad Anwar al-Sadat fi iftitah al-dawra al-istithna'iyya li-Majlis al-Sha'b, 16 October 1973, ibid.

10. Hinnebusch, *Egyptian Politics under Sadat*, 54.

11. "October Working Paper," April 1974, 7, Anwar Sadat Archives, Anwar Sadat Chair for Peace and Development, http://sadat.umd.edu/archives/written_works.htm (accessed 21 December 2013). Page numbers reflect source as reproduced.

12. 'Ali, *Al-Hawiyya w-al-ta'lim*, 173.

13. Hinnebusch, *Egyptian Politics under Sadat*, 57.

14. FBIS, 22 July 1975, "Text of Sadat Speech," D5 and D6, as numbered in FBIS.

15. Gorman, *Historians, State and Politics*, 67.

16. It was formally dissolved in 1985. See ibid., 68.

17. FBIS, 14 March 1976, "Al-Sadat Addresses People's Assembly," D16.

18. Jason Brownlee, *Authoritarianism in an Age of Democratization* (New York: Cambridge University Press, 2007), 92.

19. FBIS, 29 January 1977, "[Sadat's] Concluding Speech," D12–D14.

20. "Egypt-Israel Relations: Address by Egyptian President Anwar Sadat to the Knesset (November 20, 1977)," Jewish Virtual Library, www.jewishvirtuallibrary.org/jsource/Peace/sadat_speech.html (accessed 21 December 2013). Page numbers reflect the hard-copy printout.

21. FBIS, 8 December 1977, 8 December 1977, "Sadat Address," D23.

22. FBIS, 14 May 1978, "Sadat Speaks on Corrective Revolution Anniversary," D1.

23. Reminiscent of the 1973 "victory," the Islamic calendar's 10 Ramadan (but not 6 October) is used as the anniversary of the founding of the National Democratic Party. For more on the evolution of the party and its role, see Brownlee, *Authoritarianism*, and Joshua Stacher, *Adaptable Autocrats: Regime Power in Egypt and Syria* (Stanford: Stanford University Press, 2012).

24. FBIS, 14 May 1978, "Sadat Speaks on Corrective Revolution Anniversary," D14.

25. "Kalimat al-Ra'is Muhammad Anwar al-Sadat ba'd mu'ahidat al-salam," 26 March 1979, in "President Anwar Sadat: Speeches," Bibliotheca Alexandrina, 1 and 2.

26. Egypt's 7,000-year history, its unity, its faith and morality, and its resistance to outside invaders, and so on. FBIS, 5 April 1979, "Sadat Addresses Special Session of People's Assembly," D1.

27. "Kalimat al-Ra'is Muhammad Anwar al-Sadat w-allati alqaha al-Sayyid Muhammad Husni Mubarak bi-munasibat 'Id Thawrat 23 July," 22 July 1979, 2 in "President Anwar Sadat: Speeches," Bibliotheca Alexandrina.

28. Al-Ayyubi, *Siyasat al-ta'lim fi Misr*, 41.

29. For example, the defeat of Mehmet Ali and Ibrahim Pasha was called "the collapse of the first Arab unity," in effect establishing an historical precedent for the 1961 Syrian secession, and attributing it to "weak Arab nationalist awareness" at the time (45). In the questions section, students were asked to give the reasons for "the persistence of Arab nationalism despite the length and brutality of Ottoman rule" (47).

30. Khudr, *Al-Ittijah al-qawmi*, 185 and 189.

31. There are two issues related to the translation of the title *Al-Tarbiya al-qawmiyya*. First, as noted in chapter 2, *tarbiya* has the sense of both upbringing and education. Second, the adjective that generally accompanies it in such books is *wataniyya*. Here, however, the influence of the Arab nationalism of the Nasser period is clear in the use of the adjective *qawmiyya*, referring to the larger Arab nation.

32. Andrawus, *Al-Siyasat al-ta'limiyya*, 239.

33. Khudr, *Al-Ittijah al-qawmi*, 138–39.

34. Although not directly relevant for the narrative, article 77 was also amended to remove the limit on the number of presidential terms, and an entirely new institution, the Shura Council, was introduced. 'Ashur, *Al-Dasatir al-Misriyyah*, 218.

35. FBIS, 14 May 1980, "Sadat Speech on May Corrective Revolution Anniversary."

36. FBIS, 1 October 1980, "Sadat Address," D3.

37. "Khitab al-Ra'is Muhammad Anwar al-Sadat," 5 September 1981, 2.

38. Vatikiotis, *Modern History of Egypt*, 423.

39. Ibid., 444.

40. FBIS, 8 November 1981, "Mubarak People's Assembly Speech," 1.

41. FBIS, 26 July 1982, "Mubarak Speech to National Democratic Party," 1.

42. Vatikiotis, *Modern History of Egypt*, 453.

43. FBIS, 26 February 1986, "Mubarak Speech [to] Nation," 1.

44. Vatikiotis, *Modern History of Egypt*, 452.

45. FBIS, 6 July 1987, "Mubarak Acceptance Speech," 3.

46. Hijja, *Al-Ta'rikh al-thaqafi*, 322–23.

47. Andrawus, *Al-Siyasat al-ta'limiyya*, 240 and 246.

48. "In the name of God, praise be to God and prayers and peace be on our master/lord Muhammad, the faithful prophet."

49. Deniz Cakirer, "Neo-Liberal Restructuring and Re-Construction of Islamic Community Discourses in Turkey: The Cases of the Gülen and Erenköy Communities" (PhD diss., University of Southern California, 2012).

50. 'Ali, *Al-Hawiyya w-al-ta'lim*, 233.

51. Fatema H. Sayed, *Transforming Education in Egypt: Western Influence and Domestic Policy Reform* (Cairo: American University in Cairo Press, 2006), 65.

52. Hijja, *Al-Ta'rikh al-thaqafi*, 340.

53. Linda Herrera, "Islamization and Education: Between Politics, Profit and Pluralism," in *Cultures of Arab Schooling: Critical Ethnographies from Egypt*, ed. Herrera and Carlos Alberto Torres (Albany: State University of New York Press, 2006), 29.

54. Ibid., 30 and 32.

55. The fact that exams are administered on a national level by the government has been a strong incentive for these schools to adhere to the obligatory curriculum, even when there may have been temptations to diverge from it. Herrera noted students in such a private Islamic school singing the nonsectarian patriotic national anthem "Biladi, Biladi" (My Country, My Country) each morning with the completely different words "Illahi, Illahi" (My God, My God). The substituted wording included references to martyrdom and jihad and was critical of unbelievers. Ibid., 36–38.

56. Sayed, *Transforming Education in Egypt*, 75.

57. Ibid., 63 and 81.

58. Andrawus, *Al-Siyasat al-ta'limiyya*, 310–11.

59. Sayed, *Transforming Education in Egypt*, 62.

60. Here the distinction between *watani* and *qawmi* seems to be that of "domestic patriotic" versus "national," thus again suggesting the fluidity, but also at times the lack of precision, in the use of such terms, even in official documents.

61. 'Isam al-Din 'Ali Hilal and Muhammad Ibrahim Minufi, *Al-Tarbiya al-siyasiyya l-il-tifl al-Misri* (Cairo: Dar Farha l-il-Nashr w-al-Tawzir, 2005), 56 and 60.

62. Kamal Hamid Mughayth and Ilham 'Abd al-Hamid, *Al-Ta'lim wa-huquq al-insan* (Cairo: LRRC, 1997), 71.

63. Ibid., 81.

64. FBIS, 25 January 1993, "Mubarak Speech on Confrontation of Terrorism," 2.

65. FBIS, 30 August 1993, "Mubarak Marks Prophet's Birthday with Speech," 2.

66. FBIS, 25 January 1996, "Mubarak Speech Stresses Fight against 'Terror' in Egypt," 3.

67. FBIS, 21 July 1994, "Mubarak Speech Stresses National Dialogue," 1.

68. *Ahram Online*, no. 604, September 2002.

69. Ibid., no. 603, September 2002.

70. Stacher, *Adaptable Autocrats*,103.

71. Ibid., 122 and 124.

72. Fayiz Murad Mina, *Al-Ta'lim fi Misr: Al-Waqi' w-al-mustaqbal hatta 'am 2020* (Cairo: Anglo-Egyptian Bookstore, 2001), 169.

73. Herrera, "Islamization and Education," 27.

74. 'Ali, *Al-Hawiyya w-al-ta'lim*, 236.

75. Sayed, *Transforming Education in Egypt*, 75.

76. Ibid., 99. Sayed also contends that to walk the fine line stipulated by the peace treaty without offending Egyptian sensibilities, placing the names Palestine and Israel on maps is avoided.

77. Ibid., 114.

78. Ibid.

79. Ibid., 109–11, 114, 118, 121.

80. 'Ashur, *Al-Dasatir al-Misriyyah*, 230.

81. *Ahram Online*, no. 870, November 2007, editorial.

82. Ibid.

83. 23 July 2010, Revolution Day speech.

84. Sadat, speech of 1 October 1980.

85. In his careful examination of the evolution of the balance of power among what he identifies as the three most important components in the post-1952 Egyptian regime(s)—the politicians, the military and the security forces—Hazem Kandil argues that Sadat's primary challenge after defeating his immediate rivals in May 1971 lay in reducing the power of the military. Kandil attributes what many analysts viewed as Sadat's squandering of the early gains of the 1973 war to the politically still insecure president's need for a high-profile political victory, while at the same time denying the armed forces a military one. See Hazem Kandil, *Soldiers, Spies, and Statesmen: Egypt's Road to Revolt* (London: Verso, 2012), chap. 4.

CHAPTER 4: ALGERIA FROM THE LIBERATION STRUGGLE THROUGH BOUMEDIENNE

1. Hugh Roberts, "The Politics of Algerian Socialism," in *North Africa: Contemporary Politics and Economic Development*, ed. Richard I. Lawless and Allan Findlay (New York: St. Martin's Press, 1984), 7.

2. Ibid., 6.

3. Most notable, and in some cases deadly, were the struggles between the FLN and the partisans of Messali Hadj (see n. 34 below), but there are also examples of intra-FLN

violence, such as the murder of Ramdane Abane in 1957 and the elimination of internal dissidents in 1960.

4. The dimensions of the question of Berber—Kabyle, Chaoui, Chenoui, Zenata, Chelha, M'zab, and Toureg—identity will be engaged further below.

5. A *wilaya* is an administrative district, such as a province or state. For the purposes of the war, the FLN had divided Algeria into six such districts, each with its own military leadership.

6. For more on the French colonial narrative see, inter alia: Abdel-Majid Hannoum, *Colonial Histories, Post-colonial Memories: The Legend of the Kahina, a North African Heroine* (New York: Heinemann, 2001); Mohammed Ghalem, "F-il-wataniyya w-al-ta'rikh: Dirasa hawl al-usus al-nathariyya li-kitab 'Ta'rikh al-Jaza'ir f-il-madi w-al-hadir' ta'lif al-Shaykh Mubarak al-Mili" (Oran: Centre de recherche en anthropologie sociale et culturelle, June 1995); Abdallah Mazouni, *Culture et enseignement en Algérie et au Maghreb* (Paris: François Maspero, 1969); Mohammed Brahim Salhi, *Algérie: Citoyenneté et identité* (Algiers: Achab, 2010).

7. In their defense, the Algerian elite had rather limited access to the kinds of sources that would have enabled them to write such an "unencumbered" history.

8. The French adopted a similar divide-and-rule, Arab vs. Berber, classificatory scheme in their subsequent colonization of Morocco.

9. For more on the origins of the designation "Berber," see Ramzi Rouighi, "Andalusi Origins of the Berbers," *Journal of Medieval Iberian Studies* 2, no. 1 (January 2010): 93–108, and id., "The Berbers of the Arabs," *Studia Islamica* 1 (2011): 67–101.

10. James McDougall explores the role of violence in both the French and the *islahi* versions of Algerian history in "Martyrdom and Destiny: The Inscription and Imagination of Algerian History," in *Memory and Violence in the Middle East and North Africa*, ed. Ussama Makdisi and Paul A. Silverstein (Bloomington: Indian University Press, 2006), 50–72.

11. The term *salafi* refers to ancestors or predecessors, and refers to a reformist trend among religious scholars that emerged at the end of the nineteenth century aimed at recapturing the pure roots of Islam in response to increasing Western encroachment in Muslim majority regions. Its increasing use to refer to an austere and puritanical form of Islam associated with the Wahhabism promoted by Saudi Arabia is much more recent development.

12. Founded by Shaykh 'Abd al-Hamid bin Badis in 1931, the Jam'iyyat al-'Ulama' al-Muslimin al-Jaza'iriyyin (Association des Uléma Musulmans Algériens [AUMA]: Association of Algerian Muslim Ulama), a group of reformist religious scholars, sought to put an end to popular religious practices it viewed as counter to the spirit and law of orthodox Islam. It also sought to revive religious and Arabic education in the colony. Although it has subsequently been portrayed as the precursor to the national movement, it was long more implicitly than explicitly anti-colonial, except as regards language and religious policy. It aligned itself with the FLN in 1955.

13. Arabic *'ulama'* is the plural of *'alim*, a man of religious learning or a religious scholar.

14. For a deeper exploration of al-Madani, see James McDougall, *History and the Culture of Nationalism in Algeria* (New York: Cambridge University Press, 2008).

15. Hannoum, *Colonial Histories*, 113–14.

16. In the Tamazight language, Amazigh (pl. Imazighen), the word used to refer to its people, means free men.

17. Masinissa (ca. 240 or 238 BC–ca. 148 BC) was the first king of the North African kingdom of Numidia. The Numidian king Jugurtha (ca. 160–ca. 104 BC) was his grandson. See Ghalem, "F-il-Wataniyya w-al-ta'rikh," 7–8.

18. Hannoum, *Colonial Histories*, 148.

19. Ibid., 137 and 149.

20. Mazouni, *Culture et enseignement*, 106.

21. Noureddine Toualbi Thaalibi, *École, idéologie et droits de l'homme*, 2nd ed. (Algiers: Casbah, 2004), 36–37.

22. On the Berber myth, see Salhi, *Algérie*; and Judith Scheele, *Village Matters: Knowledge, Politics and Community in Kabylia, Algeria* (London: James Currey, 2009).

23. The Kabyles are a Berber group primarily from the mountainous regions and along the Mediterranean Sea to the east of Algiers known as Kabilie or Kabilya. See, Jean Morizot, *Les Kabyles: Propos d'un témoin* (Paris: Centre de hautes études sur l'Afrique et l'Asie modernes, 1985), 18–19. Morizot discusses the complex evolution of this term, which in the Algerian context had long been applied simply to *montagnards*.

24. It is also the case that particularly the Kabyles were disproportionately recruited to migrate to work in France.

25. Hannoum, *Colonial Histories*, 150.

26. Mohammed Ghalem et al., "Al-Sulta w-al-ma'rifa fi-haql al-'ulum al-insaniyya—al-ta'rikh, al-falsafa, w-al-qanun," in *Actes des journées scientifiques de présentation des resultats de recherche des projects PNR: Population et Société* (Oran: Centre de recherche en anthropologie sociale et culturelle, 2006), 58.

27. See Thomas DeGeorges, "The Shifting Sands of Revolutionary Legitimacy: The Role of Former *Mujahidin* in the Shaping of Algeria's Collective Memory," *Journal of North African Studies* 14, no. 2 (2009): 273–288.

28. According to Rabah Lounisi, "Al-Sira'at al-dakhiliyya l-il-thawra al-Jaza'iriyya f-il-khitab al-ta'rikhi al-Jaza'iri," *Insaniyat* 8, nos. 25–26 (July–December 2004): 39, the revolutionary concern with secrecy and charges of *fitna* persist.

29. In *La guerre commence en Algérie* (Brussels: Éditions Complexe, 1984), Mohammed Harbi talks about three myths of the revolution: that of the tabula rasa, the negation or devalorization of all political struggles prior to 1954; that of the revolution being led by the peasantry; and that of the unanimity of the Algerian people.

30. République algérienne, Présidence de la République, "Les Textes Fondateurs de

la République," www.el-mouradia.dz/francais/symbole/textes/symbolefr.htm (accessed 21 December 2013).

31. Specifically, the references was to the Centralistes and the Messalistes in the Mouvement pour le triomphe des libertés démocratiques (MTLD).

32. République algérienne, Présidence, "Textes Fondateurs" (cited n. 30 above).

33. William B. Quandt, *Revolution and Political Leadership: Algeria, 1954–1968* (Cambridge, MA: MIT Press, 1969), 78.

34. The early nationalist leader Messali Hadj founded the Parti du peuple algérien (PPA) in 1937 and then the Mouvement pour le triomphe des libertés démocratiques (MTLD) in 1946 to replace the PPA, which had been outlawed by the French. A rift in the MTLD over the question of immediate action aimed at liberation led to a split, which ultimately produced the FLN. Shortly after the launching of the revolution, Hadj tried to compete with the FLN by establishing the Mouvement national algérien (MNA).

35. Quandt, *Revolution and Political Leadership*, 97. See also Ali Haroun, *La 7e wilaya: La guerre du FLN en France, 1954–1962* (Algiers: Casbah, 2005).

36. Being called a member of the *hizb fransa* (party of France) has retained a strong negative connotation.

37. I have decided to adopt the French terms for these groups: *arabisants* for those most comfortable using Arabic in formal and professional settings and *francisants* for those most at ease in French.

38. République algérienne, Présidence, "Textes Fondateurs" (cited n. 30 above).

39. During the Liberation War, the Fédération de France du FLN (1955–62) sought to recruit Algerian emigrants resident in France.

40. The Gouvernement provisoire de la République algérienne (GPRA) was proclaimed in Cairo by the FLN on 19 September 1958.

41. Quandt, *Revolution and Political Leadership*, 168.

42. An anti-GPRA coalition emerged behind Ben Bella, which came to be known as the Tlemcen group (named after the city in western Algeria from which or near which some of its key members came, or where they were based immediately after independence); in opposition to Ben Bella a so-called Tizi Ouzou group emerged, taking its name from the key city in Kabylia, although it would be a mistake to see this contest as being primarily Arab vs. Kabyle, since neither group could easily be classified on ethnic grounds. Ibid., 11, 168, 170.

43. Ibid., 171.

44. See Robert Parks, "Local-National Relations and the Politics of Property Rights in Algeria and Tunisia" (PhD diss., University of Texas at Austin, 2011).

45. The French term *autogestion* refers to the "self-management" that began immediately after independence when Algerians seized the factories and farms of the fleeing *pieds-noirs*. A series of decrees between October 1962 and October 1963 institutionalized this.

46. The Armée nationale populaire (ANP) was the post-independence successor of the wartime Armée de libération nationale (ALN).

47. The 1965 coup demonstrated that Ben Bella's constituencies were also quite limited.

48. John Ruedy, *Modern Algeria: The Origins and Development of a Nation* (Bloomington: Indiana University Press, 1992), 202.

49. Roberts, "Politics of Algerian Socialism," 8.

50. République algérienne, Présidence, "Textes Fondateurs" (cited n. 30 above).

51. Ibid.

52. Hadj Ben Alla was a member of the first FLN politbureau.

53. Ruedy, *Modern Algeria*, 203.

54. Ibid., 225.

55. In keeping with the *islahi* narrative, discussed above, the Charte d'Alger's presentation of these early invasions, and resistance to them, parallels the nineteenth-century French invasion.

56. The role of the Ottomans in the narrative is worthy of a separate discussion. Suffice it here to say that there is ambivalence: on the one hand, the "state" that is so central to the Algerian narrative was of Ottoman construction; yet the Turks themselves are generally referred to as outsiders, certainly not central to the identity of the state, and the collapse of the state with the advance of the French is attributed to the weakness of the Turks.

57. Ahmed Bey, the last bey of Constantine (1826–48), who, unlike 'Abd al-Qadir, did have the makings of a state bureaucracy, led a long, bitter struggle against the French. Perhaps it is because he was a *koulougli*, or half "Turk," half "Algerian," that the history of his struggle has been suppressed.

58. République algérienne, Présidence, "Textes Fondateurs" (cited n. 30 above).

59. The paramilitary Organisation de l'armée secrète (OAS: Secret Army Organization) was created in February 1961 to prevent the decolonization of Algeria.

60. Ruedy, *Modern Algeria*, 204–5.

61. Mahfoud Bennoune, *Éducation, culture et développement en Algérie: Bilan et perspectives du système éducatif* (Algiers: Marinoor-ENAG, 2000), 143.

62. Chems Eddine Chitour, *L'éducation et la culture de l'Algérie: Des origins à nos jours* (Algiers: ENAG, 1999), 215.

63. The Étoile nord-africaine (ENA), a nationalist organization founded in Europe by Algerians, among them Messali Hadj, demanded the independence of all of North Africa.

64. Bennoune, *Éducation, culture et développement en Algérie*, 167 and 169.

65. Ibid., 13.

66. Ibid., 225.

67. During my fieldwork in October 2009 in Oran, I heard stories from fifty-somethings about having teachers from Vietnam and Russia. None had Arabic language skills.

68. Mansour Khaled-Khodja, "Population et éducation en Algérie: Bilan et perspectives" (master's thesis, Université d'Essenia, Oran, 2005), 22.

69. Bennoune, *Éducation, culture et développement en Algérie*, 227.

70. In the teaching of French, texts by francophone Algerian authors were introduced for the first time. See Khaled-Khodja, "Population et éducation," 22.

71. *Journal officiel de la République algérienne*, 5 March 1963.

72. Karimah Marzuki, "Al-Adwar al-ijtima'iyya f-il-kitab al-madrasi," (master's thesis, Université d'Oran, 2005–6), 26.

73. Nouria Benghabrit-Remaoun, "École et religion," in *Où va l'Algérie?* ed. Ahmed Mahiou and Jean-Robert Henry (Paris: Karthala and Institut de recherches et d'études du monde arabe et musulman, 2001), 291.

74. Bennoune, *Éducation, culture et développement en Algérie*, 219.

75. Christiane Souriau, "La politique algérienne de l'arabisation," *Annuaire de l'Afrique du Nord, 1975* (Paris: Centre national de la recherche scientifique, 1976), 365.

76. Bennoune, *Éducation, culture et développement en Algérie*, 228–29.

77. Gilbert Grandguillaume, "Les débats et les enjeux linguistiques," in *Où va l'Algerie?* ed. Ahmed Mahiou and Jean-Robert Henry (Paris: Karthala and Institut de recherches et d'études du monde arabe et musulman, 2001), 276.

78. Ruedy, *Modern Algeria*, 224.

79. "Documents: Changement de régime du 19 juin 1965," *Annuaire de l'Afrique du Nord, 1965* (Paris: Centre national de la recherche scientifique, 1966), 627.

80. For example, one can look at the origins of the Algerian state corps via the MALG (Ministère de l'armement et des liaisons générales). Its recruits, the *malgaches*, were usually educated and francophone. After independence, one half entered the administration; the others, the Sécurité militaire, the precursor to the state intelligence service. See Mohamed Lemkani, *Les hommes de l'ombre: Mémoires d'un officier du MALG* (Algiers: ANEP, 2004).

81. Benghabrit-Remaoun, "École et religion," 289.

82. Mohammed Harbi, *L'Algérie et son destin: Croyants ou citoyens* (Paris: Arcantère, 1992), 29.

83. Grandguillaume, "Débats," 279.

84. Souriau, "Politique algérienne de l'arabisation," 373–74.

85. According to Souriau, writing in 1975, it was "an anachronism to label all the Algerian *arabisants* as salafists who lead or frequent mosques and Islamic institutes . . . and there are former madrasa students with degrees in Arabic who have a French education (ibid., 384).

86. Paul Silverstein argues in *Algeria in France: Transpolitics, Race and Nation* (Bloomington: Indiana University Press, 2004), 70, that Boumedienne's regime demonized Berber identity as backward, and as colonialist for have been privileged, if not invented, by the French.

87. Souriau, "Politique algérienne de l'arabisation," 390–91.

88. Grandguillaume, "Débats," 277.

89. Hassan Remaoun, "Pratiques historiographiques et mythes de fondation: Le cas de la Guerre de libération à travers les institutions algériennes d'éducation et de recherché," in *La guerre d'Algérie et les Algériens, 1954–1962*, ed. Charles-Robert Ageron (Paris: Armand Colin, 1997), 315.

90. Fouad Soufi, *Essai de lecture d'un évènement fondateur: Le 1er Novembre 1954* (Oran: Centre de recherche en anthropologie sociale et culturelle, 1996), 3.

91. See DeGeorges "Shifting Sands."

92. www.onm.org.dz (accessed August 12, 2011; no longer accessible).

93. Ibid.

94. Hassan Remaoun, "L'État national et sa mémoire: Le paradigme histoire," in *État des savoirs en sciences sociales et humaines, 1954–2004*, ed. Nouria Benghabrit-Remaou and Mustapha Haddab (Oran: Centre de recherche en anthropologie sociale et culturelle, 2008), 154.

95. Hassan Remaoun, "L'intervention institutionelle et son impact sur la pratique historiographique en Algérie: La politique 'd'Ecriture et de Réécriture de l'histoire,' tendances et contre-tendances" *Insaniyat* 7, nos. 19–20 (January–June 2003): 7–8.

96. Soufi, *Essai de lecture*, 6n18.

97. Ibid., 3.

98. Ibid., 3.

99. Compare with article 40 of the 1963 version noted earlier in the chapter: "Faithful to the principles of the revolution and to the souls of the martyrs, I swear . . . "

100. Fouad Soufi, "En Algérie: L'histoire et sa pratique," in *Savoirs historiques au Maghreb*, ed. Sami Bargaoui and Hassan Remaoun (Oran: Centre de recherche en anthropologie sociale et culturelle, 2006), 132.

101. Edict 72–68 of 2 December 1972.

102. Soufi, "En Algérie," 130.

103. Roberts, "Politics of Algerian Socialism,"11.

104. Ibid., 13.

105. Parks, "Local-National Relations," details how in 1967 and 1969 popular political engagement was undertaken at the local and *wilaya* levels, with disastrous results, which may also explain the reticence regarding extending participation to the national level.

106. For a fuller discussion of the political context in which the 1976 Charte nationale was discussed and issued, see John Entelis, *Algeria: The Revolution Institutionalized* (Boulder, CO: Westview Press, 1986).

107. This also marked the restoration of constitutional rule, which had been suspended since 1965.

108. For the full text, see Nicole Grimaud, *La Charte nationale algérienne (27 juin 1976)* (Paris: Documentation française, 1977).

109. No individuals or political parties of the period were specified. In this way Messali was fully banished and the internecine fighting of the summer of 1962 excised from the narrative.

110. République algérienne, Présidence, "Textes Fondateurs" (cited n. 30 above).

111. Bennoune, *Éducation, culture et développement en Algérie*, 280–82.

112. Ibid., 285.

113. Ibid., 284–5.

114. Ibid., 297.

CHAPTER 5: ALGERIA FROM BENDJEDID TO THE DARK DECADE

1. The Parti de l'avant-garde socialiste, organized in 1966, was the successor to the suppressed Parti communiste algérien (PCA: Algerian Communist Party).

2. Roberts, "Politics of Algerian Socialism," 31.

3. Ibid., 31–32.

4. Ibid., 34.

5. Ruedy, Modern Algeria, 240.

6. Roberts, "Politics of Algerian Socialism," 32.

7. Tizi Ouzou is the second-largest city in Kabylia and the capital and largest city of the Tizi Ouzou province and Greater Kabylia.

8. Roberts, "Politics of Algerian Socialism," 35.

9. Ruedy, *Modern Algeria*, 241.

10. Ibid., 242–43.

11. Mounira Charrad, *States and Women's Rights: The Making of Postcolonial Tunisia, Algeria and Morocco* (Berkeley: University of California Press, 2001), 200.

12. In the Algerian context, the term *mujahidat* refers specifically to female veterans of the 1954–62 national liberation war.

13. The Code was revised in 2005 to grant women more rights in terms of divorce, passing on citizenship to their children, and reducing the role of male guardians.

14. www.onm.org.dz/index.php?option=com_content&task=view&id=45&Item id=91 (accessed August 12, 2011; currently inaccessible).

15. The museum, which was originally dedicated in 1935 as the Musée Demaeght, named after a French commander, an archeologist and epigrapher, who first had the idea of establishing a museum in the city back in 1882, was renamed in 1986.

16. This huge concrete structure is popularly mocked as a *hubl*, a pre-Islamic god worshiped in Mecca.

17. Algerian estimates of the number killed in brutal French reprisals following nationalist demonstrations on 8 May 1945 at the towns of Sétif and Guelma, west of Constantine, run as high as 50,000. See also Alistair Horne, *A Savage War of Peace: Algeria, 1954–62* (New York: Viking, 1978), who suggests that 6,000 might be more accurate.

These bloody events constituted a watershed, leading younger nationalists especially to conclude that revolution, not reform, was the only way forward.

18. The Challe and Morice lines were barriers (consisting of land mines, barbed wire, etc.) created by the French to restrict the movements of the ALN.

19. On the OAS, see chap. 4, n. 59, above.

20. Husayn Hammad, "Dirasa tahliliyya muqarina l-kitabay al-ta'rikh l-il-sana al-niha'iyya (al-bakalawriyus) f-il-Jaza'ir wa-Tunis," in *Comment on enseigne l'histoire en Algérie*, ed. Mohammed Ghalem and Hasssan Remaoun (Oran: Centre de recherche en anthropologie sociale et culturelle, 1995), 78. The textbook he is referring to is *Al-Ta'rikh al-mu'asir* (1983). He says that even the color of the cover remained the same.

21. Its consolidation as early as the 1970s meant that the regime had less to fear from the pre-1954 narrative that valorized the historic leadership of the revolution and devalorized the winners of the 1962–65 period, according to Omar Carlier, "Entre le savant et le politique: La constitution problématique d'un champ historiographique autonome: Le cas de l'histoire nationale du nationalisme algérien" (Édition Centre de recherche en anthropologie sociale et culturelle, 1995), 17.

22. See chap. 4, n. 16.

23. The anachronism is jarring, suggesting that North Africa was Arab before the arrival of the Arabs. This is just one of many anachronisms from which this and other Algerian history texts suffer.

24. When I asked about this combination, a middle school principal told me that the two topics were nonetheless taught by different teachers. Religious education was taught by the same instructor who taught Arabic, while civics was taught by a social studies teacher.

25. *Tarbiya wataniyya* is generally translated simply as "civics." *Tarbiyya* means education or upbringing, while *wataniyya* can have the meaning of both national and patriotic.

26. It is worth noting, however, that the study questions that follow concern only the basic history of the revolution, not any religious aspects or terms (114).

27. The Arabic word *madhhab* (pl. *madhahib*) means "school," in the sense of intellectual approach. It is most often used to refer to the different schools of Islamic law.

28. For the full text, see *Journal officiel de la République algérienne*, 16 February 1986, 97–184.

29. On Sétif, see n. 17 above.

30. The words *musabbalin* and *fida'iyyin* refer to average people who aided or sacrificed themselves for the liberation cause.

31. The suggestion that ancient history can be national is, of course, extremely problematic.

32. Numidia is the name used to refer to the ancient kingdom located in what is present-day eastern Algeria.

33. Remaoun, "Intervention institutionelle," 28.

34. The use of the word *dialecte* also suggests that they are not really distinct languages from Arabic.

35. In a religious frame, *'asabiyya* refers to prejudice produced by group affiliation such as tribalism, racism, or nationalism. It is not always used with a negative connotation.

36. "Maghrib," which refers to the broad region and is the name in Arabic of Morocco, most basically means in Arabic "where the sun sets."

37. Again, note that talking about the Amazigh in the past was now acceptable. The present, however, remained problematic.

38. These are the first four successors to the Prophet Muhammad in leading the Muslim community: Abu Bakr, 'Umar, 'Uthman, and 'Ali.

39. The Rustumid dynasty ruled the central Maghreb from their capital Tahert (or Tiaret) in present-day western Algeria, 777–909 CE.

40. Ruedy, *Modern Algeria*, 251, notes the 1989 Constitution's more explicit language about the Islamic nature of the Algerian state and society than that found in the 1976 Constitution. However, it is a retreat from what was contained in the 1986 Charte nationale.

41. The French term is *ayants droits*, literally, those having rights, as a result of a particular relationship with a specified category of individuals.

42. This is the textbook referred to in n. 20 above. I have to accept Hammad's assessment, since I did not find an earlier version of this book during my research. The fact that it does not discuss anything after the French withdrawal in 1968 from the naval base at Mers-el-Kébir, just west of Oran, would tend to confirm this.

43. The international airport at Tlemcen was inaugurated as the Aéroport international Messali Hadj de Tlemcen during Bouteflika's presidency.

44. The French end-of-high-school baccalauréat exam (*le bac*) determines, not only whether one graduates, but also whether one may go on to college, and in which faculty.

45. Outsiders have generally referred to this period as a civil war in Algeria, but this characterization is not accepted or used by Algerians. Instead, the terms *décennie noire* or *al-'ashriyya al-sawda'*(the dark decade) or *le terrorisme* (terrorism) are used.

46. The assassin, who was one of Boudiaf's bodyguards, claimed he had acted alone, but the episode unleashed myriad conspiracy theories regarding motive and the possibility of military involvement.

47. Rabah Lounissi, "Al-Sira'at al-dakhiliyya l-il-thawra al-Jaza'iriyya f-il-khitab al-ta'rikhi al-Jaza'iri," *Insaniyat* 8, nos. 25–26 (July–December 2004): 33–34.

48. Noureddine Toualbi Thaalibi, *École, idéologie et droits de l'homme*, 2nd ed. (Algiers: Casbah, 2004), 54.

49. *Ta'lim asli* in Arabic.

50. Benghabrit-Remaoun, "École et religion," 291.

51. See Hassan Remaoun, "L'État national et sa mémoire: Le paradigme histoire,"

in *État des savoirs en sciences sociales et humaines, 1954–2004*, ed. Nouria Benghabrit-Remaou and Mustapha Haddab (Oran: Centre de recherche en anthropologie sociale et culturelle, 2008).

52. Ibid., 156.

53. Hassan Remaoun, "Sur l'enseignement de l'histoire en Algérie ou de la crise identitaire à travers (et par) l'école," in *Comment on enseigne l'histoire en Algérie*, ed. Mohammed Ghalem and Hasssan Remaoun (Oran: Centre de recherche en anthropologie sociale et culturelle, 1995), 47–68. Remaoun also shows here that Moroccan texts give much more space to specifically Moroccan history than is the case with Algerian texts and Algerian history.

54. E.g., the 1988–89 first-year secondary text *Al-Mukhtar f-il-tarbiya al-Islamiyya w-al-wataniyya*, which was still in use in 1995; the 1995 eighth-year basic text *Al-Tarbiya al-Islamiyya*; and the 1997–98 seventh-year basic text *Al-Tarbiya al-Islamiyya.*

55. Prior to the introduction of the *école fondamentale* model, pre-secondary texts merged Islamic and civic education, but as this system was implemented, they were separated.

56. Kafi had been appointed HCE president following the assassination of Mohamed Boudiaf in June 1992.

57. The new holidays were 19 March, Victory Day (after 19 March 1962, the proclamation of the cease-fire ending the liberation war); 19 May, Students' Day (after 19 May 1956, when the Union générale des étudiants musulmans algériens, UGEMA, called a national strike); 20 August, National Mujahid Day (after the strikes of 20 August 1955 and 1956); 17 October, Emigration Day (after 17 October 1961, when the French police brutally suppressed Algerian demonstrators in Paris); and 11 December, People's Demonstration Day (after the demonstrations during President de Gaulle's visit to Algiers on 11 December 1960).

58. Guy Pervillé, "Histoire de l'Algérie et mythes politiques algériens: De 'parti de la France' aux 'anciens et nouveaux harkis,'" in *La guerre d'Algérie et les Algériens 1954–1962*, ed. Charles-Robert Ageron (Paris: Armand Colin, 1997), 323.

59. Ibid., 324.

60. Ibid., 325–26.

61. The Aurès is a mountainous region in southeastern Algeria where the Chaoui Berbers live. The Mzab is a plateau region in the northern Algerian Sahara inhabited by tribes who were converted to the Ibadi sect of Islam.

62. Nora Akrouf, "The High Commission for Amazighity (HCA)," www.ee.umd.edu/~sellami/DEC95/HCA.html (accessed 24 February 2014).

63. In the 1980s and early 1990s, the idea that society could demand that the state conform to *shari'a* had gained currency. See Ramdane Babadji, "De la religion comme instrument à l'identité comme sanctuaire: Quelques remarques sur la constitution algérienne du 28 novembre 1996," in *Où va l'Algérie?* ed. Ahmed Mahiou and Jean-Robert

Henry (Paris: Karthala and Institut de recherches et d'études du monde arabe et musulman, 2001), 59 and 66–67.

64. Known as *la famille revolutionnaire*, the members of the Organisation nationale des moudjahidines can be counted on to turn out to vote.

65. Abderrahmane Moussaoui, "La concorde civile en Algérie: Entre mémoire et histoire," in *Où va l'Algérie?* (cited n. 63 above), 73.

66. Remaoun, "État national," 157n12.

67. Another piece of legislation, Law no. 08–04 of 23 January 2008, also concerned the orientation of national education (*Journal officiel de la République algérienne*, 27 January 2008). I was told in March 2011 by a group of Algerian scholars who were working on textbooks that the earlier reform had been pushed through hastily, and that more careful reflection had been needed; hence the 2008 law. That said, a new set of textbooks was issued beginning in 2003. The text of the 2008 law does not represent a significant departure from the 2003 law in terms of elements pertinent to this discussion.

68. Tamazight was elevated to national (but still not official) status according to Law 02–03 of 10 April 2002, promulgated on the same day as the constitutional amendment.

69. *L'éducateur*, no. 1, April–May 2004, "Dossier: La réforme du système éducatif," 7.

70. Ordonnance 03–09 of 13 August 2003 modified article 2 of a 1976 law to read: "the educational system has as a mission—in the framework of the fundamental components of the identity of the Algerian people, which are Islam, Arabism *and Amazighism*" (*Journal officiel de la République algérienne*, 13 August 2003; my emphasis).

71. *L'éducateur*, "Dossier," 7.

72. Ibid., 6.

CHAPTER 6: NARRATIVE RESCRIPTINGS AND LEGITIMACY CRISES

1. I have not included a separate discussion here of the assassination of HCE President Mohamed Boudiaf in 1992 or the transition from the Haut comité d'État to the presidency of Liamine Zeroual in 1994 because these occurred during the period of the internal insurgency.

2. The Algerian army's termination of the democratic experiment in Algeria in 1992 is considered below under the heading "Internal Instability."

3. Johnson, *Islam and the Politics of Meaning*, 4.

4. Articles in *Liberté* on the fifty-eighth anniversary of the launching of the revolution (1 November 2012) suggest that even just a few years out of high school, Algerian students remembered shockingly little from their history courses.

5. Gregory Starrett, *Putting Islam to Work: Education, Politics, and Religious Transformation in Egypt* (Berkeley: University of California Press, 1998); Linda Herrera, "Islamization and Education: Between Politics, Profit and Pluralism," in *Cultures of Arab Schooling: Critical Ethnographies from Egypt, ed.* Herrera and Carlos Alberto Torres (Albany: State University of New York Press, 2006), 25–52; Fida J. Adely, *Gendered Paradoxes: Educating*

Jordanian Women in Nation, Faith and Progress (Chicago: University of Chicago Press, 2012).

6. "According to the World Economic Forum's Global Competitiveness Report 2012–13, Egypt ranked 139th out of 144 countries in the quality of its educational system and 129th in staff training" (www.csmonitor.com/World/Middle-East/2013/0116/Egyptians-begin-to-take-back-their-clunker-classrooms [accessed 9 January 2014]).

EPILOGUE: THE OFFICIAL NARRATIVE AND THE ARAB SPRING

1. *El Watan,* 5 and 8 May 2012.

2. *Liberté,* 21 January 2012. Analyzing the images on the front page of the official *El Moujahid*'s special anniversary (5 July 2012) issue, Thomas Serres argued that they confirmed the traditional place of authority of the "revolutionary family" and the obedience it was owed. On the question of identity, he also noted the presence of an obviously (from her dress) Kabyle woman on the cover, but the portrayal smacked more of folklore than serious identity engagement. See Thomas Serres, "Euphémiser la domination, ce qu'une première page nous apprend sur le régime algérien," *Jadaliyya,* July 22, 2012, www.jadaliyya.com/pages/index/6521/euph%C3%A9miser-la-domination-ce-quune-premi%C3%A8re-page-no (accessed 5 January 2014).

3. Muriam Haleh Davis, "Borders and Bobbing Heads: Postcoloniality and Algeria's Fiftieth Anniversary of Independence," *Jadaliyya,* July 7, 2012, www.jadaliyya.com/pages/index/6330/borders-and-bobbing-heads_postcoloniality-and-alge (accessed 24 February 2014); *El Watan,* 6 July 2012.

4. *El Watan,* 5 July 2012. My translation.

5. Malika Rahal in *El Watan,* 6 July 2012.

6. The demonstrators' chanting of "One, two, where is the Egyptian army?" rhymes in Arabic: "*Wahid, itnayn, al-gaysh al-Masri fayn?*" It is not my intention here to engage in the debate regarding whether what has transpired in Egypt to date constitutes a revolution (cf. Paul Sedra et al., "Roundtable on the Language of Revolution in Egypt," *Jadaliyya,* August 12, 2012, www.jadaliyya.com/pages/index/6552/roundtable-on-the-language-of-revolution-in-egypt [accessed 5 January 2014]). My concern is with the way the story of 25 January–11 February is being presented and configured by state elites.

7. See, e.g., Mary Mourad, "We Will Document Egypt's Revolution, not Dictate the Story: AUC Professor," *Ahram Online,* May 28, 2011, http://english.ahram.org.eg/News/13026.aspx (discussing the work of Khaled Fahmy and others in archiving recent events in Egypt; accessed January 9, 2014).

8. Judy Barsalou, "Recalling the Past: The Battle over History, Collective Memory and Memorialization in Egypt," *Jadaliyya,* June 22, 2012, www.jadaliyya.com/pages/index/6007/recalling-the-past_the-battle-over-history-collect (accessed January 9, 2014).

9. Interview with Dr. Salah 'Arafa, director of the Center for Curriculum and Instructional Materials Development (CCIM), Cairo, 8 June 2011.

10. *Al-Masri al-Yawm*, 12 June 2011.

11. Barsalou, "Recalling the Past."

12. While not on an official level, it is worth noting that the family of General Sa'ad al-Shazly, who had been disgraced by Sadat's claims that he had collapsed during the battle, published his memoirs as a means of trying to set this record straight. Ibid.

13. *Al-Sharq al-Awsat*, 9 October 2011.

14. www.masress.com/tahrirnews/232986; in Arabic (accessed 5 January 2014).

15. *Egypt Independent*, 23 July 2012.

16. *Al-Ahram*, 23 July 2012.

17. *Egypt Independent*, 23 July 2012.

18. *Al-Akhbar English*, 4 October 2012.

19. *Egypt Independent*, 27 November 2012.

20. This is a scarf worn by pious/conservative Muslim women that covers the head, hair, and neck.

21. Al-Masry Al-Youm, "Education Ministry Faces Heat after Deleting Unveiled Feminist from Textbooks," www.egyptindependent.com/print/1382971 (accessed 24 February 2014).

22. The referendum on the new Constitution secured a 63.8 percent favorable vote, but less than one-third of the electorate participated.

23. Article 64 included the martyrs of the 25 January revolution among those whom the state was to honor and whose families were to be supported.

24. Paul Sedra, "Copts and the Power over Personal Status," *Jadaliyya*, December 3, 2012, www.jadaliyya.com/pages/index/8741/copts-and-the-power-over-personal-status (accessed 5 January 2014). Sedra also notes, however, that "those who have expressed concern about the provision largely cite the document's failure to acknowledge members of faith communities apart from Muslims, Christians, and Jews, or those who practice no faith."

25. Rime Naguib, "The President Speaks," www.egyptindependent.com/print/1317751 (accessed 5 January 2014).

SELECT BIBLIOGRAPHY

GENERAL

Adely, Fida J. *Gendered Paradoxes: Educating Jordanian Women in Nation, Faith and Progress.* Chicago: University of Chicago Press, 2012.

Alayan, Samira, and Achim Rohde, eds. *The Politics of Education Reform in the Middle East: Self and Other in Textbooks and Curricula.* New York: Berghahn Books, 2012.

Altinay, Ayşe Gül. *The Myth of the Military-Nation: Militarism, Gender, and Education in Turkey.* New York: Palgrave Macmillan, 2004.

Anagnost, Ann. *National Past-Times: Narrative, Representation and Power in Modern China.* Durham, NC: Duke University Press, 1997.

Anderson, Betty S. *Nationalist Voices in Jordan: The Street and the State.* Austin: University of Texas Press, 2005.

———. "Writing the Nation: Textbooks of the Hashemite Kingdom of Jordan." *Comparative Studies of South Asia, Africa and the Middle East* 21, no. 1 (2005): 5–14.

Bengio, Ofra. *Saddam's Word: Political Discourse in Iraq.* New York: Oxford University Press, 1998.

Berkhoff, Karel C. *Motherland in Danger: Soviet Propaganda during World War II.* Cambridge, MA: Harvard University Press, 2012.

Bhabha, Homi K. *Nation and Narration.* London: Routledge, 1990.

Bora, Tanil. "Nationalist Discourses in Turkey." *South Atlantic Quarterly* 102, no. 2 (2003): 433–51.

Brady, Anne-Marie, ed. *China's Thought Management.* New York: Routledge, 2012.

Burke, Edmund, III. "Theorizing the Histories of Colonialism and Nationalism in the Arab Maghrib." *Arab Studies Quarterly* 20, no. 2 (1998).

Chatterjee, Partha. *The Nation and Its Fragments: Colonial and Postcolonial Histories.* Princeton, NJ: Princeton University Press, 1993.

Davis, Eric. *Memories of State: Politics, History and Collective Identity in Modern Iraq.* Berkeley: University of California Press, 2005.

Dijk, Teun Adrianus van. *Discourse and Power.* New York: Palgrave Macmillan, 2008.

Doumato, Eleanor Abdella, and Gregory Starrett. *Teaching Islam: Textbooks and Religion in the Middle East.* Boulder, CO: Lynne Rienner, 2007.

Duara, Prasenjit. *Rescuing History from the Nation: Questioning Narratives of Modern China.* Chicago: University of Chicago Press, 1995.

Gellner, Ernest. "The Coming of Nationalism and Its Interpretation: The Myths of Nation and Class." In *Mapping the Nation*, ed. Gopal Balakrishnan, 98–145. New York: Verso, 1996.

Guerra, Lillian. *Visions of Power in Cuba: Revolution, Redemption, and Resistance, 1959–1971.* Chapel Hill: University of North Carolina Press, 2012.

Hechter, Michael. *Containing Nationalism.* New York: Oxford University Press, 2001.

Hobsbawm, E. J., and T. O. Ranger, eds. *The Invention of Tradition.* Cambridge: Cambridge University Press, 1984.

İnce, Başak. *Citizenship and Identity in Turkey: From Atatürk's Republic to the Present Day.* New York: I. B. Tauris, 2012.

Johnson, Nels. *Islam and the Politics of Meaning in Palestinian Nationalism.* Boston: Kegan Paul International, 1982.

Kaplan, Sam. *The Pedagogical State: Education and the Politics of National Culture in Post-1980 Turkey.* Stanford: Stanford University Press, 2006.

Kenez, Peter. *The Birth of the Propaganda State: Soviet Methods of Mass Mobilization, 1917–1929.* Cambridge: Cambridge University Press, 1985.

Monger, David. *Patriotism and Propaganda in First World War Britain: The National War Aims Committee and Civilian Morale.* Liverpool: Liverpool University Press, 2012.

Nasser, Riad M. *Palestinian Identity in Jordan and Israel: The Necessary "Others" in the Making of a Nation.* New York: Routledge, 2005.

Peled-Elhanan, Nurit. *Palestine in Israeli School Books: Ideology and Propaganda in Education.* New York: Tauris Academic Studies, 2012.

Perrie, Maureen. *The Cult of Ivan the Terrible in Stalin's Russia.* New York: Palgrave, 2001.

Podeh, Elie. *The Arab-Israeli Conflict in Israeli History Textbooks, 1948–2000.* Westport, CT: Bergin & Garvey, 2002.

———. *The Politics of National Celebrations in the Arab Middle East.* New York: Cambridge University Press, 2011.

Posusney, Marsha Pripstein, and Michele Penner Angrist. *Authoritarianism in the Middle East: Regimes and Resistance.* Boulder, CO: Lynne Rienner, 2005.

Salibi, Kamal. *A House of Many Mansions: The History of Lebanon Reconsidered.* Berkeley: University of California Press, 1988.

Sassoon, Anne Showstack. *Gramsci's Politics.* Minneapolis: University of Minnesota Press, 1987.

Shlaim, Avi. "The Debate about 1948." *International Journal of Middle East Studies* 27, no. 3 (1995): 287–304.

Smith, Anthony D. "Nationalism and the Historians." In *Mapping the Nation*, ed. Gopal Balakrishnan, 175–97. New York: Verso, 1996.

Stanard, Matthew G. *Selling the Congo: A History of European Pro-Empire Propaganda and the Making of Belgian Imperialism.* Lincoln: University of Nebraska Press, 2011.

Sutherland, Claire. "Nation-Building through Discourse Theory." *Nations and Nationalism* 11, no. 2 (2005): 185–202.

Verdery, Kathleen. "Whither 'Nation' and 'Nationalism.'" In *Mapping the Nation*, ed. Gopal Balakrishnan, 226–34. New York: Verso, 1996.

Weber, Max. *The Theory of Social and Economic Organization.* Translated by Alexander Morell Henderson and Talcott Parsons. New York: Free Press, 1964.

Wedeen, Lisa. *Ambiguities of Domination: Politics, Rhetoric, and Symbols in Contemporary Syria.* Chicago: University of Chicago Press, 1999.

Wertsch, James V. *Voices of Collective Remembering.* Cambridge: Cambridge University Press, 2002.

Yadgar, Yaacov. "From the Particularistic to the Universalistic: National Narratives in Israel's Mainstream Press, 1967–97." *Nations and Nationalism* 8, no. 1 (2002): 55–72.

Zerubavel, Yael. *Recovered Roots: Collective Memory and the Making of Israeli National Tradition.* Chicago: University of Chicago Press, 1995.

ALGERIA

Books and Articles

Abdoun, Rabah. "Algeria: The Problem of Nation-Building." In *Adjustment or Delinking: The African Experience*, ed. A. Mahjoub. London: Zed Books, 1990.

Abi 'Ayad, Ahmed. "Al-Ta'rikh Al-Jaza'iri - taqyim wa-naqd: Halat Al-Jaza'ir Al-'Uthmaniyya." *Insaniyat* 14, no. 47–48 (January–June 2010): 57–75.

Ainad Tabet, Redouane. "Manuels d'histoire et discours idéologique véhiculé." In *Comment on enseigne l'histoire en Algérie*, ed. Mohamed Ghalem and Hassan Remaoun, 35–45. Oran: Centre de recherche en anthropologie sociale et culturelle, 1995.

Ait Amara, Hamid. "La nation et l'État." In *État des savoirs en sciences sociales et humaines, 1954–2004*, ed. Nouria Benghabrit-Remaou and Mustapha Haddab, 247–52. Oran: Centre de recherche en anthropologie sociale et culturelle, 2008.

Babadji, Ramdane. "De la religion comme instrument à l'identité comme sanctuaire: Quelques remarques sur la constitution algérienne du 28 novembre 1996." In *Où va l'Algérie?* ed. Ahmed Mahiou and Jean-Robert Henry, 53–70. Paris: Karthala and Institut de recherches et d'études du monde arabe et musulman, 2001.

Benghabrit-Remaoun, Nouria. "École et religion." In *Où va l'Algérie?* ed. Ahmed Mahiou and Jean-Robert Henry, 289–302. Paris: Karthala and Institut de recherches et d'études du monde arabe et musulman, 2001.

Bennoune, Mahfoud. *Éducation, culture et développement en Algérie: Bilan et perspectives du système éducatif. Étude des modèles Allemagne, Amérique, Japon. . . .* 2 vols. Algiers: Marinoor-ENAG, 2000.

Carlier, Omar. "Mémoire, mythe et doxa de l'État en Algérie." *XXème Siècle*, no. 30 (1991): 82–91.

———. "Entre le savant et le politique: La constitution problématique d'un champ historiographique autonome: Le cas de l'histoire nationale du nationalisme algérien." Édition Centre de recherche en anthropologie sociale et culturelle, 1995.

Cheriet, Abdellah. *Opinion sur la politique de l'enseignement et de l'arabisation.* Algiers: Société nationale d'édition et de diffusion, 1983.

Chitour, Chems Eddine. *L'éducation et la culture de l'Algérie: Des origins à nos jours.* Algiers: ENAG, 1999.

DeGeorges, Thomas. "The Shifting Sands of Revolutionary Legitimacy: The Role of Former *Mujahidin* in the Shaping of Algeria's Collective Memory." *Journal of North African Studies* 14, no. 2 (2009): 273–88.

Entelis, John P. *Algeria: The Revolution Institutionalized.* Boulder, CO: Westview Press, 1986.

Ghalem, Mohammed. "F-il-wataniyya w-al-ta'rikh: Dirasa hawl al-usus al-nazariyya li-kitab: 'Ta'rikh Al-Jaza'ir f-il-madi w-al-hadir,' ta'lif al-Shaykh Mubarak al-Mili." Oran: Centre de recherche en anthropologie sociale et culturelle, 1995.

———. "Historiographie algérienne du XVIIIème siècle: Savoir historique et mode de légitimation politique." In *Savoirs historiques au Maghreb*, ed. Sami Bargaoui and Hassan Remaoun, 115–21. Oran: Centre de recherche en anthropologie sociale et culturelle, 2006.

Ghalem, Mohammed, Ahmad Karrumi, and Muhammad 'Addah Jalul. "Al-Sulta w-al-ma'rifa fi haql al-'ulum al-insaniyya—al-ta'rikh, al-falsafa, w-al-qanun." In *Actes des journées scientifiques de présentation des résultats de recherche des projets PNR: Population et société*, 45–77. Oran: Centre de recherche en anthropologie sociale et culturelle, 2006.

Grandguillaume, Gilbert. "Les débats et les enjeux linguistiques." In *Où va l'Algerie?* ed. Ahmed Mahiou and Jean-Robert Henry, 273–87. Paris: Karthala and Institut de recherches et d'études du monde arabe et musulman, 2001.

Grimaud, Nicole. *La Charte nationale algérienne (27 juin 1976).* Paris: Documentation française, 1977.

Haddab, Mustapha. "Statut social de l'histoire: Éléments de réflexion." In *Comment on enseigne l'histoire en Algérie*, ed. Mohamed Ghalem and Hassan Remaoun, 15–33. Oran: Centre de recherche en anthropologie sociale et culturelle, 1995.

Hammad, Husayn. "Dirasa tahliliyya muqarana li-kitabay al-ta'rikh l-il-sana al-niha'iyya (al-bakalawriyus) f-il-Jaza'ir wa-Tunis." In *Comment on enseigne l'histoire en Algérie*, ed. Mohammed Ghalem and Hassan Remaoun, 77–95. Oran: Centre de recherche en anthropologie sociale et culturelle, 1995.

Hannoum, Abdel-Majid. *Colonial Histories, Post-Colonial Memories: The Legend of the Kahina, a North African Heroine.* New York: Heinemann, 2001.

———. "Faut-il brûler l'Orientalisme? On French Scholarship of North Africa." *Cultural Dynamics* 16, no. 1 (2004): 71–91.

———. "Writing Algeria: On the History and Culture of Colonialism." *Maghreb Center Journal*, no. 1 (Spring–Summer 2010): 1–19.

Harbi, Mohammed. *L'Algérie et son destin: Croyants ou citoyens*. Paris: Arcantère, 1992.

Haroun, Ali. *La 7e wilaya: La guerre du FLN en France, 1954–1962*. Algiers: Casbah, 2005.

Horne, Alistair. *A Savage War of Peace: Algeria, 1954–62* (New York: Viking, 1978).

Khaled-Khodja, Mansour. "Population et éducation en Algérie: Bilan et perspectives." Master's thesis, Université d'Essenia, Oran, 2005.

Lemkani, Mohamed. *Les hommes de l'ombre: Mémoires d'un officier du MALG*. Algiers: ANEP, 2004.

Lounissi, Rabah. "Al-Sira'at al-dakhiliyya l-il-thawra al-Jaza'iriyya f-il-khitab al-ta'rikhi al-Jaza'iri." *Insaniyat* 8, no. 25–26 (July–December 2004): 27–42.

Marzuki, Karimah. "Al-Adwar al-ijtima'iyya f-il-kitab al-madrasi." Master's thesis, Université d'Oran, 2005–2006.

Mazouni, Abdallah. *Culture et enseignement en Algérie et au Maghreb*. Paris: François Maspero, 1969.

McDougall, James. *History and the Culture of Nationalism in Algeria*. New York: Cambridge University Press, 2006.

———. "Martyrdom and Destiny: The Inscription and Imagination of Algerian History." In *Memory and Violence in the Middle East and North Africa*, ed. Ussama Makdisi and Paul A. Silverstein, 50–72. Bloomington: Indiana University Press, 2006.

Morizot, Jean. *Les Kabyles: Propos d'un témoin*. Paris: Centre de hautes études sur l'Afrique et l'Asie modernes, 1985.

Moussaoui, Abderrahmane. "La concorde civile en Algérie: Entre mémoire et histoire." In *Où va l'Algérie?* ed. Ahmed Mahiou and Jean-Robert Henry, 71–92. Paris: Karthala and Institut de recherches et d'études du monde arabe et musulman, 2001.

Naylor, Phillip C. *Historical Dictionary of Algeria*. 3rd ed. Lanham, MD: Scarecrow Press, 2006.

Parks, Robert P. "Local-National Relations and the Politics of Property Rights in Algeria and Tunisia." PhD diss., University of Texas at Austin, 2011.

Pervillé, Guy. "Histoire de l'Algérie et mythes politiques algériens: De 'parti de la France' aux 'anciens et nouveaux harkis.'" In *La guerre d'Algérie et les Algériens, 1954–1962*, ed. Charles-Robert Ageron, 323–31. Paris: Armand Colin, 1997.

Quandt, William B. *Revolution and Political Leadership: Algeria 1954–1968*. Cambridge, MA: MIT Press, 1969.

Quraynik (Guerinik), Ahmad. "Mawqif al-talmidh min maddat al-ta'rikh f-il-sana al-tasi'a asasi." In *Comment on enseigne l'histoire en Algérie*, ed. Mohamed Ghalem and Hassan Remaoun, 27–66. Oran: Centre de recherche en anthropologie sociale et culturelle, 1995.

Remaoun, Hassan. "Sur l'enseignement de l'histoire en Algérie ou de la crise identitaire à travers (et par) l'école." In *Comment on enseigne l'histoire en Algérie*, ed. Mohammed Ghalem and Hasssan Remaoun, 47–68. Oran: Centre de recherche en anthropologie sociale et culturelle, 1995.

———. "Al-Ta'rikh al-watani w-al-mumarisat al-siyasiyya w-al-intima' al-hawiyyatiyya: qira'a f-il-kutub al-madrasiyya al-mutadawila f-il-madrasa al-Jaza'iriyya." *Insaniyat*, no. 3 (Winter 1997): 7–33.

———. "Pratiques historiographiques et mythes de fondation: Le cas de la Guerre de libération à travers les institutions algériennes d'éducation et de recherche." In *La guerre d'Algérie et les Algériens, 1954–1962*, ed. Charles-Robert Ageron, 305–21. Paris: Armand Colin, 1997.

———. "La question de l'histoire dans le débat sur la violence en Algérie." *Insaniyat*, no. 10 (January–June 2000): 31–44.

———. "L'intervention institutionelle et son impact sur la pratique historiographique en Algérie: La politique 'd'Écriture et de Réécriture de l'histoire,' tendances et contre-tendances." *Insaniyat*, nos. 19–20 (January–June 2003): 7–40.

———. "Les historiens algériens issus du Mouvement national." *Insaniyat*, no. 25–26 (July–December 2004): 225–38.

———. "Les pratiques historiographiques dans l'Algérie post-independante et leurs relations aux traditions historiographiques coloniale et nationaliste." In *Savoirs historiques au Maghreb*, ed. Sami Bargaoui and Hassan Remaoun, 147–58. Oran: Centre de recherche en anthropologie sociale et culturelle, 2006.

———. "Sciences sociales, pratiques historiographiques et politique dans le monde arabe contemporain: Le cas de l'Algérie." *Insaniyat*, no. 32–33 (April–September 2006): 231–46.

———. "L'enseignement de la Guerre de libération nationale (1954–1962) dans les anciens et nouveaux manuels algériens d'histoire. Un enjeu pour l'affirmation d'une culture de la citoyenneté." *Tréma*, no. 29 (March 2008): 1–13.

———. "L'État national et sa mémoire: Le paradigme histoire." In *État des savoirs en sciences sociales et humaines, 1954–2004*, ed. Nouria Benghabrit-Remaoun and Mustapha Haddab, 149–66. Oran: Centre de recherche en anthropologie sociale et culturelle, 2008.

Roberts, Hugh. "The Politics of Algerian Socialism." In *North Africa: Contemporary Politics and Economic Development*, ed. Richard I. Lawless and Allan Findlay, 5–49. New York: St. Martin's Press, 1984.

Rouadjia, Ahmed. *Les frères et la mosquée: Enquête sur le movement islamiste en Algérie.* Paris: Karthala, 1990.

Rouighi, Ramzi. "Andalusi Origins of the Berbers." *Journal of Medieval Iberian Studies* 2, no. 1 (January 2010): 93–108.

———. "The Berbers of the Arabs." *Studia Islamica*, no. 1 (2011): 67–101.

Ruedy, John. *Modern Algeria: The Origins and Development of a Nation*. Bloomington: Indiana University Press, 1992.

Salhi, Mohammed Brahim. *Algérie: Citoyenneté et identité*. Algiers: Achab, 2010.

Scheele, Judith. *Village Matters: Knowledge, Politics and Community in Kabylia, Algeria*. London: James Currey, 2009.

Silverstein, Paul A. *Algeria in France: Transpolitics, Race and Nation*. Bloomington: Indiana University Press, 2004.

Soufi, Fouad. *Essai de lecture d'un évènement fondateur: Le 1er Novembre 1954*. Oran: Centre de recherche en anthropologie sociale et culturelle, 1996.

———. "Les archives: Une problématique patrimonialisation." *Insaniyat*, no. 12 (September–December 2000): 129–48.

———. "En Algérie: L'histoire et sa pratique." In *Savoirs historiques au Maghreb*, ed. Sami Bargaoui and Hassan Remaoun, 123–57. Oran: Centre de recherche en anthropologie sociale et culturelle, 2006.

Souriau, Christiane. "La politique algérienne de l'arabisation." *Annuaire de l'Afrique du Nord* 14 (1975): 363–401.

Stora, Benjamin. "Algérie: Les retours de la mémoire de la guerre d'indépendence." *Modern and Contemporary France* 10, no. 4 (2002): 461–73.

———. "L'historie de l'Algérie, sources, problèmes, écritures." *Insaniyat* 8, no. 25–26 (July–December 2004): 215–24.

Tengour, Ouanassa Siari. "Dits et non dits dans les mémoires de quelques acteurs de la guerre d'Algérie." In *Savoirs historiques au Maghreb*, ed. Sami Bargaoui and Hassan Remaoun, 159–80. Oran: Centre de recherche en anthropologie sociale et culturelle, 2006.

Thaalibi, Noureddine Toualbi. *École, idéologie et droits de l'homme*. 2nd ed. Algiers: Casbah, 2004.

Werenfels, Isabelle. *Managing Instability in Algeria: Elites and Political Change since 1995*. New York: Routledge, 2007.

Zayid, Mustafa. *Al-Tanmiya al-ijtima'iyya wa-nizam al-ta'lim al-rasmi f-il-Jaza'ir, 1962–1980*. Algiers: Diwan al-Matbu'at al-Jami'iyya, 1986.

Algerian School Textbooks

Al-Ta'rikh al-hadith, 1453–1815. Third-year secondary school, 1970.

Ta'rikh al-'Arab al-hadith. Sixth-year secondary school, 1970s.

Ta'rikh al-'Arab al-hadith w-al-'alam. Second-year secondary school, 1979–80.

Ta'rikh al-'alam al-hadith. First-year secondary school, 1979–80.

Ta'rikh al-Qurūn al-Wusta. Second-year middle school, 1983–84.

Al-Ta'rikh al-hadith, 1453–1815. Third-year middle school, 1983–84.

Kitab al-ta'rikh. First-year middle school, 1980s.

Ta'rikh al-hadarat al-qadimah. First-year middle school, date uncertain, early 1980s.

Al-Mukhtar f-il-tarbiya al-Islamiyya w-al-wataniyya. Third-year middle school, 1984–85.
Al-Mukhtar f-il-tarbiya al-Islamiyya w-al-wataniyya. Fourth-year middle school, 1985–86.
Al-Mukhtar f-il-tarbiya al-Islamiyya w-al-wataniyya. Seventh-year basic school, 1985–86.
Al-Ta'rikh. Seventh-year basic school, 1986–87.
Al-Ta'rikh. Eighth-year basic school, 1986–-87.
Al-Tarbiya al-Islamiyya. Ninth-year basic school, 1987 or 1988.
Ta'rikh al-'Arab al-hadith w-al-'alam, 1516–1939. Second-year secondary school, 1987–88.
Al-Mukhtar f-il-tarbiya al-Islamiyya w-al-wataniyya. First-year secondary school, 1988–89.
Ta'rikh al-'alam al-hadith. First-year secondary school, 1988–89.
Ta'rikh al-Maghrib al-'Arabi al-hadith. Ninth-year basic school, 1988–89.
Al-Ta'rikh al-mu'asir. Final-year secondary school, 1990–91.
Al-Ta'rikh. Fifth-year basic school, 1992–93.
Al-Ta'rikh. Sixth-year basic school, 1992–93.
Al-Ta'rikh. Ninth-year basic school, 1992–93.
Al-Tarbiya al-Islamiyya. Eighth-year basic school, 1995.
Al-Tarbiya al-Islamiyya. Seventh-year basic school, 1997–98.
Kitab al-ta'rikh. Seventh-year basic school, 1998–99.
Al-Tarbiya al-Islamiyya. Seventh-year basic school, 2001–2.
Al-Tarbiya al-Islamiyya. Eighth-year basic school, 2001–2.
Al-Tarbiya al-wataniyya. Ninth-year basic school, 2002–2003.
Al-Tarbiya al-wataniyya. First-year middle school, 2003.
Al-Tarbiya al-Islamiyya. First-year middle school, 2003.
Kitab al-'ulum al-shar'iyya. Second-year secondary school, 2003–4.
Al-Tarbiya al-wataniyya. Second-year middle school, 2004.
Al-Mufid f-il-tarbiya al-Islamiyya. Second-year middle school, 2004.
Kitab f-il-ta'rikh. Fifth-year basic school, 2004–2005.
Kitab al-ta'rikh. First-year middle school, 2004, 2008–9.
Kitab al-ta'rikh, parts one and two. Second-year middle school, 2004.
Al-Jadid f-il-tarbiya al-madaniyya. Third-year middle school, 2005.
Al-Mufid f-il-tarbiya al-Islamiyya. Third-year middle school, 2005.
Kitab al-ta'rikh. Third-year secondary school, 2005.
Al-Tarbiya al-Islamiyya. Third-year middle school, 2005.
Al-Munir f-il-'ulum al-Islamiyya. First-year secondary school, 2005–6.
Kitab al-ta'rikh. Fourth-year middle school, 2006.
Al-Ta'rikh. Second-year secondary school, 2006.
Al-Jadid f-il-tarbiya al-madaniyya. Fourth-year middle school, 2006.
Al-Tarbiya al-Islamiyya. Fourth-year middle school, 2006.
Al-Wadih f-il-'ulum al-Islamiyya. Second-year secondary school, 2006.
Al-Tarbiya al-Islamiyya. Sixth-year basic, school 2006–8.

Al-Mufid f-il-tarbiya al-Islamiyya. Second-year middle school, 2006–7.
Al-Mufid f-il-tarbiya al-Islamiyya. Fourth-year middle school, 2006–7.
Al-Mufid f-il-'ulum al-Islamiyya. Third-year secondary school, 2007.
Kitab al-ta'rikh. Third-year middle school, 2007–8.
Kitab al-ta'rikh. Second-year middle school, 2008–9.

Algerian Speeches and Government Documents

République algérienne, Secrétariat général du gouvernement. Texts of all laws and the National Charters of 1976 and 1986, www.joradp.dz/HFR/Index.htm (accessed 21 December 2013).

———. Présidence de la République. "Les Textes Fondateurs de la République," www.el-mouradia.dz/francais/symbole/textes/symbolefr.htm (accessed 21 December 2013):
La proclamation du 1er Novembre 1954
La Déclaration du Congrès de la Soummam (1956)
La Déclaration du Congrès de Tripoli (June 1962)
La Charte d'Alger (April 1964)
Constitution de 1963
Constitution de 1976
Révision constitutionnelle de 1988
Constitution de 1989
Constitution de 1996
Révision constitutionnelle de 2002
Révision constitutionnelle de 2008

EGYPT

Books and Articles

'Abd al-Ghaffar, Ihlam Rajab. *Ta'rikh al-tarbiya wa-nizam al-ta'lim fi Misr.* Cairo: Dar al-Thaqafa l-il-Tiba'a w-al-Nashr, 1991.

'Abd al-Naṣir, Gamal. *Falsafat al-thawra.* 1953. Cairo: Maktabat Madbuli, 2005.

'Ali, Sa'id Isma'il. *Al-Hawiyya w-al-ta'lim.* Cairo: 'Alam al-Kitab, 2005.

'Ammar, Hamid. *Al-Siyaq al-ta'rikhi li-tatwir al-ta'lim al-Misri.* Cairo: Maktabat al-Dar al-'Arabiyya li-l-Kitab, 2005.

'Ashur, 'Isam. *Al-Dasatir al-Misriyya 'abr al-ta'rikh, 1837–2011 rihlat nidal.* Cairo: Dar Mirit, 2011.

Al-Ayyubi, Nazih Nasif. *Siyasat al-ta'lim fi Misr: dirasa siyasiyya wa-idariyya.* Cairo: Al-Ahram Center for Political and Strategic Studies, 1978.

Al-Dasatir al-Misriyya, 1805–1971: nusus wa tahlil. Cairo: Al-Ahram, Markaz al-Tanzim w-al-Mikrufilm, 1977.

Al-Qabbani, Isma'il Mahmud. *Dirasat fi tanzim al-ta'lim bi-Misr.* Cairo: Maktabat al-Nahda al-Misriyya, 1958.

Andrawus, Amal. *Al-Siyasat al-ta'limiyya fi Misr*. Cairo: Dar Farha l-il-Nashr w-al-Tawzi', 2004.

Baker, Raymond William. *Egypt's Uncertain Revolution under Nasser and Sadat*. Cambridge, MA: Harvard University Press, 1978.

Beattie, Kirk J. *Egypt during the Nasser Years: Ideology, Politics and Civil Society*. Boulder, CO: Westview Press, 1994.

Boktor, Amir. *The Development and Expansion of Education in the United Arab Republic*. Cairo: American University in Cairo Press, 1963.

Brownlee, Jason. *Authoritarianism in an Age of Democratization*. New York: Cambridge University Press, 2007.

———. *Democracy Prevention: The Politics of the U.S.-Egyptian Alliance*. New York: Cambridge University Press, 2012.

Cochran, Judith. *Educational Roots of Political Crisis in Egypt*. Lanham, MD: Lexington Books, 2008.

Colla, Elliott. *Conflicted Antiquities: Egyptology, Egyptomania, Egyptian Modernity*. Durham, NC: Duke University Press, 2007.

Dekmejian, R. Hrair. *Egypt under Nasir: A Study in Political Dynamics*. Albany: State University of New York Press, 1971.

Di-Capua, Yoav. *Gatekeepers of the Arab Past: Historians and History Writing in Twentieth-Century Egypt*. Berkeley: University of California Press, 2009.

El Shakry, Omnia. *The Great Social Laboratory: Subjects of Knowledge in Colonial and Postcolonial Egypt*. Stanford: Stanford University Press, 2007.

Fahmy, Khaled. *All the Pasha's Men: Mehmed Ali, His Army and the Making of Modern Egypt*. Cairo: American University in Cairo Press, 2002.

Farag, Iman. "La construction sociale d'une éducation nationale: Enjeux politiques et trajectoires éducatives." PhD diss., École des hautes études en sciences sociales, 1999.

Gershoni, Israel, and James P. Jankowski. *Redefining the Egyptian Nation 1930–1945*. New York: Cambridge University Press, 1995.

Gordon, Joel. *Revolutionary Melodrama: Popular Film and Civic Identity in Nasser's Egypt*. Chicago: Middle East Documentation Center, 2002.

Gorman, Anthony. *Historians, State and Politics in Twentieth Century Egypt: Contesting the Nation*. New York: Routledge Curzon, 2010.

Hegazy, Hoda Abdel Samea. "Values and Attitudes Expressed in Egyptian Primary School Readers: A Comparative Study of the Pre-1952 and the 1970 Readers." PhD diss., Rutgers University, 1980.

Herrera, Linda. "Islamization and Education: Between Politics, Profit and Pluralism." In *Cultures of Arab Schooling: Critical Ethnographies from Egypt*, ed. Linda Herrera and Carolos Alberto Torres, 25–52. Albany: State University of New York Press, 2006.

Hijja, Ahmad Isma'il. *Al-Ta'rikh al-thaqafi l-il-ta'lim fi Misr*. Cairo: Dar al-Fikr al-'Arabi, 2002.

Hilal, 'Isam al-Din 'Ali, and Muhammad Ibrahim al-Minufi. *Al-Tarbiya al-siyasiyya l-il-tifl al-Misri.* Cairo: Dar Farha l-il-Nashr w-al-Tawzi', 2005.

Hinnebusch, Raymond A. *Egyptian Politics under Sadat: The Post-Populist Development of an Authoritarian-Modernizing State.* New York: Cambridge University Press, 1985.

Hyde, Georgie D.M. *Education in Modern Egypt: Ideals and Realities.* Boston: Routledge & Kegan Paul, 1978.

Ibrahim, Majdi 'Aziz. *Tatwir al-ta'lim fi 'asr al-'awlama.* Cairo: Anglo-Egyptian, 2000.

Kandil, Hazem. *Soldiers, Spies, and Statesmen: Egypt's Road to Revolt.* London: Verso, 2012.

Khudr, Muhsin. *Al-Ittijah al-qawmi al-'Arabi f-il-ta'lim al-Misri 1952–1981.* Cairo: Al-Hay'a al-Misriyya al-'Amma l-il-Kitab, 1992.

Mina, Fayiz Murad. *Al-Ta'lim fi Misr: al-waqi' w-al-mustaqbal hatta 'Am 2020.* Cairo: Anglo-Egyptian Bookstore, 2001.

Mughayth, Kamal, ed. *Al-Ta'lim wa-tahaddiyat al-hawiyya al-qawmiyya.* Cairo: Dar al-Mahrusa, 1998.

Mughayth, Kamal, and Ilham 'Abd al-Hamid. *Al-Ta'lim wa-huquq al-insan.* Cairo: LRRC, 1997.

Qandil, Amani. *Siyasat al-ta'lim fi Wadi al-Nil w-al-Sumal wa-Jibuti.* Cairo: Muntada al-Fikr al-'Arabi, 1989.

Reid, Donald Malcolm. *Whose Pharaohs? Archaeology, Museums and Egyptian National Identity from Napoleon to World War I.* Berkeley: University of California Press, 2002.

Sayed, Fatema H. *Transforming Education in Egypt: Western Influence and Domestic Policy Reform.* Cairo: American University in Cairo Press, 2006.

Shivtel, Shlomit Shraybom. "Language and Political Change in Modern Egypt." *International Journal of the Sociology of Language,* no. 137 (1999): 131–40.

Smith, Charles D. "Imagined Identities, Imagined Nationalism: Print Culture and Egyptian Nationalism in Light of Recent Scholarship." Review of *Redefining the Egyptian Nation, 1930–1945,* by Israel Gershoni and James P. Jankowski. *International Journal of Middle East Studies* 29, no. 4 (November 1997): 607–22.

Stacher, Joshua. *Adaptable Autocrats: Regime Power in Egypt and Syria.* Stanford: Stanford University Press, 2012.

Starrett, Gregory. *Putting Islam to Work: Education, Politics, and Religious Transformation in Egypt.* Berkeley: University of California Press, 1998.

Vatikiotis, P. J. *The Modern History of Egypt: From Muhammad Ali to Mubarak.* 4th ed. Baltimore: Johns Hopkins University Press, 1991.

Egyptian School Textbooks

Ta'rikh Misr f-il-'asr al-hadith. Secondary school, 1954.

Al-Tarbiya al-wataniyya. Fifth-year elementary school, 1956.

Ta'rikh al-'alam al-'Arabi f-il-'asr al-hadith. Secondary school, 1956.

Al-Tarbiya al-wataniyya. Sixth-year elementary school, 1957.

Al-Tarbiya al-wataniyya. Fourth-year preparatory school, 1957.
Al-Talmidh wa-watanuhu. Second-year preparatory school, 1961.
Ta'rikh al-'Arab al-hadith w-al-mu'asir. Third-year secondary school, 1962.
Al-Talmidh wa-watanuhu. Second-year preparatory school, 1964.
Al-Mawwad al-ijtima'iyya, al-jiyughrafiya w-al-ta'rikh w-al-tarbiya al-wataniyya. Fifth-year elementary school, 1967.
Ta'rikh al-'Arab al-hadith w-al-mu'asir. Third-year secondary school, 1969.
Al-Tarbiya al-qawmiyya. Third-year preparatory school, 1971.
Ta'rikh al-'Arab al-hadith w-al-mu'asir. Third-year secondary school, 1974.
Ta'rikh al-'Arab al-hadith w-al-mu'asir. Third-year secondary school, 1975.
Ta'rikh al-'Arab al-hadith w-al-mu'asir. Third-year secondary school, 1977.
Al-Tarbiya al-qawmiyya, Jumhuriyyat Misr al-'Arabiyya w-al-'alam al-mu'asir. Third-year preparatory school, 1978.
Al-Tarbiya al-qawmiyya, Jumhuriyyat Misr al-'Arabiyya w-al-'alam al-mu'asir. Third-year preparatory school, 1980.
Ta'rikh al-'Arab al-hadith w-al-mu'asir. Third-year secondary school, 1986.
Al-Tarbiya al-wataniyya, al-dawla al-'asriyya, dawlat al-'ilm w-al-tanmiya. Part one. First-year secondary school, 1987–88.
Al-Tarbiya al-wataniyya, al-dawla al-'asriyya. Part two. First-year secondary school, 1987–88.
Al-Tarbiya al-wataniyya, tanmiyat al-mujtama' al-Misri. First-year secondary school, 1988–89.
Al-Tarbiya al-wataniyya, al-shakhsiyya al-Misriyya. Part three. Third-year secondary school, 1988–89.
Al-Tarbiya al-wataniyya, yaqizat al-mujtami' al-Misri. Second-year secondary school, 1990–91.
Ta'rikh Misr w-al-'Arab al-hadith. Third-year secondary school, 1991–92.
Al-Tarbiya al-wataniyya, Misr wa-dawruha al-hadari. First-year secondary school, 1994–95.
Al-Ta'rikh. General secondary school (*thanawiyya 'ammah*), 1995–96.
Al-Tarbiya al-wataniyya, al-dawr al-hadari l-il-mujtami' al-Misri. Second-year secondary school, 2005–6.
Al-Dirasat al-ijtima'iyya, zawahir tabi'iyya wa-hadara Misriyya. First-year preparatory school, first semester, 2008–9.
Al-Dirasat al-ijtima'iyya, zawahir tabi'iyya wa-hadara Misriyya. First-year preparatory, school second semester, 2008–9.
Al-Dirasat al-ijtima'iyya, watanuna al-'Arabi, zawahir jiyughrafiyya wa-hadara Islamiyya. Second-year preparatory school, first semester, 2009–10.
Al-Dirasat al-ijtima'iyya, watanuna al-'Arabi, zawahir jiyughrafiyya wa-hadara Islamiyya. Second-year preparatory school, second semester, 2009–10.

Al-Dirasat al-ijtima'iyya, jiyughrafiyat al-'alam wa-ta'rikh Misr al-hadith. Third-year preparatory school, first semester, 2010.
Al-Dirasat al-ijtima'iyya: jiyughrafiyat al-'alam wa-ta'rikh Misr al-hadith. Third-year preparatory school, second semester, 2010.

Egyptian Speeches and Government Documents

Mubarak, President Muhammad Husni. 1997. Speech on the occasion of the 45th anniversary of the July 23rd revolution.
———. 2000. Address to the nation on the occasion of 23rd July 1952 Revolution.
———. 2003. Statement on the 51st anniversary of the 23 July Revolution.
———. 2006. Statement on the 54th anniversary of the July Revolution.
———. 2010. Speech at the 58th anniversary of the Glorious July 23rd Revolution.
Abdel Nasser, President Gamal. "President Gamal Abd El Nasser: Plastic and Applied Arts." Bibliotheca Alexandrina. All referenced stamps. http://nasser.bibalex.org/NasserCulture/Arts_Main.aspx?x=7&TP=0&CS=0&lang=en (accessed 21 December 2013).
———. "President Gamal Abd El Nasser: Speeches." *Bibliotheca Alexandrina.* http://nasser.bibalex.org/Speeches/SpeechesAll.aspx?CS=0&lang=ar (accessed 21 December 2013):
26 July 1956, "Khitab al-Ra'is Gamal 'Abd al-Nasir, khitab ta'mim Qanat al-Suways"
5 February 1958, "Kalimat al-Ra'is Gamal 'Abd al-Nasir fi Majlis al-Umma bi-munasibat i'lan usus al-wahda bayna Misr wa-Suriya"
22 July 1961, "Khitab al-Ra'is Gamal 'Abd al-Nasir fi 'Id al-Thawra al-tasi'"
28 September 1961, "Bayan al-Ra'is Gamal 'Abd al-Nasir, al-bayan al-awwal yawm al-infisal 'an Suriya"
28 September 1961, "Bayan al-Ra'is Gamal 'Abd al-Nasir, al-bayan al-thani yawm al-infisal 'an Suriya"
29 September 1961, "Kalimat al-Ra'is Gamal 'Abd al-Nasir fi Maydan al-Jumhuriyya bi-sha'n al-infisal 'an Suriya"
5 October 1961, "Bayan al- Ra'is Gamal 'Abd al-Nasir bi-sha'n al-infisal 'an Suriya"
16 October 1961, "Khitab al- Ra'is Gamal 'Abd al-Nasir"
9 June 1967, "Bayan al- Ra'is Gamal 'Abd al-Nasir ila al-sha'b w-al-umma bi-i'lan al-tanahhi 'an ri'sat al-jumhuriyya"
10 June 1967, "Bayan al-Ra'is Gamal 'Abd al-Nasir b-il-'udul 'an al-tanahhi 'an al-hukm"
23 July 1967, Khitab al-Ra'is Gamal 'Abd al-Nasir.
23 July 1969, "Khitab al-Ra'is Gamal 'Abd al-Nasir"
23 July 1970, "Khitab al-Ra'is Gamal 'Abd al-Nasir"
National Democratic Party. 2000. "Al-Mashru' al-watani li-tahdith al-dawla wa-tarsikh dawr al-mu'sssasat, barnamij al- Hizb al-Watani al-Dimuqrayi."
———. September 2004. "Al-Mu'tamar al-sanawi al-thani: awraq siyasat."
———. September 2005. "Min awraq al-mu'tamar al-sanawi al-thalith."
———. November 2008. "Awraq al-siyasat l-il-mu'tamar al-khamis."

———. November 2008. "Al-Ru'ya al-istratijiyya li-siyasat al-Hizb al-Watani: khamis sanawat min al-fikr al-jadid."

Sadat, President Anwar el-. Anwar Sadat Archives. *Anwar Sadat Chair for Peace and Development.* http://sadat.umd.edu/archives/written_works.htm (accessed 21 December 2013):

Address by the U.A.R. President Designate Anwar El Sadat before the National Assembly, 7 October 1970.

Policy on Coming Tasks, 19 November 1970.

The Arab Socialist Union, 39–51.

Building the Socialist Society, 17–21.

October Working Paper, April 1974.

Message to the People's Assembly on the Anniversary of the Rectification Revolution, 15 May 1976.

———. "Egypt-Israel Relations: Address by Egyptian President Anwar Sadat to the Knesset (November 20, 1977)." Jewish Virtual Library. www.jewishvirtuallibrary.org/jsource/Peace/sadat_speech.html (accessed 21 December 2013).

———. "President Anwar Sadat: Speeches." Bibliotheca Alexandrina, http://sadat.bibalex.org/speeches/speechesall.aspx?CS=0 (accessed 21 December 2013):

28 September 1970, "Bayan al-Ra'is Muhammad Anwar al-Sadat ila al-umma"

6 November 1970, "Bayan al-Ra'is Anwar al-Sadat fi dhikr arbi'in il-za'im al-khalid Gamal 'Abd al-Nasir"

14 May 1971, "Bayan al-Ra'is Muhammad Anwar al-Sadat ila al-umma"

23 July 1972, "Khitab al-Ra'is Muhammad Anwar al-Sadat fi iftitah al-dawra al-jadida l-il-mu'tamar al-qawmi al-'amm l-il-Ittihad al-Ishtiraki al-'Arabi"

28 December 1972, "Bayan al-Ra'is Muhammad Anwar al-Sadat"

16 October 1973, "Khitab al-Ra'is Muhammad Anwar al-Sadat fi iftitah al-dawra al-istithna'iyya li-Majlis al-Sha'b"

17 September 1978, "Kalimat al-Ra'is Muhammad Anwar al-Sadat ila al-sha'b al-Misri ba'd tawqi' Camp David"

26 March 1979, "Kalimat al-Ra'is Muhammad Anwar al-Sadat ba'd mu'ahidat al-salam"

22 July 1979, "Kalimat al-Ra'is Muhammad Anwar al-Sadat w-allati alqaha al-Sayyid Muhammad Husni Mubarak bi-munasibat 'Id Thawrat 23 July"

26 July 1980, "Hadith al-Ra'is Muhammad Anwar al-Sadat bi-munasibat al-dhikra 28 li-Thawrat Yuliyu"

14 May 1981, "Khitab al-Ra'is Muhammad Anwar al-Sadat"

23 July 1981, "Khitab al-Ra'is Muhammad Anwar al-Sadat"

5 September 1981, "Khitab al-Ra'is Muhammad Anwar al-Sadat"

United Arab Republic. *Al-Mithaq al-watani* [The National Charter]. N.p.: Maslahat al-Isti'lamat, 1962.

Foreign Broadcast Information Service (FBIS)
29 March 1975, "Text of Sadat Address"
5 June 1975, "Sadat Speech"
22 July 1975, "Text of Sadat Speech"
14 March 1976, "Sadat Addresses People's Assembly Session"
26 July 1976, "Sadat Addresses Alexandria University Students"
29 January 1977, "Concluding Speech"
22 July 1977, "Sadat Raps Libya in 23 July Revolution Anniversary Speech"
8 December 1977, "Sadat Address"
21 January 1978, "Text of Sadat Speech"
14 May 1978, "Sadat Speaks on Corrective Revolution Anniversary"
23 November 1978, "Sadat Addresses Session"
5 April 1979, "Sadat Addresses Special Session of People's Assembly"
14 May 1980, "Sadat Speech on May Corrective Revolution Anniversary"
22 July 1980, "Sadat Speech on NDP, War, Revolution Anniversaries"
1 October 1980, "Sadat Address"
8 November 1981, "Mubarak People's Assembly Speech"
26 January 1982, "Mubarak Outlines Economic Plans in Party Speech"
26 July 1982, "Mubarak Speech to National Democratic Party"
23 April 1983, "Mubarak Speech on Sinai Return Anniversary"
25 January 1984, "Mubarak Law Enforcement Conference Speech"
6 October 1984, "Mubarak October War Anniversary Speech"
22 July 1985, "Mubarak Revolution Anniversary Speech"
26 February 1986, "Mubarak Speech [to] Nation"
6 July 1987, "Mubarak Acceptance Speech"
20 July 1988, "Mubarak 23 July Revolution Anniversary Speech"
25 January 1989, "Mubarak Speech on Police Day"
25 January 1990, "Mubarak Speech on Police Day"
11 February 1991, "Mubarak Comments on Crisis during Religious Speech"
22 July 1991, "Mubarak Revolution Anniversary Speech"
25 January 1993, "Mubarak Speech on Confrontation of Terrorism"
30 August 1993, "Mubarak Marks Prophet's Birthday with Speech"
21 July 1994, "Mubarak Speech Stresses National Dialogue"
25 January 1996, "Mubarak Speech Stresses Fight against 'Terror' in Egypt"

INDEX

Kabir Tambar, *The Reckoning of Pluralism: Political Belonging and the Demands of History in Turkey*
2014

Diana Allan, *Refugees of the Revolution: Experiences of Palestinian Exile*
2013

Shira Robinson, *Citizen Strangers: Palestinians and the Birth of Israel's Liberal Settler State*
2013

Joel Beinin and Frédéric Vairel, editors, *Social Movements, Mobilization, and Contestation in the Middle East and North Africa*
2013 (Second Edition), 2011

Ariella Azoulay and Adi Ophir, *The One-State Condition: Occupation and Democracy in Israel/Palestine*
2012

Steven Heydemann and Reinoud Leenders, editors, *Middle East Authoritarianisms: Governance, Contestation, and Regime Resilience in Syria and Iran*
2012

Jonathan Marshall, *The Lebanese Connection: Corruption, Civil War, and the International Drug Traffic*
2012

Joshua Stacher, *Adaptable Autocrats: Regime Power in Egypt and Syria*
2012

Bassam Haddad, *Business Networks in Syria: The Political Economy of Authoritarian Resilience*
2011

Noah Coburn, *Bazaar Politics: Power and Pottery in an Afghan Market Town*
2011

Laura Bier, *Revolutionary Womanhood: Feminisms, Modernity, and the State in Nasser's Egypt*
2011

Samer Soliman, *The Autumn of Dictatorship: Fiscal Crisis and Political Change in Egypt under Mubarak*
2011

Rochelle A. Davis, *Palestinian Village Histories: Geographies of the Displaced*
2010

Haggai Ram, *Iranophobia: The Logic of an Israeli Obsession*
2009

John Chalcraft, *The Invisible Cage: Syrian Migrant Workers in Lebanon*
2008

Rhoda Kanaaneh, *Surrounded: Palestinian Soldiers in the Israeli Military*
2008

Asef Bayat, *Making Islam Democratic: Social Movements and the Post-Islamist Turn*
2007

Robert Vitalis, *America's Kingdom: Mythmaking on the Saudi Oil Frontier*
2006

Jessica Winegar, *Creative Reckonings: The Politics of Art and Culture in Contemporary Egypt*
2006

Joel Beinin and Rebecca L. Stein, editors, *The Struggle for Sovereignty: Palestine and Israel, 1993–2005*
2006

The authorized representative in the EU for product safety and compliance is:
Mare Nostrum Group
B.V Doelen 72
4831 GR Breda
The Netherlands

www.ingramcontent.com/pod-product-compliance
Lightning Source LLC
Chambersburg PA
CBHW020512270326
41926CB00008B/837

* 9 7 8 0 8 0 4 7 9 2 1 6 5 *